Education and Psychology of the Gifted Series

JAMES H. BO⸱⸱⸱⸱⸱⸱ EDITOR

Multicultural
DONNA Y. FORD

Reversing Underachievemen⸱⸱⸱
Promising Prac⸱⸱⸱
DONNA Y. FORD

Out of Our Minds:
Anti-Intellectualism and Talent Development in American Schooling
CRAIG B. HOWLEY, AIMEE HOWLEY, and EDWINA D. PENDARVIS

The Hunter College Campus Schools for the Gifted:
The Challenge of Equity and Excellence
ELIZABETH STONE

Recommended Practices in Gifted Education:
A Critical Analysis
BRUCE M. SHORE, DEWEY G. CORNELL, ANN W. ROBINSON, and VIRGIL S. WARD

Conducting Research and Evaluation in Gifted Education:
A Handbook of Methods and Applications
NINA K. BUCHANAN and JOHN F FELDHUSEN, Editors

The Academic Acceleration of Gifted Children
W. THOMAS SOUTHERN and ERIC D. JONES, Editors

Reaching the Gifted Underachiever:
Program Strategy and Design
PATRICIA L. SUPPLEE

Planning and Implementing Programs for the Gifted
JAMES H. BORLAND

MULTICULTURAL
GIFTED
EDUCATION

Donna Y. Ford • J. John Harris III

Teachers College, Columbia University
New York and London

Published by Teachers College Press, 1234 Amsterdam Avenue, New York, NY 10027

Library of Congress Cataloging-in-Publication Data

Ford, Donna Y.
    Multicultural gifted education / Donna Y. Ford, J. John Harris III.
       p.   cm. — (Education and psychology of the gifted series)
    Includes bibliographical references (p.) and index.
    ISBN 0-8077-3851-4 (alk. paper). — ISBN 0-8077-3850-6 (pbk. : alk. paper)
       1. Gifted children — Education — United States.   2. Multicultural education — United States.   3. Minorities — Education — United States.   I. Harris, J. John.   II. Title.   III. Series.
    LC3993.9.F658   1999
    371.95'0973 — DC21   98-56046

ISBN 0-8077-3850-6 (paper)
ISBN 0-8077-3851-4 (cloth)

Printed on acid-free paper
Manufactured in the United States of America

06   05   04   03   02   01   00   99   8   7   6   5   4   3   2   1

Contents

Preface

The body is the hardware.
Culture is the software.

We are living in a nation (and a world) of unparalleled diversity. Given the nation's changing demographics, issues of diversity must occupy center stage in much of what is currently being discussed, written, and taught in education. Demographic data indicate that minority[1] students represent an increasingly large proportion of the school population. In some U.S. cities and schools, "minority" groups are actually the numerical majority[2].

By 2020, projections are that minority students will comprise almost half (46%) of all public school students (National Center for Education Statistics, 1994). This increase of minority students in the national school population, however, has not been mirrored in gifted education. Table P.1 reflects demographic shifts in schools and gifted education programs since 1978. Specifically, the increase in students of color nationally is not matched by increases in gifted education. In fact, depending on the year and the particular ethnic group, there are declines in minority representation in gifted education. This is both ironic and troubling given increased efforts and initiatives (e.g., the Javits Act) to recruit more minority students into gifted education.

Many efforts are underway to seek parity by increasing the representation of minority students in gifted education. These efforts include: (1) finding more valid, reliable, and *useful* instruments to assess giftedness and *potential* among minority students, and (2) increasing teacher training in identification and assessment so as to ultimately increase the referral of minority students for gifted education services (e.g., D. Y. Ford, 1994a, 1994b; Frasier, Garcia, & Passow, 1995; Frasier & Passow, 1994; Frasier, Martin, et al., 1995). Similarly, the Javits Act of 1988 (Title IV, Part B, 1988) gives highest priority to the identification of gifted racial minority, economically disadvantaged, limited English proficient, and handicapped students. In its most recent call for applications (1997), the Javits Act targets students in Empowerment Zones — the poorest school districts targeted by the USDE for intervention; most are urban. Should these initiatives obtain their goals of recruiting more minority students in gifted education, educators will have to give greater at-

**Table P.1 Trends in the Representation of Minority Students in Gifted
Education Programs from 1978 to 1992**

Student Population	1978	1980	1982	1984	1992
	6.8	9.0	8.6	13.2	13.7
Hispanic	5.15	5.4	4.0	7.2	7.9
Americans	(U=25%)	(U=40%)	(U=53%)	(U=45%)	(U=42%)
	.8	.7	.5	.8	1.0
American	.3	.3	.3	.3	.5
Indians	(U=62%)	(U=57%)	(U=40%)	(U=62%)	(U=50%)
	1.4	2.2	2.6	3.7	4.0
Asian	3.4	4.4	4.7	6.8	7.0
Americans	(O=59%)	(O=50%)	(O=45%)	(O=46%)	(O=43%)
	15.7	20.1	25.8	24.5	21.1
African	10.3	11.1	11.0	12.9	12.0
Americans	(U=33%)	(U=45%)	(U=57%)	(U=47%)	(U=41%)

Source: Ford (1998)

Notes: Percentages are rounded; top number indicates percentage of student population; middle
number represents percentage of gifted education.
"O" indicates overrepresentation; "U" indicates underrepresentation. Percentage of
underrepresentation calculated using the following: 1 minus (percent of gifted education program
divided by percent of school district).
Source for 1978 to 1984 Office for Civil Rights data—Chinn & Hughes (1987); Source for 1992
data—Office for Civil Rights Elementary and Secondary School Civil Rights Compliance Report
(1992).

tention to multicultural education, and to the *retention* of minority students
in gifted education.

More than two decades ago, the American Association of Colleges for
Teacher Education (1973) advised that effective implementation of multicultural education has four major objectives: teaching values that support
cultural diversity and individual uniqueness; encouraging the qualitative ex-
pansion of existing ethnic cultures and their incorporation into the mainstream of American socio-economic and political life; exploring alternative
and emerging lifestyles; and encouraging a philosophy of multiculturalism
and equity. Banks and Banks (1993) defined multicultural education as

> an educational reform movement designed to change the total educational envi-
> ronment so that students from diverse racial and ethnic groups, both gender
> groups, exceptional students, and students from each social-class group will ex-
> perience equal educational opportunities in schools, colleges and universities.
> (p. 359)

The integration of multiculturalism into such fields as education, counseling, and research is not widespread, but efforts have increased in recent years. This work has pointed to the significance of multicultural education[3] to the psychological, affective, and educational well-being of racially and culturally diverse students. Although less often discussed, non-minority children also benefit from an education that is multicultural. Noticeably absent in gifted education, however, has been the focus on multicultural education. This book represents a call to professionals in gifted education to give greater attention to multicultural education, and those in multicultural education to raise the level of cognitive instruction.

In raising this call, we have listened to Black students express their concerns about the lack of diversity in the curriculum. As part of a larger study, Ford (1995a) interviewed 43 gifted Black students[4] in grades 6 through 9 about their curricular needs and concerns. Specifically, 41% of the students agreed or strongly agreed that "I get tired of learning about White people in class"; 87% agreed or strongly agreed that "I get more interested in school when we learn about Black people"; and all students supported the statement "I want to learn more about Black people in school."

Most of the Black students indicated that schools have adopted the most basic, simplistic approaches to multicultural education. An 8th grade male implores:

> You get tired of learning about the same White people and the same things. We need to broaden our horizons and learn about other people, even other countries. The White people are just trying to advance other White people and leave Blacks behind and ignorant. . . . I feel like being in the class more when I learn about Blacks and my heritage. It gives me encouragement and lets me know that I have rights. It helps to improve my grades. Learning about White people doesn't help me know about myself. . . . I'd like to educate my children about my heritage when I get older. I want to feel good about who I am. Why shouldn't I want to learn more about Black people?

Students' comments reveal their displeasure with and disinterest in the traditional curriculum offered in their schools and gifted programs. From their comments, it is clear that the gifted Black students see education as teaching the culturally different (or assimilation), human relations, and single-group studies approaches, as described by Sleeter and Grant (1993). Similarly, students' comments indicate that teachers practice lower levels of multicultural education as described by Banks (1997), namely, the additive and contributions levels. These two approaches and two levels are simplistic and, thus, easily implemented, but they are inadequate and insufficient. The gifted

Black students want more from their educational experiences than is currently offered. Their comments reveal that the students desire an education that is multicultural; they seek self-affirmation and self-understanding from the school and its curriculum. Just as important, the gifted Black students indicate that educational engagement *increases* when the curriculum is relevant, that is, multicultural.

Our interviews with these students have several implications: gifted Black students are not being educated to live in a racially and culturally diverse society; the curriculum does not enhance their racial and cultural identities; and, for some gifted Black students, school subjects lack relevance and meaning. These negative attitudes toward school help to explain why Black students, including gifted Black students, are represented disproportionately among underachievers. The lack of educational relevance can decrease student motivation and interest in school.

Teachers must listen to students and work to provide a learning environment that promotes a multicultural philosophy, as well as curricular, instructional, assessment, and structural changes. High on this agenda is the need: (a) to recruit and retain a more diverse teaching force in gifted education; (b) to make curricular changes relative to goals, content, and process; (c) to adopt more culturally sensitive instruments for the identification and assessment of minority students; (d) to have ongoing preparation in multicultural education for teachers and school personnel, including multicultural resources and consultants; and (e) to have ongoing evaluations of the status of multicultural education in gifted programs and services.

Just as we have argued for the desegregation of gifted education relative to increasing student diversity (Ford & Webb, 1995), we ask for desegregation of the curriculum. It is our position, and those of many Black students with whom we have worked, that gifted education, like all of education, must provide all students with mirrors and windows. In terms of mirrors, students must see themselves reflected in the curriculum; likewise, in terms of windows, students must see others reflected in the curriculum. Neither mirrors nor windows need be distorted images of people of color. People of color must not be devalued, ignored, or negated. An honest and open portrayal of minority groups empowers White and minority children by giving them a vision of hope. Thus, education must also provide ropes and ladders, particularly for minority children, so that they can pull themselves up and rise to the challenge that education has to offer. These apparatuses — mirrors, windows, ropes, and ladders — help all children to succeed.

Too often, students are presented a homogenized curriculum, one that is most likely to meet the academic and affective needs of White students in upper-income brackets. In this type of curriculum, little (if any) material and discussion address multicultural perspectives. Minority groups are ignored, trivialized, or negated in various ways. This treatment of diversity often

Figure P.1 Four Dimensions of Multicultural Teaching

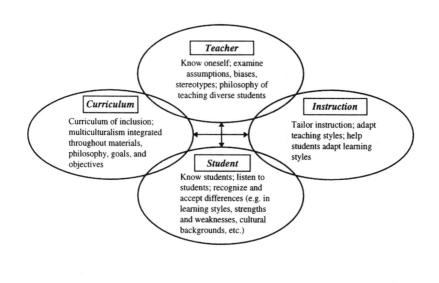

Source: Adapted from Banks & Banks (1993)

affirms, directly and indirectly, White students, while devaluing students of color. Likewise, homogenization espouses a color-blind and "culture-blind" philosophy, which is equally offensive to students of color. In gifted education, we work diligently to ensure gender equity; likewise, we must ensure equity relative to race and culture. Our efforts must not be color-blind or culture-blind, which robs minority students of essential opportunities to be valued and respected as diverse cultural groups. When we seek such blindness, often considered an ideal, equality is equated with sameness, but students are not the same; they are equally human, but they are different. That is, in the process to achieve such blindness, we negate, minimize, or trivialize the richness of diversity.

In seeking to create gifted education that is multicultural, we address the following questions: Why do students (including White students) need multicultural education? Who needs an education that is multicultural? What is an education that is multicultural? Which components are most important? When is multicultural education needed? Where is this type of education needed? How can we implement multicultural education so that it becomes not an add-on, but an integral and integrated aspect of the educational process? Finally, we offer recommendations for educators of gifted students to become more culturally aware, responsive, and skilled. A unique feature of the book is its use of case studies and scenarios. The cases are of actual children, and they are designed to help readers to put research and theory to practice. They put life into the theory and facilitate practice.

Figure P.1 presents a visual illustration of one multicultural education model that guides our work. Throughout the book, we urge educators: (1) to take part in self-evaluation relative to working with racially and culturally diverse students; (2) to seek an increased understanding of their students such that learning and teaching are based on students' needs; and (3) to adopt an education that is multicultural, that requires modifying curriculum and instruction, counseling, and identification and assessment.

This book addresses what is needed in gifted education if it is to truly become multicultural, and if education is to affirm the dignity and humanity of minority students. Thus, school personnel in gifted education must explore the need and rationale for multicultural perspectives in assessment, research, curriculum and instruction, and counseling. Just as we address academic and intellectual diversity, educators of gifted students must attend to racial and cultural diversity. We must seek excellence and equity for *all* students, acknowledging in the process that all students are the future and are worth educating. Educators of gifted students must be proactive rather than reactive in addressing this increasing diversity; they must seek both excellence and equity — the two are inextricably bound.

CHAPTER 1

Racially and Culturally Diverse Students and Families

INTRODUCTION AND OVERVIEW

That our songs are different is nowhere near as important as the fact that we all have a song to sing.
—Siccone (1995)

Culture is defined as those values, beliefs, attitudes, and norms unique to a group bound by race, gender, location, religion, or social class. It is the collective consciousness of a community with its own unique customs, rituals, communication style, coping patterns, social organization, and childbearing attitudes and patterns (Shade & Edwards, 1987; Shade, Kelly, & Oberg, 1997). Culture is the aggregation of beliefs, attitudes, habits, values, and practices that form a view of reality. These patterns function as a filter through which a group or individual views and responds to the environment. Learning styles are experienced by individuals in terms of acting, feeling, and being.

Cultural orientations represent patterns learned at an early age, as one grows up in a given family and community context. As people move out of the context of this primary socialization, they respond to new situations with previously learned behaviors and styles. When individuals encounter cultural patterns that are different in the new situation, they may have difficulty making a cultural transition. For minority students, this new situation may include being placed in a gifted program where teachers and school personnel may not understand their cultural styles and orientations. The less cultural congruence between the home and school, the more difficult the cultural transition and the more negative will be students' educational outcomes.

WHY CULTURE MATTERS

One of the obstacles to the full development of talent in our society is that we have yet to make the most of the potential and abilities of racially and culturally diverse students.

Interpretations of cultural characteristics take on one of three perspectives — cultural difference, deficits and inferiority, and cultural incongruence or conflict. All of these perspectives carry different implications for the educational experiences and outcomes of gifted minority students.

By the end of the century, we will be teaching children who are growing up in a country of unparalleled diversity. Projections are that minority students will soon represent more than one-third of public school children. Already, several of the largest school districts are teaching majority minority students — that is, schools where 50% or more of the students are Black and Hispanic. Specifically, by 2050, the U.S. Census projects that 52% of students will be Latino, and 10% Asian. Data also indicate the following:

1. Blacks currently comprise 12% of the U.S. population; Hispanics comprise 9%, and Asians comprise 3%;
2. In 1992, 37% of U.S. immigrants came from Asia; 44% came from Latin America and the Caribbean Islands;
3. Thirteen percent of Americans speak a language other than English at home;
4. Between 1985 and 1991, enrollments in the public school increased by just 4%, yet the number of students with little or no English language skills increased by 50% (U.S. Bureau of the Census, 1993).

Not long ago, a colleague forwarded the senior author an e-mail that places the world into perspective (see Figure 1.1). When one considers our world from such an incredibly compressed perspective, the need for both tolerance and understanding becomes glaringly apparent. That is, in addition to recognizing the increase in diversity nationally, it is important to recognize diversity globally. The figure emphasizes that globally, White populations are the "minority."

EXAMINING RACIAL AND CULTURAL DIVERSITY

As with much of what will be discussed in this chapter and book, a critical examination of both the nation and world is essential if we are to prepare students to live in a multicultural, pluralistic society. When we view the world

Figure 1.1 The World Metric: A Profile

*If we could shrink the Earth's population to a village of precisely 100 people, with all
existing human ratios remaining the same, it would look something like this*:

- There would be 57 Asians, 21 Europeans, 14 from the Western Hemisphere (North and South), and 8 Africans.

- 51 would be female; 49 would be male.

- 70 would be nonwhite; 30 would be white.

- 70 would be non-Christian; 30 would be Christian.

- 50 percent of the entire world's wealth would be in the hands of only 6.

through myopic lenses, it is difficult to see the richness of differences and diversity. Contrary to what many students (and adults) may believe, most of the world is comprised of people of color. Who are these people of color, and what must educators know about these groups to promote effective educational opportunities for them?

The following sections present profiles of minority groups in the United States relative to demographic variables, history, and cultural values and norms. The descriptors are presented as guidelines from which to better understand the academic, intellectual, affective, and cultural needs of minority groups. We maintain, as do many advocates of multicultural education, that students are both individuals and members of their respective racial and cultural groups. We must also recognize and understand within- and between-group differences, for there is similarity, but also tremendous diversity. Unfortunately, space limitations do not allow for an in-depth discussion of each minority group; however, more detailed information appears in Banks (1997) and Gollnick and Chinn (1998).

American Indians and Native Hawaiians

The first Americans—American Indians and Native Hawaiians—are the nation's smallest racial groups, representing approximately 1% of the U.S. population (1,878,000 and 211,000, respectively). Although once referred to as the "vanishing Americans," these groups have increased steadily since the 1940 Census (Banks, 1997). For example, the Census has identified approximately 500 American Indian tribes and bands (U.S. Bureau of the Census, 1993). Only the Cherokee (16% of the total American Indian population), the Navajo (12%), the Chippewa (6%), and the Sioux (6%) total more than 100,000 members. Most American Indians live in Oklahoma, California, Arizona, and New Mexico. Census data indicate that 60% live in urban areas and 22% live on reservations. Poverty runs rampant among American Indian populations. Specifically, in 1990, the median family income of American Indians was 62% of that of the total U.S. population. For those living on reservations, 51% lived in poverty.

Educational Data. According to Plisko and Stern (1985), in 1980 and 1981, a higher percentage of American Indians attended colleges or had received undergraduate degrees than Hispanic Americans and African Americans (.25%, .20%, and .23%, respectively). This slightly higher success in colleges is not mirrored in gifted education. American Indians represent 1% of the school population, but .3% of those in gifted education programs — a 70% underrepresentation (U.S. Department of Education, 1993).

Negative images of American Indians are widespread, contributing in significant ways to the difficulties these students confront in U.S. educational settings. In schools, American Indians face a great disservice. For example, they are taught (as are most children) that Columbus "discovered" America, and White Europeans' migration from the eastern to western part of the United States continues to be called the "Western Movement." As Banks (1997) noted, both perspectives foster the (mis)belief that American civilization was nonexistent until Europeans arrived. Such a belief does little to promote racial and cultural pride among American Indian students, and it has the potential for promoting misguided notions of superiority or supremacy among other students. In both cases, students are misinformed (at best) and miseducated (at worst). Whose story is told?

Cultural Values. In general, American Indians from different tribes share some values. Particularly important to American Indians is the collective identity, that is, one's belonging to the tribe. Sisk (1989) also noted that American Indian values also include idealism, nonaggressiveness, and nonmaterialism. Some of these values are highlighted in Figure 1.2.

Kirschenbaum (1989), Gardner, Kornhaber, and Wake (1996), Sternberg (1985), and many others have reminded readers that what is valued and respected as gifted in one culture is not necessarily valued in another[5]. For instance, the Navajo conception of giftedness includes talent for working in the crafts or performing in cultural rituals. Further, being gifted means doing things considered constructive, taking on leadership roles when necessary, and helping one's family. These values are not to be measured by traditional standardized tests of achievement and intelligence.

Hawaiians are very heterogeneous, which has made it difficult to classify them in recent years. Specifically, many Hawaiians have varied backgrounds, including Korean, Chinese, Japanese, and African ancestry. According to Banks (1997), only 1% can be considered "pure-blooded."

Figure 1.2 Comparative Framework: American Indian and White American Values and Traditions

Traditional American Indian Cultural Values	Traditional White American Cultural Values
Collective identity (tribal identity); anonymity	Individual identity
Cooperation, both social and familial	Competition
Nonaggressive	Aggressive
Nonmaterialistic; nature valued	Materialistic; things and possessions highly valued
Spiritual—religion is a way of life; respect persons with spiritual powers	Religion is one more institution; respect persons with social status
Maternalistic	Paternalistic
Nonverbal and verbal expressiveness	Verbal expressiveness
Bilingual	Monolingual
Seeks harmony, maintains traditions; present-time oriented	Seeks progress, change; future-oriented
Idealism	Realism

As with all diverse groups, Hawaiians have many cultural values and norms that can be used to create an educational framework. For instance, the spirit of *Aloha Aina* (love for the land) persists, as does the value of *Ohana,* a cooperative system of social relationships and extended family networks. The value of *Ohana* can conflict with school values and contribute to problems for Hawaiian children. For example, these students may not wish to participate in competitive situations with classmates; likewise, working with others may be perceived as cheating and dependency by school personnel who are unfamiliar with this cultural value and other values (i.e., strong family relations, a respect for and love of nature, creativity and expressiveness).

Effective and appropriate programming and instruction for gifted American Indians must incorporate their beliefs, values, and traditions. As Garrison (1989) asserted, "the goal of such a program is not to make American Indian students 'Anglo-American,' but to make them bicultural by giving them the skills, pride, and self-confidence to enable them to move between cultures" (p. 116). Thus, the teacher's responsibility is to help build bridges rather than destroy cultures. Building bridges results, in part, from providing students with cultural understanding and respect.

In meeting the needs of American Indian students, teachers might decrease competition via cooperative/collaborative teaching methods and groupings, as well as modify instructional styles. For instance, these students might benefit from increased use of visual aids, increased opportunities for storytelling, increased use of multisensory approaches to instruction, more open-ended or divergent assignments, and increased use of culturally relevant and affirming materials (see Garrison, 1989).

African Americans

In general education, gifted education, and special education, African Americans have received more attention than other minority groups, perhaps because they are the largest minority group in the United States. Currently, Black students represent 12% of the U.S. population and 16% of the school population. Ogbu (1988) noted that African Americans are the only minority group to come to the United States in chains; other groups have come by choice — to search for the American dream, or to escape horrendous conditions in their homelands. Thus, African Americans are considered the only "involuntary" minority group in the United States. While differing from other minority groups in this regard, African Americans, nonetheless, share dismal educational and employment outcomes with some Asian Americans, and many Hispanic Americans and Indian Americans. For example, in 1992, the median income for Black families was 54% that of White families, one-third lived below the poverty level, and their rate of unemployment was 13% — more than twice that of Whites (6%) (U.S. Bureau of the Census, 1993).

Cultural Characteristics and Values. As a cultural group, Black students are socially oriented, as reflected in strong fictive kinship networks and large, extended families (e.g., McAdoo, 1993). There is a strong need to belong and for affiliation, and a need to bond with others who share similar concerns and interests (Figure 1.3). In many ways, group support represents a mechanism for cultural preservation and social identity. However, social identity can be an important source of vulnerability for Black students. Black students confronted with racism who respond with anger and rebelliousness may develop an *oppositional social identity* (Ogbu, 1988). They may deliberately perform poorly in school, rebel against authority figures (e.g., teachers and school administrators) who are perceived as agents of oppression, and rebel against any behavior associated with mainstream society. To protect their self-esteem, African American students may develop ineffective coping styles that

Figure 1.3 Comparative Framework: African American and White American Values and Traditions

Traditional African American Values	Traditional White American Values
Extended family—strong family and fictive kinship bonds	Nuclear family
Spiritual	Religious
Cooperation; social-oriented; mutual interdependence; collectiveness	Competition; task-oriented; independence; individuality
Multilingual (Ebonics)	Monolingual
Situation oriented	Time oriented
High context communication; verbal and non-verbal	Low context communication; verbal
Obedience to elders	Obedience to authority

alienate them from school and hinder academic achievement. For instance, in a predominantly White gifted program, Black students may limit or avoid completely any contact with their White peers, and they may deliberately exert little effort in school because it is associated with the White culture. Many Black children hide their academic abilities by becoming class clowns, dropping out, and suppressing effort.

Other Black students may have a *diffused identity,* characterized by low self-esteem and alienation from both the Black culture and the mainstream. Their poor academic and social competencies result in educational, social, and psychological adjustment problems. This identity is most likely to develop when the values, attitudes, and behaviors espoused in the home and school are incongruent; this incompatibility or dissonance between the home and school can cause considerable stress for Black students, particularly if the schools attempt to assimilate Black students by ignoring, trivializing, or eliminating their cultural differences. While schools require a high degree of mainstream socialization from students, they do not always provide the environments necessary for Black youth to gain mainstream skills while remaining connected to their home and community environments. The result is increased or more intense barriers to Black students' academic success.

Hispanic Americans

Hispanic Americans represent the fastest-growing minority group in the United States. Between 1980 and 1990, this country witnessed a 53% increase in the number of Hispanic Americans nationally. Projections indicate that this trend will continue; by 2020, Hispanic Americans are expected to make up 25% of the nation's school-age population. The largest groups of Hispanic Americans include Mexican Americans (62%), followed by Puerto Ricans (12%). These groups are highly concentrated in California, Texas, New York, and Florida (U.S. Bureau of the Census, 1993).

Like most minority groups, Hispanic Americans are confronted by high poverty and unemployment rates, as well as poor educational outcomes. Dropout rates among Hispanic Americans are alarming, with some reports indicating that one in two leave the public school system without a degree. In 1993, a little more than half of Hispanic Americans completed high school (53%). Equally disturbing, these students are underrepresented in gifted education programs nationally—they comprise 9.4% of the school population, but 4.7% of those in gifted education programs (U.S. Department of Education, 1993).

Educational Data. Many efforts have targeted Hispanic students relative to language acquisition—bilingual programs, Spanish immersion programs, English as a Second Language (ESL) or Limited English Proficiency programs. Language is a major barrier for students of color in U.S. schools, and teachers' beliefs about foreign languages can play a role in their inability to see the verbal strengths of these students. The irony here is that verbal skills have been used as the hallmark of giftedness, yet students who speak two languages (bilingual) are often poorly identified in verbal areas of ability or giftedness.

Cultural Characteristics and Values. Udall (1989) and many others have summarized values inherent in Hispanic cultures, as reflected in Figure 1.4. In general, Hispanic Americans value nonmaterial possessions, family bonds, real-world learning experiences, social and cooperative learning, student-centered classrooms, and active learning experiences. Educating and empowering Hispanic American students for school success necessitates developing students' appreciation for their own culture, adapting teaching styles to learning styles, increasing students' sense of belonging in school settings, and focusing on strengths while remediating weaknesses.

Asian Americans

Unlike most minority groups, Asian Americans often suffer from the image of the "model minority." They are often used to illustrate how an ethnic group of color can succeed in the United States. Yet conspicuously absent is a discussion of why Asian Americans outperform White students in school.

**Figure 1.4 Comparative Framework: Hispanic American and White
American Values and Traditions**

Traditional Hispanic American Values	Traditional White American Values
Family bonds	Individualistic
Relaxed/permissive child-rearing practices	Authoritative child-rearing practices
Interdependence cooperation; emphasis on social relations	Independence; competition; emphasis on task
Concrete thinking and learning experiences	Abstract thinking
Active learning	Passive learning
Social learning (pairs, small groups)	Individual, independent learning
Present-time orientation	Future orientation
Bilingual	Monolingual

In 1989, Maker and Shiever reported that Asian Americans comprised 2.1%
of the U.S. population, but 8% of the student body at Harvard, 19% at MIT,
25% at UC-Berkeley, and over 33% at UC-Irvine. Further, while representing
2.5% of the school population, they represent 5% of those in gifted education
(U.S. Department of Education, 1993). Consequent to this positive stereotype, little attention is given to Asian Americans in textbooks and popular
media; yet several authors have noted the harm that comes with stereotypical
images of perfection, dedication, and hard work (e.g., Lee, 1996). Few studies and articles discuss the mental stresses facing Asian Americans, so many of
whom covet the model minority image.

As with all groups, the ravages of poverty have not escaped Asian Americans. When between-group differences are examined, Banks (1997) reports
that harsh realities set in. For example, in 1990, 42% of Chinese Americans
had menial service, low-skilled, and blue-collar jobs. About 52% had manage-
rial and technical jobs.

Asians have immigrated to the United States from various countries—
the Philippines, China, Japan, Korea, Vietnam, Laos, and so forth. In 1990,
Chinese Americans represented the largest Asian American group (approximately 24%), followed by Filipinos (20%), Japanese, Asian Indians, and Koreans (approximately 12% each) (U.S. Bureau of the Census, 1993). As a
group, Asian Americans increased faster than any other racial group in the
United States. Specifically, there was a 99% increase from 1980 to 1990,

**Figure 1.5 Comparative Framework: Asian American and White American
Values and Traditions**

Traditional Asian American Values	Traditional White American Values
Confucian ethic—strong work ethic centered on effort and persistence	Protestant work ethic—Strong work ethic centered on ability and personal characteristics
Academic orientation— status by effort	Academic orientation—status by ability
Family honor and tradition	Individualistic
Past, tradition	Future, change
Nonaggressive, cooperation	Aggressive, competition
Multilingual	Monolingual
Mutual interdependence, collectiveness, group welfare, public conscience	Independence, self-reliance, individuality, privacy
Harmony with nature	Mastery of nature
Conformity, correctness, obedience to adult authority and elders	Challenge, question adult authority

compared to an increase of 53% for Hispanic students in this same time frame
(U.S. Bureau of the Census, 1993).

Cultural Characteristics and Values. Each group has its unique cultural values, as well as similar values. In general, Asian American values include mature self-control, a Confucian ethic (the belief that people can be
improved by effort and instruction), a strong work or achievement ethic,
strong family bonds, a respect for obedience and authority, and a strong commitment to education and achievement (See Figure 1.5).

Educational Data. Although many Asian groups are excelling in U.S.
schools, Tanaka (1989) argued for a reevaluation of education for Asian
Americans, one that addresses the development of talents in leadership, the
arts, and creativity. Woo (1989) recommended an emphasis on cooperative
learning, self-paced instruction, and values awareness. Like other students of
color, it is essential that Asian Americans address issues of assimilation and
acculturation (i.e., dual identities as American and Asian) in positive and proactive ways.

BETWEEN-GROUP COMPARISONS

The previous sections addressed within-group diversity, emphasizing that there is much variation among different groups of Asian Americans, different groups of American Indians, and so forth. In this section, we discuss between-group similarities and differences. We must have a framework from which to meet the needs of minority students as individuals and members of their respective groups. Further, although each group is distinctive in its own right, many minority cultures share common cultural characteristics and values.

Between-Group Similarities

Numerous similarities exist between the four major minority groups just described. In fact, the similarities seem to outweigh the differences. At its worst, almost every group has confronted racial discrimination, and they share the burden of poor educational outcomes, high unemployment rates, and high poverty rates. Conversely, they share cultural values that can serve as strengths in identification and assessment, research, and curriculum and instruction (Figure 1.6). Namely, the value that minority groups place on family bonds goes unparalleled, as does the preference for cooperation and social learning. Bell (1997) noted that approximately 70% of the world's population lives in collective cultures.

Expressive communication — physical and creative expressiveness — is also an important value for each group, to varying degrees. For instance, African Americans and Hispanic Americans are known for their creative expression and aesthetic appreciation. Other methods of communication also cross cultures for students of color, many of whom are bilingual. Debates regarding Black English (recently referred to as "Ebonics") have resurfaced for African Americans. While critics contend that Black English is not a legitimate language, that it is a dialect, others consider such a debate futile. We contend that "non-standard English" is a communication system worthy of attention in meeting students' educational needs. All efforts must be made to ensure a goodness of fit between students and schools.

Between-Group Differences

People of color have come to the U.S. for different reasons and under different circumstances. According to Ogbu (1988), voluntary and involuntary minorities have responded differently to social injustices. Specifically, involuntary minority groups — African Americans — have been less optimistic about the democratic ideals of U.S. society and have resisted assimilation.

Figure 1.6 Common Bonds: Strengths of Minority Cultures and Implications for Giftedness

Affect

This strength appears analogous to Gardner's (1983) interpersonal intelligence and intrapersonal intelligence. It is also related to Goleman's (1995) emotional intelligence. These students are often very sensitive, caring, and social (e.g., extroverted, people-oriented, humanistic). For example, affect represents an ability or potential to:

- Express feelings and emotions
- Use expressive and colorful speech
- Read and interpret the emotional cues and nonverbal behaviors of others

Physical Expressiveness

This strength is analogous to Gardner's (1983) bodily-kinesthetic intelligence. Thus, students demonstrate or have the potential to demonstrate:

- Articulateness in role-playing and storytelling
- Enjoyment of and ability in visual and performing arts
- Enjoyment of and ability in creative movement, dance, and dramatics
- Responsiveness to the kinesthetic (movement)
- Expressiveness of gestures and body language

Creativity

Creativity is represented in many definitions and theories of giftedness. It is an integral component of bodily-kinesthetic intelligence (Gardner, 1983) and Sternberg's (1985) synthetic intelligence. Renzulli (1977) also notes the important role of creativity in giftedness. Further, some creative behaviors require problem-solving, often considered an important aspect of critical thinking. Creativity represents skills of:

- Improvisation, fluency
- Originality
- Invention
- Elaboration, embellishment

Communication

Communication is an essential life skill for all students. It is an integral component of all definitions and theories of intelligence (Gardner, 1983, Sternberg, 1985; Renzulli, 1977). For instance, communication skills are important in interpersonal intelligence and creativity. They represent:

- Fluency and flexibility in nonverbal media
- Keen sense of humor
- Richness of imagery in informal language
- Enjoyment of and skill in social learning and problem-solving situations
- Quickness of "warm-up"

Adapted from Torrance (1977) and Ford (1996)

Public schools in the U.S. were originally designed for a homogeneous group of children with a common culture, values, morals, ambitions, and parental expectations. Thus, immigrants and minority groups in the U.S. were thrown into the "melting pot," where their differences were expected to boil away as they molded into true-blue Americans, living the American way and realizing the American dream (Siccone, 1995, p. xii). The dream, however, has proven elusive, sometimes a nightmare, for many, particularly those who refuse to adopt narrowly defined notions of the "American" identity. The cost of giving up one's cultural identity to achieve qualified success, to achieve second-class citizenship, is too high a price to pay for some individuals.

In recent years, the image of the melting pot has itself boiled away to be replaced by another image — that of a salad bowl. More recently, the salad bowl has been replaced by the tapestry. This new image or metaphor for cultural diversity recognizes that each group has its distinctive qualities to be valued and that different people can come together in order to create a new whole. As Martin Luther King Jr. once stated, we are all caught in an inescapable network of mutuality, tied into a single garment of destiny — whatever affects one directly affects all indirectly.

Few Americans seem to understand what lies at the heart of multicultural education. The issue is not whether our society is comprised of many cultures. It always has been and is becoming more so. The issue is whether we will create a *new* vision for how our multicultural society will function effectively. The issue is how to deal with both dimensions of the nation's motto: *E Pluribus Unum,* out of many, one (Siccone, 1995, p. xii). As Takaki (1993) noted, America's dilemma has been our resistance to ourselves — our denial of our immensely varied selves. But we have nothing to fear but fear of our own diversity.

SUMMARY

The richness in any single culture lies in its inherent differences from other cultures.
—*Montgomery (1989, p. 79)*

The U.S. has become a kaleidoscope of diverse cultures. Each minority group has a rich heritage, values, customs, and traditions. Unfortunately, these differences are often perceived as weaknesses, as disadvantages and deficits. Many groups of color have fought the tendency of U.S. schools to erase their differences through assimilation and color-blindness. Neither approach has proved effective for minority students. In fact, the more efforts aimed at forcing assimilation upon groups of color, the more these groups resist (e.g., Fordham & Ogbu, 1988). There is a strong belief among minority groups that they must hold on tightly to their uniqueness, to their heritage, to their cultural values and language. Thus, as Ogbu's (1988) research indicates, the melting pot philosophy may be valued by White Americans, but it may be rejected by minority groups. Consequently, rather than resist diversity, educators must embrace it. This is the first step toward helping to ensure that minority students reach higher levels of achievement in schools and other social settings.

CHAPTER 2

Historical and Legal Perspectives on Educating Gifted and Minority Students

Few would deny that all human beings are due equal consideration and respect. Few would deny that individuals should enjoy the opportunity to rise as far as their talents and abilities may carry them.

—*Salomone (1986, p. 17)*

INTRODUCTION AND OVERVIEW

Few students are as envied as gifted students; few students are as misunderstood as minority students. This chapter presents a historical analysis of gifted education and multicultural education, calling attention to legal issues in serving these students. As their histories indicate, securing the educational rights of gifted students and minority students has been difficult. In particular, we focus on *Brown vs. Board of Education* (1954) and the Javits Act of 1988 (Title IV, Part B), as well as court cases to shed additional light on the challenges gifted students, minority students, and gifted minority students confront in trying to secure their educational rights. This historical overview makes at least one point clear — neither gifted nor minority students can afford to be caught in the battle between excellence versus equity. These students, as do all students, require the best of what education can offer — excellence *and* equity.

THE CALL FOR EQUITY AND EXCELLENCE: MULTICULTURAL EDUCATION

The field of multicultural education, as a formal discipline, is in its infancy. It is a field of study and an emerging discipline whose major goal is to create educational opportunities for students from diverse racial, ethnic, social, and cultural groups (Banks, 1993, 1997; Banks & Banks, 1995).

One of its important goals, as described in the next chapter, is to help *all* students to acquire the knowledge, attitudes, and skills needed to function effectively in a pluralistic democratic society and to interact, negotiate, and communicate with people from diverse groups. Ultimately, multicultural education seeks to create a civic and moral community that works for the common good (Banks & Banks, 1995, p. xi). These goals are consistent with our democratic principles of equity and justice, as represented in founding documents such as the Declaration of Independence. Multicultural education seeks to put the words of these documents into reality.

Multicultural education has a rich but brief history. According to Banks and Banks (1995), it is linked directly to African American scholarship of the late 19th and early 20th centuries. One of the earliest and most urgent calls for multicultural education came from Carter G. Woodson in the *Miseducation of the Negro* (1933). The concerns expressed by Woodson more than six decades ago are still relevant today.

The struggle for educational opportunity reached a climax in the 1950s. During this time, the United States witnessed a cataclysmic event that changed the power and focus of education, namely, *Brown v. Board of Education* (1954). In *Brown,* the Court recognized that "education is perhaps the most important function of state and local governments" (p. 493). Further, the Court ruled that the "segregation of children in public schools solely on the basis of race, even though the physical facilities and other 'tangible' factors may be equal" (p. 493), not only deprived them of equal and equitable educational opportunities, but also violated their right to equal protection of laws guaranteed under the Fourteenth Amendment to the United States Constitution. *Brown* is the foundation upon which all subsequent developments ensuring the legal rights of the disenfranchised rest.

Brown represents a legal and moral imperative grounded in the principle of equality, the principle that all children should receive an education on equal terms. Not only did the case acknowledge the inherent worth of Black students, it argued that racially segregated schools are unequal. *Brown* laid the foundation for equality and guided, directly and indirectly, numerous educational decisions affecting Black students into the next century. The decision was based on the premise that racial discrimination violates our national sense of morality.

The 1960s ushered in compensatory educational programs designed to redress inequities in learning opportunities for economically disadvantaged students, particularly minority students. Such programs as Head Start and Chapter I had the expressed goal of closing the educational gap (or gulf) between economically disadvantaged and advantaged children, between poverty and plenty. The ultimate goal was to ensure the educational success of all students, regardless of their racial and socio-economic status (SES) background, by equipping them with the skills necessary to compete in the educational arena.

The mid-1960s also experienced the War on Poverty and Great Society programs, which represented dramatic calls to reform education based on the equality principle. The Great Society programs were justified by a theory of education as an "investment in human capital"; rhetoric regarding "wasted talent" flooded the educational scene, including gifted education programs. In 1964, Congress enacted the Civil Rights Act. Title VI prohibits discrimination on the basis of race, color, and national origin in federally assisted programs. The Act put teeth into the enforcement of the *Brown* mandate (Salomone, 1986) by helping to achieve substantial school desegregation, particularly in the South.

By the late 1970s, the United States witnessed a groundswell of opposition to the equality principle, specifically the reforms it generated. Salomone (1986) asserts that to a society that valued merit and talent, we added the criteria of need and social neglect. And in the process of meeting that national agenda, individual choice and community preference became all but irrelevant in the wider educational policy arena. As laws were passed to protect the rights of minority and economically challenged students, backlash mounted. Opponents demanded a greater deference to the individual rights of the majority.

Many misconceptions have permeated some reform reports, making excellence and equity for minority and economically disadvantaged students difficult. First, excellence is frequently equated with quantity rather than quality of school experiences. The reports focused extensively on cognitive performance (e.g., higher test scores and graduation rates) at the expense of the quality of students' school experiences, an issue that is particularly important when discussing underachievement among minority students.

Second, reformers often supported a common core curriculum that by its very nature promotes conformity and uniformity. A common curriculum ignores individual and group differences in learning, particularly the academic needs of gifted, minority, and underachieving students.

Third, the reports supported the erroneous belief that opportunity to achieve the recommended standards of excellence is equally distributed and within every child's reach. In essence, the reports have virtually ignored the educational limitations posed by low socio-economic status (SES), minority status, family influences, handicapping conditions, and racial and gender prejudices. The net effect has been a retreat to the belief that focusing on group differences is antidemocratic. In attempting to be democratic, reformers have ignored the importance of group differences (e.g., gender, race, socio-economic status) as general guidelines from which to educate children, especially racially and culturally diverse youth. It is a reality that children come to school with different levels of ability and readiness, and that children of the same socio-economic status background, family structure, community, age, gender, height, and weight can and do achieve differently.

Just as educators have had to confront past and current inequities in school settings, so too have the courts. A discussion of the educational status of gifted minority students would be incomplete without attention to court decisions in this area. Thus, three cases affecting the educational status of minority groups are described below.

Sample Court Cases Involving Gifted Minority Students

The first court case to directly impact gifted minority students occurred some three decades ago. *Hobson v. Hansen* (1967) was a case before the District of Columbia in which minority groups questioned the constitutionality of using group IQ tests and achievement measures in placing children in special educational tracks. Black students were overrepresented in low-ability tracks (particularly educably mentally retarded classes, EMR), and White students were placed disproportionately in upper-ability tracks (especially college preparatory classes). The court prohibited the use of tests for the purposes of grouping, holding that the tests had been standardized on primarily White, middle-class populations; therefore, the tests yielded biased results when administered to minority students.

Three years later, the courts heard *Diana v. California State Board of Education* (1970). Plaintiffs on behalf of nine Latin American students charged that the children were inappropriately placed in EMR (educably mentally retarded) classes as a result of scores on IQ tests that assumed equality of examinees' linguistic and cultural backgrounds. When the students were permitted to take the test in their primary language, there was an average increase of 15 IQ points. The case led to an out-of-court settlement stipulating that children from non-English-speaking homes would be tested in their native language. It also led to subsequent out-of-court settlements specifying that IQ tests used for special education placement must: (a) be normed on culturally and linguistically relevant groups; and (b) contain no culturally unfair content.

The final case discussed here is *Larry P. v. Wilson Riles* (1979). The plaintiffs were six Black parents who claimed that their children had been placed wrongly in EMR classes because the standardized IQ tests used for placement were racially and culturally biased. The case first appeared in 1971 against the San Francisco Unified School District. After several years of injunctions and appeals, the case finally came to trial in 1979. The court rendered a decision in favor of the plaintiffs, noting that disproportionate numbers of Black students were placed in EMR classes (Black students comprised 27% of the total student population, but over 60% of the EMR population). The court noted that "There is less than one in a million chance that the over-representation of Black children and the under-enrollment of non-Black children in the EMR classes in 1967–1977 would have resulted under a color-blind system of placement" (cited in Anderson, Stiggins, & Gordon, 1980, p. 19). The State of California appealed the decision. In 1984, an appellate court upheld the court's decision. A more detailed description of the cases appears in Worthen, Borg, and White (1993).

Implications

The emergence of multicultural education is affiliated most with the Civil Rights Movement of the 1950s, 1960s and 1970s — a period of change and progress like no other for Blacks. It was during these three decades that Blacks and other minorities took greater ownership of their destiny, and were energized in significant ways by a sense of empowerment. This sense of self-efficacy was ignited by such leaders as Martin Luther King Jr. and Malcolm X, and by groups such as the National Association for the Advancement of Colored People (NAACP) and the Black Panthers. African Americans demanded more than symbolic representations of democracy; they sought (and still seek) structural changes, particularly in education and employment. Education is viewed as many things, but primarily as the great equalizer that fosters critical thinking, socialization, upward and social mobility, and democracy. Thus, education has been elevated from a public benefit to a guaranteed right (Salomone, 1986). President Johnson affirmed that "we seek not just freedom but opportunity — not just legal equity by ability — not just equality as a right and a theory, but equality as a fact and a result" (Eastland & Bennett, 1979, cited in Salomone, 1986). As described below, however, high ability does not guarantee equitable educational opportunities; thus, the educational picture is also bleak for gifted students.

GIFTED STUDENTS: ANOTHER CALL FOR EXCELLENCE AND EQUITY

Americans have a love–hate relationship with gifted students whereby the products of talent are valued, but services to gifted students are viewed as elitist and antidemocratic. The "threats" posed by the Soviet Union and Sputnik and, more recently, by the rigorous Japanese educational system marshal reformers to redress the shortcomings in gifted education. With the most recent U.S. Department of Education (1993) report on the status of gifted education, attention to gifted students appears to have increased. The report revealed that gifted seniors in the U.S. ranked among the lowest of 13 countries studied: biology (ranked 13th), chemistry (13th), algebra (13th), physics (9th), and calculus and geometry (12th). These data were borne out even more recently with the 1998 Third International Mathematics and Science Study (TIMSS) (National Center for Education Statistics, 1998). For example, according to the National Science Foundation (NSF) Director, Neal Lane:

> The results of students in the final year of secondary school in the TIMSS science and mathematics general knowledge assessments found that our students performed less well than they did at grade 8, significantly below the international mean. In addition, our most advanced students (those taking pre-calculus or calculus, and physics) performed at low levels in advanced mathematics and at especially low levels in physics when compared with similar students in other countries. More specific findings for advanced students[6] are that:
>
> 1. The performance of U.S. physics and advanced mathematics students was among the lowest of the 16 countries which administered the physics and advanced mathematics assessments. In advanced mathematics, 11 countries outperformed the United States and no countries performed more poorly. In physics, 14 countries outperformed the United States; again, no countries performed more poorly.
> 2. In all three content areas of advanced mathematics and in all five content areas of physics, U.S. physics and advanced mathematics students' performance was among the lowest of the TIMSS nations.
> 3. In both physics and advanced mathematics, males outperformed females in the United States and most of the other TIMSS countries.
> 4. More countries outperformed the United States in physics than in advanced mathematics. This differs from the results for mathematics and science general knowledge, as well as the results at grades 4 and 8, where more countries outperformed the United States in mathematics than in science. (National Center for Education Statistics, 1998)

In reaction to the report, one can expect an onslaught of new initiatives aimed at raising test scores and targeting gifted students. High-stakes testing will increase even more. Once the threats pass, however, those programs for gifted students tend to wither away. Such reactive responses are generally inadequate and have the effect of sustaining an overall low regard for the needs of highly capable students. As described below, if gifted education is ever to receive more than cursory attention, strong support must come from the federal government and from a much greater proportion of the citizenry.

Legislation Impacting Gifted Education

The Sputnik era implicitly made gifted students the prime benefactors of major curricular reform, because it was propelled by the need to redress low achievement (compared to other countries) among highly capable U.S. students. Albert (1969) reported that among all articles published on gifted students between 1927 and 1965, more than 90% appeared after the launch of Sputnik.

The initial, sporadic, and short-lived emphasis on gifted education raised many of the problems advocates of gifted education face today: underfunding, understaffing, and a sort of studied inattention to the needs of gifted students. As Zirkel and Stevens (1987) reported, of the estimated 2.5 to 3.0 million gifted children[7] in the nation, only 1.2 million participate in special programs for gifted students. Thus, even those districts providing gifted education often fail to serve all of their qualified students.

While two in three states mandate the establishment of programs for gifted students, state guidelines tend merely to describe rather than mandate what is desirable. Gallagher (1988) identified four contributing factors: (1) narrow definitions of giftedness and subsequent identification procedures; (2) lack of offerings at certain grade levels or in certain subject areas; (3) superficial provisions rather than substantive programs; and (4) a lack of understanding of the many and varied needs of gifted students.

This scarcity of high-quality programs is exacerbated by the fact that no mechanism exists to require the many mediocre programs to improve. Compounding the problem further are the pervasive inconsistencies in the shape and comprehensiveness of existing state and local initiatives. Some gifted students receive as little as three to five hours a week of special instruction, primarily in the form of pullout programs that cannot possibly meet the diverse needs of these students.

Thus, like students of color, gifted students frequently face educational neglect. The National Commission on Excellence in Education (1983) stated that "most gifted students should be provided with a curriculum enriched and accelerated beyond the needs of other students of high ability" (pp. 8, 24). These needs extend beyond cooperative learning, heterogeneous grouping, and the "dumbing" down of the curriculum. Rather, gifted students require a more intensive and individualized curriculum, more challenging tasks, increased opportunities for creative expression and enrichment, and practical guidance and experience.

Acting on recommendations in the Marland Report (1972), which offered the first federal definition of the gifted, Congress established the United States Office of Gifted and Talented. In the same year, amendments to the ESEA, Title IV of the Special Projects Act, made categorical funding available for gifted education. But the actual amount allotted came to about one dollar a year for each eligible student.

Progress appeared to be forthcoming when the Gifted and Talented Children Act of 1978, extending the funding provisions of the Special Projects Act, became law. Yet the optimism was short-lived, as the Act was repealed by the Omnibus Budget Reconciliation Act of 1981. The Budget Act also closed the Office of Gifted and Talented, eliminated categorical funding from federal sources, and combined authorizations for gifted education and 29 other programs into a single funding block while reducing funding by more than 40% (Karnes & Marquardt, 1991).

As a wave of educational reform swept the nation in the early 1980s amid concerns over the growing tide of mediocrity, support for gifted education programs once again grew. The Jacob K. Javits Gifted and Talented Students Act of 1988, Title IV, Part B of the ESEA, marked the culmination of the efforts of gifted education proponents. The Javits Act reinstated and both expanded and updated the programs cut seven years earlier. Its goal is

> to provide financial assistance to State and local educational agencies . . . to initiate a coordinated program of research . . . designed to build a nationwide capability in elementary and secondary schools to meet the special educational needs of gifted and talented students. (Sec. 3062 (b))

It is noteworthy that the Act "shall give highest priority" to students who are economically disadvantaged, limited English proficient, or "with handicaps" (Sec. 3065 (a)(1)).

The Javits Act, however, has two major shortcomings from the perspective of gifted education advocates. First, it fails to mandate the creation of programs. Second, it includes none of the substantive or procedural due process safeguards available to students with disabilities. For substantive due process to be satisfied, a governmental (or in this case, public school) policy or action needs to be rationally related to a legitimate governmental goal.

Implications

Some four decades after the Supreme Court's monumental ruling, the promise of *Brown* also remains unfulfilled for gifted students. In many ways, gifted education finds itself in a precarious position — society values the products of gifted students, yet devalues gifted education programs and services. Should business continue as usual, the number of students served by gifted education will remain dismally small, and the current economic, educational, and social conditions of these students will remain gloomy. The reality is simple — quality education cannot be achieved without equity.

SUMMARY

The struggles for educational equity and excellence are not only being fought by students of color, but by students with different gifts and talents. It is an unfortunate reality that schools, like other social institutions, have not fully met the needs of students who have special and unique needs. For different reasons, both gifted students and minority students find themselves constantly on the defensive — struggling for their rights to an appropriate education. Professionals in gifted education and multicultural education must redirect their efforts, and move from parallel movements to one movement. Hence, our desire to write this book on "multicultural gifted education."

CHAPTER 3

Multicultural Education and Gifted Education: Goals, Objectives, and Theoretical Perspectives

INTRODUCTION AND OVERVIEW

This chapter places into perspective the complimentary nature of gifted education and multicultural education in terms of goals and objectives. We describe the theoretical perspectives of both disciplines as we lay the foundation for multicultural gifted education. Readers will notice that the goals and objectives of gifted education and multicultural education are not mutually exclusive. The National Association for Gifted Children's (1994b) position paper on mandated educational opportunities for gifted students highlights this complimentary relationship:

> Education in a democracy must respect the uniqueness of all individuals, the broad range of cultural diversity present in our society, and the similarities and differences in learning characteristics that can be found within any group of students. NAGC is fully committed to national goals that advocate both excellence and equity for all students . . . the best way to achieve these goals is through *differentiated* educational opportunities, resources, and encouragement for all students.

In comparing the complimentary goals of gifted education and multicultural education, we discuss the characteristics, goals, and objective of each. We also present theoretical models from both fields. In particular, we discuss theoretical perspective of programs commonly adopted in gifted education (e.g., the Enrichment model, Junior Great Books, and Philosophy for Children) and multicultural education (e.g., the works of Banks and Grant and Sleeter). We end the chapter by presenting a synthesis of the two fields. Thus, this chapter guides much of what follows in later chapters.

CHARACTERISTICS OF MULTICULTURAL EDUCATION

Multicultural education is a philosophy, goal, and process. It is a philosophy based on the fundamental belief that all people must be accorded respect, regardless of age, race, ethnicity, gender, socio-economic status (SES), religion, physical ability, or mental ability. It is predicated on the belief that all people have intrinsic worth. Thus, multicultural education seeks to affirm individual differences and human diversity through the elimination of prejudices, biases, and stereotypes based on socio-demographic variables. When an education is multicultural, it permeates all aspects of schooling; it is comprehensive, penetrating, and integrating rather than narrow, supplementary, restrictive, and/or assimilating.

Multicultural education gained momentum in the 1980s, with the past and current works of Banks (1997), Bennett (1990), Garcia (1994), Gollnick and Chinn (1998), Heid (1988), Grant and Sleeter (1998), and others. These authors focused on the need to reform our educational system by adopting an education that is multicultural. They recommend:

1. developing multicultural curriculum and instruction in all subject areas and courses;
2. integrating a philosophy of multiculturalism into educational practices and programs;
3. adopting multiculturalism in all educational institutions, regardless of racial and cultural composition;
4. seeking a commitment by educators, policymakers, and decisionmakers to goals of multicultural education;
5. recruiting and retaining a more racially and culturally diverse teaching force; and
6. evaluating the quality of multicultural education to ensure that it is substantive and integral rather than superficial and ancillary to the educational process.

As a process, multicultural education helps students to develop competencies relative to perceiving, evaluating, and doing. The focus is on students understanding and learning to negotiate differences across cultures. As a process, multicultural education emphasizes that individuals can *learn* to become pluralistic in their thoughts, behaviors, and affect. Similarly, individuals do not have to reject their cultural identity to function effectively in diverse settings.

Figure 3.1 Goals of Multicultural Education

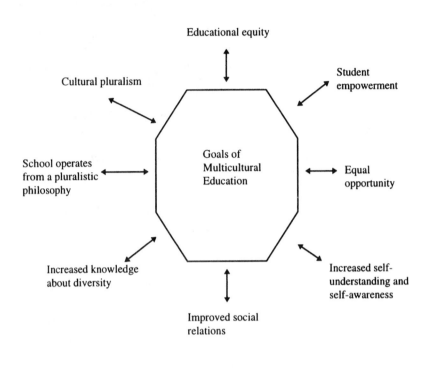

Source: Adapted from Davidman and Davidman (1994)

GOALS OF MULTICULTURAL EDUCATION

Figure 3.1 depicts the overarching goals of multicultural education, specifically, multicultural knowledge, educational equity, cultural pluralism, empowerment, improved social relations, and increased teaching from a multicultural perspective. Davidman and Davidman (1994) have summarized these goals in greater detail than we present here.

Multicultural Knowledge

Multicultural knowledge increases students' sense of self-worth and belief that they have a chance for a successful future. Multicultural knowledge lays the foundation for developing cultural pluralism, intergroup harmony, and the ability to think, work, and live with a multicultural perspective.

Educational Equity

Educational equity has three fundamental conditions: (a) an equal opportunity to learn; (b) positive educational outcomes for both individuals and groups; and (c) equal physical and financial conditions for students to grow to their fullest potential academically and affectively. These conditions are facilitated when educators seek substantive experiences in working with minority and gifted students.

Cultural Pluralism

Whereas educational equity focuses on modifying fundamental educational conditions to promote equitable learning, cultural pluralism is concerned with attitudes. It creates positive cultural attitudes in counselors, teachers, students, and decisionmakers. When school personnel support cultural pluralism, they ask themselves the important question: How can I help my students to develop understanding, respect, and appreciation for individuals who are culturally different from themselves?

Empowerment

Empowerment addresses all school members — students, teachers, administrators, families, and others. Empowerment helps students to become self-directed learners who want to grow educationally and who take more responsibility for the content and shape of their educational growth. Empowerment also helps students to become independent and interdependent learners. Just as important, empowerment connotes social action; it helps students to take an active role in improving the quality of their (and other) communities.

Educators who feel empowered are stronger advocates for students, advocates who take the steps necessary to promote positive student outcomes. They provide culturally relevant teaching and culturally responsive classrooms. Just as important, educators who feel empowered create and nurture a sense of community and interdependence.

Social Relations

To promote intergroup and intragroup harmony, educators provide knowledge, skills, and a classroom environment that prepare students to live and work with members of their own cultural group and members of other cultural groups. Instruction includes opportunities for students to work together, to learn from each other, and to rely on each other. Counselors can also work with students on lifelong skills, such as building or initiating friendships, promoting positive peer relationships, and resolving conflicts. Long-term benefits include social and cultural competence.

Teaching with a Multicultural Perspective

A multicultural perspective is a state of mind, a way of seeing and learning that is shaped by beliefs about multiculturalism (Davidman & Davidman, 1994). This belief helps teachers to see that culture, race, gender, religion, SES, and ability are powerful variables in the learning process, and that important ideas about teaching can be gained from studying cultural systems. Educators who hold this perspective utilize such information to maximize every student's learning experience. It leads administrators, curriculum developers, and teachers to select content that shows students that all of history has been decisively influenced by a wide range of cultural groups and individuals.

When teaching from a multicultural perspective, educators challenge assumptions and stereotypes; they examine curriculum from a broader point of view and in an assertive, proactive manner. They educate students for the real world by increasing students' understanding of diversity, race, and culture, for the less we know about another group, the more we make up. Further, a multicultural perspective helps to promote culturally sensitive teaching strategies because teachers are adept at collecting, interpreting, and making instructional and management decisions based on sociocultural information. Relatedly, educators endeavor to promote cultural continuity between the home and school of minority students, and attempt to eliminate culturally assaultive classrooms. Hence, the title of Shade, Kelly, and Oberg's (1997) book, *Creating Culturally Responsive Classrooms.* Ladson-Billings (1994) stated that culturally relevant and responsive teaching uses students' culture in order to maintain it and to transcend social barriers. Thus, students are empowered intellectually, socially, emotionally, and politically by using cultural referents to impart knowledge, skills, and attitudes.

STRATEGIES FOR MEETING MULTICULTURAL GOALS

A multitude of strategies is embraced under the umbrella of multicultural education (see Figure 3.2). These strategies are tied directly to the goals, objectives, and philosophies just described. For example, multicultural education strategies include using social and cooperative learning, varying teaching

Figure 3.2 Strategies for Meeting Multicultural Goals and Objectives

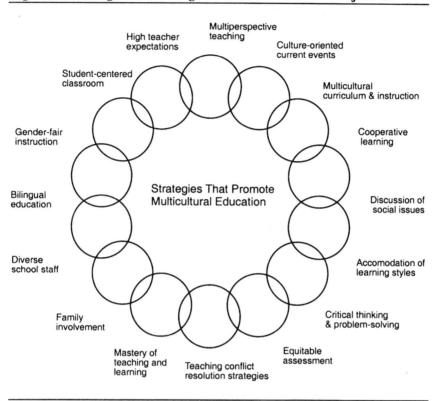

Source: Adapted from Davidman & Davidman (1994)

styles to accommodate learning styles, using equitable assessment instruments and practices, promoting student-centered classrooms, discussing social issues, setting high teacher expectations, sharing multiple perspectives, involving families, and having bilingual education programs. Many of these strategies are consistent with recommendations from educational reform reports and initiatives, and they are given greater attention and specificity in upcoming chapters.

TWO THEORIES OF MULTICULTURAL EDUCATION

In seeking to substantively alter the curriculum, multicultural education represents not only a philosophy, as described earlier, but also a process. The scholarship of Sleeter and Grant (1993) and Banks (1995, 1997) will be used to illustrate multicultural education as a process.

Sleeter and Grant's Model

As discussed below, Sleeter and Grant discussed five approaches to multicultural education (see Figure 3.3).

"Teaching the Culturally Different" Approach. The goals of this approach are to equip students with cognitive skills, concepts, information, language, and values that will enable them to function in mainstream society. According to this approach, to teach the culturally different means to teach with a notion of assimilation. Assimilationists favor the abdication of diverse students' primary culture, which is often perceived as deficient or inferior. Perhaps the most blatant example of assimilation is efforts to have limited English proficient students "give up" their primary language in favor of English. Such a belief is indicative of a melting pot philosophy, one that devalues the cultural values, beliefs, and characteristics of minority students.

Thus, minority students are expected to adapt to the values, attitudes, and behaviors of the predominant culture. Further, educators who adopt assimilationist perspectives are also likely to blame minority children for their poor achievement rather than to acknowledge the role of the educational and social system in promoting poor educational outcomes. According to the assimilationist viewpoint, children who don't succeed in schools have their families to blame. Essentially, differences (however rich) become deficits and disadvantages.

Human Relations Approach. This approach addresses individual differences and similarities. Its goal is to achieve a greater appreciation for others, and to eliminate stereotypes among students. Certain events and activities familiarize students with cultural artifacts, but students acquire a surface-level understanding of the cultural values and orientations of minority groups. In essence, students may feel good for having shared something of themselves, and classmates may enjoy the activities, but one is left to ponder what, if anything, classmates have learned. (Teachers might ask Asian American students to bring in sushi to share with students; Hispanic American students might be asked to bring in a piñata; during *Cinco de Mayo* celebrations, a Hispanic American student might be asked to teach classmates a few words of Spanish; some Black students may be asked to share a few words of Swahili, to bring in a kente cloth, or to discuss Kwanzaa during Black History Week or Month).

Single-Group Studies Approach. This approach refers to an in-depth study of a particular group of people so that the worldview of that group can be better understood. However, while students learn about one group, they may not learn about others. For instance, there may be increased understanding of Hispanic American students, but a continued lack of understanding about Black students. This "bicultural" perspective, this increased knowledge about one group, does not carry over to others. Therefore, application and transfer of knowledge are minimal. We often note, for example, that people sympathize or empathize with females facing sexual discrimination, but are less understanding of racial discrimination.

Multicultural Education Approach. This approach attempts to re-form the educational process, regardless of the predominant racial and cultural makeup of the school. It involves issues of restructuring (such as the curriculum) so that no single cultural group dominates any other cultural group in its representation. The shortcomings described with the single-group studies approach are resolved. A continued shortcoming, however, is the focus on curricular and instruction issues, without attention to larger issues affecting students' learning, such as the lack of teacher diversity in the school or poor representation of minority students in the gifted program. Thus, while teachers make curricular changes, there are few structural changes relative to the classroom and school environment.

Education That Is Multicultural and Social Reconstructionist. This approach enables students to become analytical and critical thinkers, and to participate more in a diverse environment. There is a deeper level of multicultural understanding and a commitment to bring about social change by students. Students are empowered to take learning from the classroom to the real world. For example, students join or create organizations that seek justice and equity. Martin Luther King, Malcolm X, Harriet Tubman, Rosa Parks, Gandhi, Cesar Chavez, Jaime Escalante, and many others represent the epitome of social reconstruction.

Implications

Each of these approaches has shortcomings. According to Sleeter and Grant (1993), advocates of teaching the exceptional and the culturally different approach often feel that the worst way to deal with cultural differences such as language and learning styles is to nurture them (see Figure 3.3). These advocates fail to realize the pluralistic nature of society; instead, they view society as a melting pot, a phenomenon discussed in Chapter 1.

While the human relations approach to multicultural education is impor-

Figure 3.3 Sleeter and Grant's Typology of Multicultural Education

TEACHING THE CULTURALLY DIFFERENT
Main purposes are to counter a cultural "deficiency" orientation while assisting students in developing and maintaining their own cultural identity. Efforts designed to help students develop competence in the dominant culture while developing a positive identity. Efforts focus on aspects of the cultural and language of targeted groups, with little attention to power and social relations. Few efforts extend beyond attention to culture, race, and ethnicity. While this approach communicates much culture-specific information, it may mask an assimilationist perspective.

HUMAN RELATIONS
Students of different backgrounds learn to communicate more effectively with others while learning to feel good about themselves. The emphasis on communications and relationships is narrow.

SINGLE-GROUP STUDIES
Instruction focuses on the experiences and cultures of one specific group. Black History Week/Month, and courses in African American literature, Chicano literature, Asian cultures, and American Indian culture are developed. These monoethnic courses and activities are not integrated throughout the curriculum, but rather isolated, piecemeal efforts. These efforts tend to perpetuate stereotypes and segregated curricula.

INCLUSIVE MULTICULTURAL EDUCATION
Materials, concepts, and perspectives of many different groups are adopted and infused throughout the curriculum.

EDUCATION THAT IS MULTICULTURAL and RECONSTRUCTIONIST
Helps students to critically analyze their circumstances and the social stratification that keeps them from full participation in the society at large. The entire education program is designed to address the needs of diverse groups, regardless of race, ethnicity, culture, gender, and other socio-demographic variables. Seeks to provide students with the skills necessary to become socially active in creating changes.

Democracy is put into action. Students learn to analyze their life situations and become more aware of inequalities and inequities. Students learn social action skills in order to put knowledge into action. Students learn to work collaboratively and cooperatively for change.

Source: Adapted from Grant & Sleeter (1989)

tant, a disadvantage is that it fails to move beyond a level of respect and understanding to a level of social action whereby students not only internalize appreciation, respect, and harmony, but also get involved and promote changes. In the single-group studies approach, educators often treat single groups (e.g., gender, cultural groups, etc.) as separate entities and fail to connect the group with the larger social and cultural context.

In the multicultural education approach, many educators become interested in one form of oppression, such as sexism, and fail to resolve their biases in other forms, such as racism. In addition, the integration of topics such as race, gender, and disability is neglected (Sleeter & Grant, 1993). Education that is multicultural and social reconstructionist has been criticized for not acknowledging the social inequities that accompany the issue of culture (Sleeter & Grant, 1993). However, among the various approaches, this approach best describes our view of multicultural education in that it embodies a more comprehensive view of culture — the awareness of group similarities and differences; it allows students to see how cultures, such as race and gender, interact together rather than as separate entities; and it provides opportunities for students to develop ways of thinking and analyzing that allow them to become proactive in making a change in society.

Banks's Model

Banks has written a number of books on multicultural education. In this chapter, we focus on one of those. Banks has (1993, 1995, 1997) reported on four levels of integration of multicultural content into the curriculum (see Table 3.1). In level 1, the *Contributions Approach,* educators focus on heroes, holidays, and discrete elements. This is the most frequently adopted and extensively used approach to multiculturalism in the schools. An important characteristic of this approach is that the traditional ethnocentric curriculum remains unchanged in its basic structure, goals, and salient characteristics. Students are introduced to minority heroes such as Crispus Attucks, Sojourner Truth, and Booker T. Washington. These individuals, however, are usually discussed in relation to White heroes such as George Washington and Thomas Jefferson. Furthermore, individuals who challenged the predominant culture's ideologies, values, and conceptions and who advocated radical social, political, and economic reform are often ignored in this approach. As a result, Martin Luther King Jr. is more likely to be discussed than Malcolm X; and Booker T. Washington is more likely to be discussed than W. E. B. DuBois. Subsequently, students acquire a distorted or incomplete view of history and reality.

Another characteristic of this rudimentary approach is that cultural traditions, foods, music, and dance may be discussed, but little or no attention is given to their meaning and significance to minority groups. What is the significance of Kwanzaa to African Americans? Why do Blacks celebrate this holiday? Why is there a need for alternative holidays and celebrations by diverse cultural groups? These questions would not be addressed at this stage. Also, ethnic content is limited primarily to special days, weeks, and months related to minority groups. Students learn little to nothing about the occa-

Table 3.1 Four Approaches to Integrating Multicultural Content into the Curriculum

APPROACH	DESCRIPTION	EXAMPLES	STRENGTHS	PROBLEMS
CONTRIBUTIONS	Heroes, cultural components, holidays, and other discrete elements related to ethnic groups are added to the curriculum on special days, occasions, and celebrations.	Famous minorities are studied only during certain times. Little attention is devoted the cultures in which the artifacts are embedded.	Provides a quick and easy way to put ethnic content into the curriculum. Gives ethnic heroes visibility in the curriculum, alongside mainstream heroes. Most frequently adopted in schools.	Results in a superficial understanding of ethnic cultures. Focuses on the lifestyles and artifacts of ethnic groups; reinforces stereotypes and misperceptions. Mainstream criteria used to select heroes and cultural elements for inclusion in the curriculum.
ADDITIVE	Consists of additions to the content, concepts, themes, and perspectives to the curriculum without changing its structure.	Adding books and materials without reconceptualizing the unit or giving the students the background knowledge to understand the books or materials. Adding a unit on an ethnic group without focusing on the group in other units. Leaving the core curriculum intact but adding an ethnic studies course as an elective.	Makes it possible to add ethnic content into the curriculum without changing its structure. Can be implemented within the existing curriculum.	Reinforces the idea that ethnic history and culture are not integral parts of the U.S. mainstream culture. Students view ethnic groups from a Eurocentric perspective. Fails to help students understand how the dominant culture and ethnic cultures are interconnected and interrelated.

TRANS-FORMATION	The basic goals, structure, and nature of the curriculum are changed to enable students to view concepts, events, issues, problems, and themes from the perspectives of diverse groups.	Units describe the meaning of events, issues, etc., to all groups involved. All voices are heard.	Enables students to understand the complex ways in which diverse groups participated in the formation of the U.S. society and culture. Helps reduce racial and ethnic encapsulation. Enables diverse groups to see their cultures, ethos, and perspectives in the school curriculum. Gives students a balanced view of the nature and development of U.S. culture and society. Helps to empower minority groups.	Requires substantial curriculum revision, inservice training, and the identification and development of materials written from the perspectives of diverse groups. Staff development for the institutionalization of this approach must be ongoing and continual.
SOCIAL ACTION	Students identify important social problems and issues, gather pertinent data, clarify their values on the issues, make decisions, and take reflective actions to help resolve the issues or problem.	Students study prejudice and discrimination in their school and take action to improve race relations. Students study the treatment of minority groups and take action to redress inequities.	Enables students to improve their thinking, value analysis, decision-making skills, and social-action skills. Enables students to improve their data-gathering, social-action, and problem-solving skills. Helps students to develop a sense of political efficacy. Helps students to improve their skills in working with diverse groups.	Requires a considerable amount of curriculum planning and materials. Longer in duration than more traditional teaching units. May focus on problems and issues considered controversial. Students may be unable to take meaningful actions that contribute to the resolution of some social issues and problems

sion, group, or individuals being "celebrated." The Contributions Approach is cosmetic; it provides teachers with a quick, nonthreatening way to "integrate" the curriculum, and teachers themselves can adopt this approach without knowing much about racially and culturally diverse groups. It also reinforces stereotypes about minority groups, while using safe, nonthreatening heroes found acceptable to the mainstream.

In the *Additive Approach* (level 2), the content, concepts, themes, and perspectives of minority groups are added to the curriculum without changing its structure. For instance, teachers may add a book, unit, or course to the curriculum that focuses on diverse groups or topics. While the content changes slightly, there is little restructuring of the curriculum relative to purposes and characteristics. Minority students learn little of their own history, and White students learn little of the history and contributions of other racial and cultural groups to American society. For instance, students reading *The Autobiography of Malcolm X; Roll of Thunder, Hear My Cry; The Bluest Eye; The Invisible Man; I Know Why the Caged Bird Sings; The Color Purple;* or *Native Son* lack the concepts, content background, and emotional maturity to understand, appreciate, respect, and cope effectively with the concepts and issues discussed in the books. The additive approach fails to help all students view society from diverse perspectives and to understand the ways in which the histories of the nation's diverse racial, cultural, ethnic, and religious groups are interconnected (Banks & Banks, 1993, p. 202). In essence, this superficial approach requires little commitment—little time, effort, training, and re-thinking of curriculum and instruction. Students reading Malcolm X are not required to understand the Black Nationalist Movement; they do not analyze racial identity; and they may not compare the philosophy of Martin Luther King Jr. and Malcolm X. Students fail to discuss events of the 1960s and the current social and cultural conditions today.

In the third level, the *Transformational Approach,* two types of changes occur. In one instance, the structure of the curriculum is changed to enable students to view concepts, issues, events, and themes from the perspectives of minority groups. This is a fundamental change from the previous levels; one now sees changes in the basic assumptions, goals, nature, and structure of the curriculum. The second fundamental change is that students are provided with the knowledge and skills to better understand the perspectives of minority groups (e.g., empathy). Essentially, students are informed and empowered. According to Banks and Banks (1993, 1995), the curriculum should not focus on the ways that minority groups have contributed to mainstream society and culture; instead, it must focus on how the common U.S. culture and society emerged from a complex synthesis and interaction of the diverse cultural elements that make up the U.S. This approach requires extensive curriculum revision, changes in teacher preparation, changes in student thinking, and much time, effort, and commitment.

To illustrate, we will use the topic of slavery. To increase the depth of students' understanding regarding slavery, they have experiences that promote empathy (not sympathy). For instance, students may participate in a simulation on slavery; they hold in-depth discussions of the rationale for and injustice of slavery. Lessons are not presented in which slaves are portrayed as helpless and passive; instead, slaves are depicted as people who took their lives into their own hand through revolts and other forms of resistance. Students acquire, therefore, the cognitive tools and insights to walk in the shoes of captive people.

In level 4, the *Social Action Approach,* students make decisions about important social issues and take action to help solve them. Students are not socialized to accept mainstream ideologies, practices, and institutions. Instead, students feel empowered and are proactive; they are provided with the knowledge, values, and skills necessary to participate in social change. Student self-examination becomes central in this approach through value analysis, decision-making, problem-solving, and social action skills. For example, students examine issues surrounding prejudice and discrimination, and they develop ways to improve race relations. This approach is least likely to be adopted by educators, primarily because teachers lack formal training, experience, understanding, and personal knowledge of other racial and cultural groups (e.g., histories, values, beliefs, customs). Teachers understand that knowledge without action does not improve social and cultural relations.

At the highest levels, the models described by Banks (1993, 1995, 1997) and Sleeter and Grant (1993) require extensive philosophical and curricular changes. Certainly, the most important reasons for multicultural education are its benefits to students and to our future. Multicultural education helps students to accept their culture as an essential component of their personal development. While increasing their knowledge about cultural and racial diversity, students acquire an ethic of social justice—their sense of personal independence, social interdependence, personal responsibility, and social responsibility increases interest, as well as motivation and learning (Gay, 1993, 1997). Below, we present several scholars whose efforts have reached the highest levels of multicultural education—social action.

PROFILES OF MULTICULTURAL EDUCATORS— SOCIAL ACTIVISTS

Many educators have been noted for their work in promoting equity and excellence in teaching students of color. Like Davidman and Davidman (1994), we are particularly interested in the works of Philip Uri Treisman, James P. Comer, and Jaime Escalante, all of whom demonstrated that excel-

lence and equity can coexist in harmony, and that high expectations are powerful components of multicultural teaching.

Philip Uri Treisman. A professor at the University of Texas, Austin,
and a former math educator, Treisman dramatically improved the academic
achievement of Black students after analyzing and studying the differential
math achievement of two different racial groups. In 1975, while working
with teaching assistants at the University of California at Berkeley, Treisman
found that 60% of the Black students were failing freshman calculus, compared to 12% of Chinese students. His search for an explanation for this large
discrepancy led to a doctoral dissertation in which he observed and video-
taped 20 Black and 20 Chinese students in their dorms and other settings as
they worked on math assignments.

After 18 months of observation and interviewing, Treisman discovered
that the major difference in their pattern of success was the way students inter-
acted with each other when studying. The majority of the Black students (18
out of 20) never studied with other students and attributed their success to
studying in isolation, that is, separating studying from socialization. Conversely, 13 out of 20 Chinese students adopted support-oriented study patterns that included socialization.

Based on these findings, Treisman developed and refined an equity workshop strategy that allowed students to study math under the guidance of skilled
teachers and within a community of peers. Results indicated that the 60%
failure rate of minority students dropped to 4% and that over the last decade
the minority students in the workshops have performed better than other
students. Thirty colleges and universities have adopted the workshop in such
courses as physics, chemistry, engineering, and math.

Treisman personifies multicultural education (social activism) by not accepting the failure rates of minority students and by taking active steps to
reverse the failure rates. By not accepting the students' failure and by seeking
to understand the outcomes, Treisman attributed poor outcomes to external
rather than internal factors.

James P. Comer. In 1968 Comer noted that two Black elementary
schools ranked near the bottom in terms of achievement and attendance out
of 33 New Haven elementary schools. Further, teacher attrition was among
the highest in the state, with 25% leaving per year, and parents were described
as dejected, angry, distrustful, and alienated. Within 7 years, Comer and his
colleagues at Yale University developed a comprehensive and systemic prevention and intervention plan that included mental health professionals, parents,
administrators, and teachers. Like Treisman, Comer did not blame the children for their failures; he did not perceive the major problem as low achieve-

ment, low attendance, and low morale. Instead, these variables were perceived as *symptoms* of the larger problem. Comer's team diagnosed the major problem as the schools' failure to pay attention to the psychological development of students, and the lack of positive relationships between the school and home (i.e., cultural discontinuity). Having identified the problem and symptoms, Comer developed a governance and management team that included all stakeholders in the decisions affecting students; hence, all partners had a sense of ownership in the school and its operations. By 1979, the students who had ranked the lowest in achievement among the 33 schools had caught up to their grade level by the fourth grade; by 1984, students in the fourth grade ranked third- and fourth-highest on the Iowa Test of Basic Skills.

Functioning from a multicultural perspective, Comer noted that race, culture, SES, and self-esteem were powerful variables in the learning process. Equally important, he recognized that socio-cultural forces, including a mismatch between the home and school, can wreak havoc on minority students' achievement. This cultural discontinuity resulted in student failures and conflicts. Comer was able to see the cultural nature of the problem from a proactive view rather than adopting a cultural deficit perspective.

Jaime Escalante. Escalante is a mathematics teacher. When he began teaching in Los Angeles, Escalante worked with a predominantly Latino student body. Approximately three-fourths of the students were eligible for free or reduced lunch. Most students failed to pass the AP calculus exam in 1977. One year later, four in seven students passed; by 1989, 66% passed — no comparable high school in the nation performed as well.

In raising test scores and operating from a multicultural perspective, Escalante addressed the goals of educational equity and the creation of collaborative, empowering relationships among families, educators, and students. Escalante sought to demonstrate, to prove, that Mexican American students whose parents had low educational levels could perform as well as middle-class, highly educated students. Escalante also adopted the role of mentor and role model. Escalante was available prior to school, during lunch hours, and after school; he provided educational services, with parental permission, to students up to three hours after school ended, without additional pay. For Escalante, student achievement was the reward. The primary message communicated to students was high expectations and self-affirmation: "You want to make your parents proud. You want to make your school proud. Think how good it will feel to go to college and know that you did the Calculus AP." This statement reminds us of James Baldwin's (1962) comments: "The streets of my native city were filled with youngsters searching desperately for the limits which would tell them who they are, and create for them a challenge to which they could rise."

GIFTED EDUCATION: GOALS AND OBJECTIVES

Developing a philosophy of gifted education is a challenge for many school districts. The curriculum will depend heavily on a district's belief about all students and its commitment to gifted students. According to VanTassel-Baska (1992), any statement of curriculum philosophy for gifted students must include three fundamental ideas:

1. gifted students have a right to an appropriate education, one grounded in the recognition of individual differences and unique learning needs;
2. gifted students need a curriculum responsive to their individual learning rate, style, and complexity; and
3. gifted students learn best in an instructional environment that encourages and nurtures inquiry, flexibility, and divergent thinking (p. 63).

More specifically, VanTassel-Baska describes five goals that support the fundamental ideals just described. In terms of cognitive goals, gifted programs are designed to help students to: (a) develop high-level proficiency in all core subject areas; (b) to become independent investigators; (c) to appreciate the world of ideas; (d) to enhance higher-level thinking skills; and (e) to encourage a spirit of inquiry. Affective goals of gifted programs might include: (a) the enhancement of self-understanding and the development of effective coping strategies (e.g., when pressured about being labeled gifted). Social goals might include the development of social skills (e.g., building peer relationships). Finally, aesthetic goals might center on helping students to develop an appreciation of the arts and enhancing creative expression. These goals and objectives are consistent with those set forth by the U.S. Department of Education in 1976 (pp. 18665–18666) and in its most recent report, *National Excellence: A Case for Developing America's Talent* (U.S. Department of Education, 1993). The USDE presented a proactive and bold definition of giftedness, a definition that can leave no doubt that the nation must meet the needs of its gifted students, regardless of their race, culture, or SES:

Children and youth with outstanding talent perform or show the potential for performing at remarkably high levels of accomplishment when compared with others of their age, experience, or environment. These children and youth exhibit high performance capacity in intellectual, creative, and/or artistic areas, and unusual leadership capacity, or excel in specific academic fields. They require services or activities not ordinarily provided by the schools. Outstanding talents are present in children and youth from all cultural groups, across all economic strata, and in all areas of human endeavor. (p. 26)

Relative to meeting gifted education goals, the U.S. Department of Education (1993) set forth several recommendations for action:

(1) to establish standards of performance that are high enough to challenge gifted and potentially gifted students;

(2) to establish learning opportunities that are accelerated, comprehensive, advanced, and diverse enough to meet the needs of gifted and potentially gifted students;

(3) to improve access to programs in the early years for all children, particularly students of color and low SES students; and

(4) to develop increased opportunities for minority and low SES students to participate in advanced learning experiences.

Along with identifying and assessing gifted children in more equitable ways, the definition and recommendations compel educators to find more equitable ways to *serve* gifted students. Multicultural education holds some promises here.

Gifted Education Models in Profile

Several models or programs exist for meeting the needs of gifted students. Space limitations do not permit a discussion of every model and program; thus, we focus on seven of the more common ones: (1) Bloom's Taxonomy of Cognitive Educational Objectives; (2) Renzulli's Enrichment Triad and Schoolwide Enrichment Program; (3) Philosophy for Children; (4) Higher Order Thinking Skills (HOTS); (5) Junior Great Books; (6) Odyssey of the Mind; and (7) Future Problem Solving.

Bloom's Taxonomy of Educational Objectives. Many educators believe that gifted students must be taught at higher levels of thinking. Thus, regardless of the specific program adopted, most, if not all schools, use Bloom's Taxonomy of Cognitive Educational Objectives (Bloom, 1956; see Figure 3.4). Whether gifted students are served in resource rooms, pullout programs, independent study, or special classes, an underlying premise is the need to challenge students intellectually and academically, and the highest levels of Bloom's Taxonomy — analysis, synthesis, and evaluation — are often adopted to help meet this goal. Further, there is the belief that gifted students should receive more instruction in higher-order thinking and problem-solving than other students. We differ with this perspective. Higher-level think-

Figure 3.4 Bloom's Taxonomy of Educational Objectives

Category/Level	Definition
Knowledge	Students can remember and recall what has been taught.
Comprehension	Students can demonstrate basic understanding of concepts, information, and facts.
Application	Students can transfer knowledge learned in one situation to another. They can apply what they have learned.
Analysis	Students can understand how parts relate to the whole. Students can understand structure and motive by examining, comparing and contrasting.
Synthesis	Students can change, (re)form, remake, or rebuild parts to make a new whole.
Evaluation	Students can judge the value of something using relevant criteria; students can support belief, judgment, opinion, perspective, and point of view.

ing, creative thinking, and problem-solving skills are not the sole prerogative of gifted children. *All* children must be taught to think at higher levels and to solve problems. All children should have these skills and strategies at their disposal. However, gifted children may need exposure to more complex types of problems, analogies, and other skills involved in thinking at higher levels, and they may need to be exposed to these skills at an earlier age than other students. Thus, we believe there is a continuum of higher-order thinking that goes from concrete to abstract, from simple to complex, at *all* levels in Bloom's Taxonomy. Specifically, some critical thinking tasks can be more challenging than others, just as some problems are more difficult to solve than others. Nonetheless, all children should be exposed to problem-solving and critical thinking at appropriate levels of complexity and pacing.

Table 3.2, developed by Kaplan (1979), presents a matrix of Bloom's Taxonomy to help teachers implement higher-level thinking skills in their classrooms. The matrix demonstrates that the type of questions asked and products generated facilitate different levels of complexity in thinking.

Renzulli's Enrichment Triad. This model (more recently called the Schoolwide Enrichment Program) also has qualitative and quantitative goals for gifted students. Renzulli's (Renzulli & Reis, 1977, 1997) models have played a major role in developing and nurturing talent, particularly among minority and low SES students. It represents one of the most inclusive gifted

Table 3.2 Kaplan Matrix Using Bloom's Taxonomy

Content or Concepts	Knowledge	Comprehension	Application	Analysis	Synthesis	Evaluation
Volcanoes	List facts about Mt. Saint Helens' devastation.	Compare Mt. Saint Helens to the volcanoes of Hawaii.	How could we use the piles of ash?	What do the people near Mt. Saint Helens feel?	Make a volcano model for class.	Are all things about Mt. Saint Helens bad? Why?
Minerals	Name the important gems found in the Northeast.	Contrast the hardness of the minerals found in the Northeast.	Field-test the hardness of 10 minerals.	What would happen if the government imposed tougher mining regulations?	Grow crystals of various shapes and colors.	What do you think of people who hoard gems? Why?
Space travel	Name all the people who have gone to the moon.	Compare the Russian space program to the U.S. program.	If you were an astronaut, what would you study about space?	What do you think would happen if we found life elsewhere?	Make a rocket and fly it.	What are some of the negative things about being an astronaut and why?
Weather and climate	Describe the different types of clouds.	Contrast the climates of the Southeast and the Southwest.	Chart the amount of rainfall for the next week.	What effect does acid rain have on the weather?	Create a wind generator.	Which climate best suits your lifestyle and why?

education models. For example, the Triad model targets the top 15% to 25% of the student population, compared to many programs that serve 3% to 5%. Further, the Schoolwide model targets talent development in all students, thereby giving every child an opportunity for enrichment experiences that focus on interests and hidden abilities. At its highest level, the models are designed:

1. to assist students in becoming actual investigators of real problems or topics using an inquiry method;
2. to provide students with opportunities for taking an active part in formulating problems to be investigated, along with methods for attacking problems;
3. to provide students with information (raw data) rather than reporting about conclusions reached by others;
4. to provide students with opportunities for inquiry directed toward some tangible product; and
5. to provide students with an opportunity to apply thinking and feeling processes to real situations rather than structured exercises.

The Schoolwide Enrichment Model represents the essence of talent development, which raises the level of instruction for students who might otherwise be underchallenged (or unchallenged) by traditional teaching methods. This type of philosophy and program is essential in urban settings where social conditions (e.g., economics) hinder optimal development.

Philosophy for Children. The main goal of Philosophy for Children is to promote excellent thinking, thinking that is creative, critical, imaginative, and logical (Lipman, 1991). The program, therefore, focuses on improving students' reasoning skills (inductive, deductive, analogical), inquiry skills (observation, description, narration), concept formation skills (definition, classification), translation skills (comprehension, listening, writing), and critical dispositions (questioning, judging, wondering). The program is interdisciplinary, but relies heavily on literature to teach these skills. This literature-based approach, by its very nature, promotes literacy, an essential life skill.

Lipman's program is based on two major assumptions: (1) children are by nature interested in philosophical issues, such as truth, fairness, and personal identity; and (2) children should learn to think for themselves, to explore alternatives to their own points of view, to consider evidence, to make careful distinctions, and to become aware of the objectives of the educational process.

Higher Order Thinking Skills. HOTS is based on cognitive psychology theories on the brain. Its goal is to develop students' higher-order thinking skills in order to improve basic skill achievement, problem-solving, and social confidence. HOTS targets such skills as: (a) developing and testing strategies for the solution of problems; (b) interpreting computer-generated feedback to determine the quality of problem-solving strategies; (c) integrating and synthesizing information from a variety of sources for solving problems; and (d) generalizing information across content areas (Pogrow, 1991). An important assumption is that "most compensatory education students are bright and should be challenged intellectually, and the key to improving students' problem-solving ability is to get them to internalize thinking strategies" (p. 63). HOTS employs Socratic teaching strategies; teachers are trained to probe student answers and to act as coaches who guide students to construct their own understanding in solving the problems posed. Therefore, like the work of Escalante and Treisman, HOTS recognizes that students cannot achieve at higher levels without higher expectations and increased exposure to quality curriculum and instruction.

Junior Great Books. Like many programs used in gifted education, Junior Great Books is directed at improving students' critical thinking skills. This goal is accomplished through literature, primarily folk tales, and thematic and metaphorical structures. Substantive and early reading of folk tales, contends Junior Great Books, lays the foundation for students to better understand the nuances associated with more traditional literary forms, such as works by Shakespeare and Dickens.

In adopting folk tales as the foundation for its literature, Junior Great Books gives students the opportunity to "grapple with profound and sustaining truths that have stood the test of untold ages" (website, p. 2). Its shared inquiry approach allows students to take possession of these truths for themselves, to internalize the essential meanings of humankind. Further, because folk tales speak on an emotional and moral level, they contribute to students' intellectual and imaginative development.

Students read such books as *Beauty and the Beast, The Magic Flute, The Winter's Tale, Cinderella, The Ugly Duckling,* and *Death in Venice.* Our review of the booklists for the three age groups (emerging readers, middle school, and high school) reveals that Junior Great Books includes many multicultural books that represent the four major minority groups. The organization also includes books from international writers. Thus, students also read *Coyote Rides the Sun, The Singing Tortoise, The Terrible Leak,* and *Anansi's Fishing Expedition.*

Junior Great Books has five learning objectives—reading, thinking, writing, speaking, and listening. Reading strategies include citing specific passages, comparing passages, and considering different interpretations; reading comprehension targets recall of details, understanding cause and effect, and analyzing an author's tone and purpose. Reading vocabulary helps students to comprehend through content, to understand multiple-meaning words, and to understand metaphors and figures of speech.

The two thinking objectives focus on improving students' ability to generate and support ideas (e.g., identify a problem, clarify an argument, support an argument, and use inference), and helping students to evaluate and revise ideas (e.g., consider more than one perspective, question and test an argument, draw conclusions, and revise and improve an argument).

Writing objectives target note-taking, persuasive writing, relating personal experiences to ideas, using story themes in writing, and writing creatively. Speaking objectives include stating ideas clearly and fully, explaining and defending concepts, agreeing and disagreeing in constructive ways, and maintaining purposeful discussions. Finally, the program helps to improve students' listening skills. Students learn to listen for different ideas, to ask for clarification, and to synthesize and build on the ideas of others. Just as important, Junior Great Books promotes literacy.

Odyssey of the Mind. This program promotes creative team-based problem-solving for students of all ages. Students learn divergent thinking and problem-solving skills while participating in a series of activities that lead to an annual competition. Students solve problems in a variety of areas—from building mechanical devices to giving their interpretation of literary classics. OM's philosophy is that students can learn lifelong skills (such as working as a team, evaluating ideas, making decisions, and creating solutions) while developing self-confidence. OM's mission includes nurturing creativity, cooperation, self-respect, and respect for others. These are essential skills that help students in school and life.

Future Problem Solving Program. The FPSP was founded by E. Paul Torrance in 1974. The FPSP has been adopted in many school districts, with virtually every state having an affiliation. Participants in the programs discover diverse ways of thinking, and the challenge of solving open-ended problems. The focus is on how to think (not what to think). It assists students in: (a) thinking more creatively and enthusiastically; (b) developing an interactive interest in the future; (c) improving oral and written communication skills; and (d) solving difficult problems using the FPSP Six-Step process. Students work cooperatively with their teammates, learn about complex societal issues, develop important research skills, and think critically and analytically. The six-step foundation to building dynamic, creative thinking processes includes:

1. brainstorming topic-related problems;
2. identifying an underlying problem;
3. brainstorming potential solutions to the underlying problem;
4. developing criteria to judge solutions;
5. evaluating all solutions to determine the best solution; and
6. describing the best solution to develop an action plan.

Being receptive to varying skill levels, FPSP offers competitive and non-competitive programs. There are three components to FPSP: Future Problem Solving, Community Problem Solving, and Scenario Writing.

Community problem solving component. Students apply the problem-solving process to real community problems. Through Community Problem Solving, students implement a wide range of solutions. CPS helps students to:

1. Develop creative thinking; exercise critical and analytical thought; engage in research; evaluate information for truth, clarity, and worth; improve verbal and written communication skills;
2. Determine and utilize problem-solving strategies; convert-problem solving from the hypothetical to the practical;
3. Bridge the gap between school and community through involvement; increase awareness of and interest in the future; and
4. Develop teamwork skills; develop self-confidence; and demonstrate and evaluate the impact students' efforts can have on problems around them.

Future problem-solving component. This component challenges students to apply information to complicated issues. By researching, thinking, and making decisions creatively, students are expected to become proficient problem-solvers. Ideally, the skills learned can be applied to any curriculum and in real-world situations. The program targets increased interactive skills, vocabulary, and decision-making. FPS has both a curricular and competitive component.

Scenario writing component. This component encourages students to develop futuristic scenarios. As information is gathered and integrated into scenarios, students personally experience the impact of applying what they learn to their respective futures.

For the purposes of the Future Problem Solving Program, a scenario is a story that might take place as a logical outgrowth of actions or events that took place earlier. It is a prediction of the future and is written as though the

Table 3.3 Multicultural Gifted Education: A Synthesis of Goals and Objectives

Goals & Rationale	Gifted Education	Multicultural Education	Multicultural Gifted Education
Needs	Meet individual needs of students based on ability and interests	Meet individual needs of students based on ethnicity and culture	Meet individual needs of students based on ability and socio-demographic variables—SES, culture, ethnicity, and gender
Equity	Gifted students have a right to an education that is non-discriminatory, to educational programs and services that meet their cognitive and academic needs	Culturally and ethnically diverse students have a right to an education that is non-discriminatory, an education that meets their needs as cultural and ethnic beings	Gifted students have a right to an education that is nondiscriminatory; and to educational programs and services that meet their cognitive and academic needs, regardless of culture, ethnicity, gender, and SES
Excellence	Gifted students cannot achieve their potential when educational standards fail to challenge these students Curricular and instructional modifications are essential for meeting the needs of highly able students	Minority students cannot achieve to their potential when expectations are low, or fail to consider their culture and ethnicity Curricular and instructional modifications are essential for meeting the needs of ethnically and culturally diverse students	Gifted students cannot achieve to their potential when educational standards and expectations are low based on culture, ethnicity, gender, and SES Curricular and instructional modifications are essential for meeting the needs of highly able students of all racial/ethnic backgrounds, both gender groups, and all SES levels
Grouping	Ability grouping facilitates the academic and cognitive development of gifted students; gifted students perform better when taught with true peers (cognitive and social)	Cooperative and peer grouping provides social support and builds relationships; ethnically and culturally diverse students perform better academically and socio-emotionally when the learning environment is supportive, nurturing, and affirming	Grouping promotes academic and social development; all students perform best academically and socio-emotionally when the learning environment is supportive, nurturing, and affirming

Under-achievement	Underachievement must be prevented or reversed so that gifted students reach their potential in school and life	Underachievement must be prevented or reversed so that culturally and ethnically diverse students reach their potential in school and life	Underachievement must be prevented or reversed so that gifted students reach their potential in school and life, regardless of culture, ethnicity, gender, and SES
Affective & supportive services	Supportive services must be present in schools to help gifted students to adjust psychologically and socially, and to increase gifted students' self-understanding and appreciation of abilities	Supportive services must be present in schools to help ethnically and culturally diverse students to adjust psychologically and socially—to increase their self-understanding and appreciation of culture and ethnicity	Supportive services must be present in schools to help all students to adjust psychologically and socially, regardless of socio-demographic variables; students must have self-understanding, and appreciate and respect their ethnicity/culture and gender
Teacher training	Teachers must be trained to work effectively with gifted students; to provide a relevant and rigorous education	Teachers must be trained to work effectively with minority students; to provide a culturally relevant and appropriate education	Teachers must be trained to work effectively with all gifted students; to provide an academically rigorous and culturally relevant education
Lifelong goals	Gifted education helps children to become responsible adults who make a contribution to society	Education helps minority children to become responsible adults who make a contribution to society	Education helps gifted children from all backgrounds become responsible adults who make a contribution to society; citizens who are culturally competent, as well as socially active, responsive, and responsible

future were the present. The scenario is a very short story in which one possible outcome of the future is developed through characters and plot. Each scenario is set at least 20 years in the future and must have a recognizable relationship to one of the FPS topics for the current year.

A SYNTHESIS OF GOALS AND OBJECTIVES: MULTICULTURAL GIFTED EDUCATION

To educate all our children and allow America to compete in a global economy and all fields of human endeavor, the nation must provide an environment in which gifted and talented students, along with all of our children, can reach their full potential
—National Association for Gifted Children
Position Paper (1994b)

The goals, objectives, and theoretical perspectives of multicultural education and gifted education are more similar and complimentary than different. As described in Table 3.3, both fields seek equity and excellence for its students. Themes of meeting needs—intellectual, academic, academic, and aesthetic—run through both fields, validating the need for programs and services for each particular student population.

In Table 3.3, we have highlighted the themes underlying both fields and then combined the two fields, resulting in multicultural gifted education. This book operates from the fundamental belief that (1) gifted education must integrate the goals and philosophies of multicultural education into its curriculum, namely attending more issues of diversity; and (2) multicultural education must incorporate goals and philosophies of gifted education into its curriculum, namely by challenging children cognitively and academically. Multicultural gifted education supports and challenges children intellectually, academically, affectively, and aesthetically.

CHAPTER 4

Assessment: Multicultural Considerations

OVERVIEW

Before minority students can be identified and served as gifted students, they must be assessed; hence, this chapter. Virtually every school district is wrestling with issues surrounding the underrepresentation of minority students in gifted education. Assessment instruments and practices are often blamed for minority students' poor presence in gifted education. This chapter, therefore, addresses the assessment of minority students. We pay considerable attention to ethical principles and test standards relative to racially and culturally diverse students. Recommendations for ensuring and safeguarding equity in assessment on behalf of gifted minority students are presented. We also present a case study that helps to highlight, reinforce, and extend information presented in this chapter.

ETHICS AND EQUITY IN THE ASSESSMENT OF DIVERSE STUDENTS

Educators today are faced with standards and ethical guidelines that demand a higher level of practice than was the case a decade ago. Educators are also being held to higher standards of multicultural practices that compel them to develop specific competencies for more appropriately interacting with and assessing a culturally, racially, and linguistically diverse student population. The overwhelming issues surrounding minority student underrepresentation in gifted programs focus on assessment. The central issue is how to identify more diverse students for gifted programs, often translated as, "What is the best test to identify minority students?"

In July 1997, the National Association for Gifted Children (NAGC, 1997) adopted its policy statement on testing and assessment of gifted students (Figure 4.1). The statement calls for more equitable identification and

**Figure 4.1 NAGC Position Paper: The Use of Tests in the Identification
and Assessment of Gifted Students**

Most school districts use some form of standardized achievement, intelligence, or
creativity tests in the identification and screening process for gifted programs and
services. When used properly and when selected with care, these instruments may
provide valuable information about students' abilities, including their strengths and
weaknesses. Tests are also valuable for assessing students' needs, and for designing
programs and services based on these needs. Despite their potential usefulness, tests also
have limitations. Testing instruments are not perfect or infallible predictors of
intelligence, achievement or ability and, thus, should be selected and used carefully.
While critically important in all assessment, this precaution must be given even greater
consideration when assessing underserved gifted students (i.e., young children, culturally
diverse students, linguistically diverse students, economically disadvantaged students,
and students with other special educational needs).

Given the limitations of all tests, *no single measure* should be used to make identification
and placement decisions. That is, no single test or instrument should be used to include a
child in or exclude a child from gifted education services. The most effective and
equitable means of serving gifted students is to *assess* them—to identify their strengths
and weaknesses, and to prescribe services based on these needs. Testing situations should
not hinder students' performance. Students must feel comfortable, relaxed, and have a
good rapport with the examiner. Best practices indicate that multiple measures and
different types of indicators from multiple sources must be used to assess and serve gifted
students. Information should be gathered from multiple sources (caregivers/families,
teachers, students, and others with significant knowledge of the students), in different
ways (e.g., observations, performances, products, portfolios, interviews), and in different
contexts (e.g., in-school and out-of-school settings).

Any school personnel who administer, use, or advise others in the use of standardized
tests should be qualified to do so. They should:

(1)   Understand measurement principles, including how to evaluate the test's
        technical claims (e.g., validity and reliability);

(2)   Know about the particular test used, its appropriate uses, and its limitations,
        including possible consequences resulting from scores;

(3)   Administer, score, and interpret results in a professional and responsible
        manner;

(4)   Employ procedures necessary to reduce or eliminate bias in test selection,
        administration, and interpretation;

(5)   Understand the influence of cultural diversity, linguistic diversity, and socio-
        economic disadvantages on test performance; and

(6)   Weigh the results of tests carefully with other information.

NAGC advocates that all school personnel continue to explore, adapt, and evaluate
comprehensive assessment alternatives to ensure that *all* gifted students are given an
equal opportunity to develop their potential.

assessment instruments and procedures. Underlying the paper are notions of equity and accountability.

Issues of Test Bias

One of the more prominent issues in the testing of minority students is test bias. Three types of biases are described here: (a) content validity; (b) construct validity; and (c) predictive validity. The perception that bias is inherent in psychological testing has a long history, which will not be discussed here. However, Gould (1981) offers a comprehensive and substantive discussion of the topic. Concerns associated with test biases have spurred numerous debates, challenges, and accusations, the most recent being by Murray and Herrnstein (1994). To ensure equity on behalf of minority students, educators must be aware of these issues; more important, they must act upon them.

Content validity bias is the most frequent accusation of bias. Content validity is the degree to which an instrument measures an intended content area. It is determined by expert judgment and requires both item validity and sampling validity. Thus, when bias is considered, it is directed at items that seem inappropriate or offensive to a group. Specifically, Reynolds and Kamphaus (1990) describe content validity bias in the following manner:

> An item or subscale of a test is considered to be biased in content when it is demonstrated to be relatively more difficult for members of one group than for members of another in a situation where the general ability level of the groups being compared is held constant and no reasonable theoretical rationale exists to explain groups differences on the item (or subscale) in question. (p. 625)

For instance, a popular achievement test asks students the following: "What is a minority group?" Students choose from the following: (1) a group that is thought of as different; (2) a group of poor people; (3) a group that cannot vote; or (4) a group that is treated unfairly. And on many intelligence tests, students are asked to respond to questions assumed to be shared by all, questions thought to reflect common knowledge and experiences. Thus, on a famous intelligence test, students are asked: "Why do people wear sunglasses?" "Why do people go to the doctor?" " Why do we put postage on envelopes?" Unfortunately, many children do not have sunglasses, nor have many been to the doctor or mailed letters. In essence, certain sections of standardized tests tap experiences, social skills and middle class values.

Construct validity is the degree to which an instrument measures an intended hypothetical construct, or nonobservable trait, which explains behavior. A construct cannot be seen; one makes inferences based on behaviors. Intelligence, achievement, and many other variables in the social sciences represent constructs. Intelligence cannot be observed; rather, one makes inferences based on behaviors. Thus, if intelligence is defined as having a large vocabulary, a child with an extensive vocabulary will be considered intelligent. Similarly, if intelligence is defined as learning quickly, a child who learns faster than others will be considered intelligent. When different groups hold different notions or definitions of a construct, concerns over construct bias become evident. Thus, students who hold different notions or definitions of "intelligence" often find themselves at a disadvantage in school.

Finally, predictive validity is the degree to which an instrument is able to predict how well an individual will do in a future situation. Bias exists when there is error in the inference for prediction as a function of membership in a particular group. For instance, if a student scores low on an intelligence test, it is often interpreted to mean that he or she will not do well in school. Compounding this prediction is that when the student is from a minority group, the low test results may be used to confirm a teacher's perception or prediction that the student is not able. The test results may contribute to low teacher expectations and, thereby, contribute to low student achievement (Rosenthal & Jacobson, 1968). Relatedly, low teacher expectations may contribute to low teacher referral of minority students for gifted education services (Ford, 1996; Frasier, Martin, et al., 1995; High & Udall, 1983). Several studies on gifted and minority students present troubling findings. For instance, Moody (1990) reported that teachers treat Black and White students differently. Their data indicate that when White students ask questions, explore, and touch, teachers see them as gifted and smart; however, when Black students behave in this way, teachers see them as behavioral problems. Similarly, Grossman (1991) noted that research has found that even if Black children are identified as gifted, teachers give them less praise, less attention, and more negative feedback.

Educators have several options from which to choose when considering how best to assess ability and potential in linguistically, racially, and culturally diverse students: (a) adapt instruments (e.g., modify the instruments relative to language); (b) renorm the selected instruments based on local norms and needs; (c) modify predetermined cutoff scores for minority students; and (d) use alternative instruments thought to measure the same construct (e.g., Kaufman Assessment Battery for Children or the Raven's Matrices is used instead of the WISCIII as a measure of intelligence). Beyond making such accommodations, educators can also adopt certain guidelines when providing services to linguistically and culturally diverse students. This set of governing principles is described below[8].

1. Educators are cognizant of relevant research and practice issues regarding the population being assessed.
   a. Educators acknowledge that ethnicity and culture impact behavior and performance, and they take these factors into account when working with various racially and culturally diverse students.
   b. Educators seek educational and training experiences to enhance their understanding and competence, thereby addressing the needs of minority students more effectively and appropriately. These experiences include cultural, sociological, psychological, economic, political, and historical materials specific to the groups being served.
   c. Educators recognize the limits of their competencies and expertise. Those who do not possess knowledge and training about diverse students seek consultation and make referrals to experts as necessary.
   d. Educators consider the validity of a given instrument and interpret results with the cultural and linguistic characteristics of minority students in mind.
2. Educators recognize diversity and culture as significant parameters in understanding psychological processes.
   a. Educators are aware of how their own racial and cultural background, experience, attitudes, values, and biases influence psychological processes. They make efforts to correct any prejudices and biases.
   b. Educators increase students' awareness of their own cultural values and norms; they help students apply this awareness to their own lives and society at large.
   c. Educators recognize that because cultural groups differ in the extent to which they share the values that underlie testing, the imposition of tests raises questions regarding equity.
3. Educators respect the roles of family members as well as community structures, hierarchies, values, and beliefs within the student's culture. Thus, educators:
   a. identify resources in the family and community of diverse students.
   b. ensure that family members have a clear understanding of testing and how results will be used.
   c. respect the religious or spiritual beliefs and values of diverse families.
   d. become familiar with indigenous beliefs and practices of diverse students.
4. Educators interact in the language requested by students; if not feasible, they make appropriate referral or find a translator.
   a. Educators communicate results and interpretations so they are understood by students and their families.
   b. Educators recognize that assessing linguistically diverse students with

instruments written in English and normed on monolingual English-speaking students yields data of unknown validity, as well as data that cannot be meaningfully aggregated.

5. Educators consider the impact of adverse social, environmental, and political factors in assessment and intervention (e.g., curriculum and instruction, programming).

    a. Educators help ensure that the type of intervention recommended matches the student's particular needs.

    b. Educators acknowledge and attempt to eliminate practices that are discriminatory, biased, or otherwise unethical.

    c. Educators are aware of sociopolitical contexts in conducting evaluations and providing interventions.

    d. Educators document culturally and sociopolitically relevant factors in students' records (e.g., number of years or generations in the U.S.; fluency in English; nature and extent of family support and community resources; level of education of family members; socio-economic status (SES); relations with people of different racial and cultural groups).

    e. Educators give students adequate preparation to know the content being assessed.

The aforementioned set of governing principles has important implications for educators seeking equity in the assessment process. The principles hold that educators — professionals — must be responsible for test outcomes, and assume professional responsibility for acquiring the needed competencies to be most effective.

In many ways, admittance to gifted programs is based on high-stakes testing — those who meet the designated cutoff test score are identified as gifted and receive services; those who fail to meet the criteria do not receive services. We must not forget about the needs of students who have failed to score high on these tests and, subsequently, have been denied gifted education services — too often, these are racially, culturally, and linguistically diverse students.

ASSESSMENT ISSUES WITH LIMITED ENGLISH PROFICIENT STUDENTS

At least seven issues have serious implications for the boundaries of competence within which educators can work, such as maintaining expertise, basis for making judgments, communicating effectively, understanding human diversity, and other competencies that influence test results.

Boundaries of Competence

Included in the boundaries are competencies related to working with linguistically, racially, and culturally diverse populations. Essentially, this standard holds that psychologists should provide psychological assessment services only within the boundaries of their competence — based on their education, training, and appropriate professional experience. When training does not yet exist, professionals take reasonable steps to ensure the competence of their work and to protect students, their families, and others from harm. Thus, not only must educators focus on their competencies in skills, but also their efficacy in applying these skills to diverse students.

Maintaining Expertise

Educators who engage in assessment, teaching, and other professional activities should maintain a reasonable level of awareness of current scientific and professional information in their field, and engage in ongoing efforts to maintain competence in the skills they use. These efforts must include increasing competencies in working with minority students, gifted students, and other students in the school system who require or seek the guidance and assistance of educators.

Basis for Scientific and Professional Judgments

Educators rely on scientifically and professionally derived knowledge when making scientific or professional judgments or when engaging in scholarly or professional endeavors. This standard highlights the need for educators to be objective in their work, to avoid making decisions based on personal opinions, attitudes, and values.

Describing the Nature and Results of Testing

When educators provide services (e.g., assessment, evaluation, and teaching), they must do so using language that is reasonably understandable to the recipient of those services. In so doing, the students feel comfortable and receptive to the services offered.

Human Differences

In their work, educators are being increasingly required to address human differences in ability, ethnicity, culture, language, socio-economic status (SES), and other socio-demographic variables. Hence, educators must obtain the training, experience, and supervision necessary to ensure the competence of their services where differences in age, gender, race, ethnicity, national origin, language, SES, disability, and so forth significantly affect the educators' work with a particular individual or member of the respective group. If educators lack competencies in working with individual differences, they make appropriate referrals.

Respecting Others

In their work and work-related activities, educators respect the rights of others to hold values, attitudes, and opinions that differ from their own. It is essential that the values of minority groups regarding tests be examined. Albeit implicit, the predominant values associated with tests and testing are those of policymakers, test developers, and test users. We cannot assume or deny the social and interpersonal meanings associated with tests. Stated differently, too many tests tap factual information and knowledge, looking for the "right" answers; too few tests value subjectivity—feelings, reflection, and introspection (Madaus, 1994).

Nondiscrimination. In their work and work-related activities, educators must not engage in discrimination based on race, ethnicity, language, SES, gender, and other socio-demographic variables. Much of the literature on testing and diverse populations focuses on allegations of discrimination from the test itself to interpretations of results to intervention and decision-making. Educators must pay careful attention, as discussed in this chapter, to ensure that minority students are treated fairly throughout the assessment process.

Other Forms of Harassment. Educators must not knowingly engage in behavior that is harassing or demeaning to students based on factors such as the students' age, gender, race, ethnicity, language, SES, and other socio-demographic variables. Educators, for example, must not knowingly deny a student academic admittance to programs or advancement based solely on socio-demographic variables.

Personal Problems and Conflicts

Educators are human beings and, hence, not infallible. This standard addresses problems and conflicts at two stages—prior to initiating a professional relationship and during or throughout the relationship. Educators concerned about ethical conduct recognize that their personal problems and conflicts may interfere with their effectiveness. Accordingly, they must refrain from undertaking an activity when they know or should know that their personal problems are likely to lead to harming a student or the group to whom they owe a professional obligation.

Educators also have an obligation to be alert to signs of their personal problems early in the professional relationship, and to seek assistance in order to prevent impairing their effectiveness and performance. For instance, if a teacher is not familiar with the values and traditions of a diverse group, he/she should seek guidance and support from a representative of that group. Finally, when educators become aware of personal problems that interfere with their work and effectiveness, they take appropriate steps to determine how to proceed (e.g., should they limit, suspend, or terminate the professional relationship and related duties?).

SUMMARY OF ASSESSMENT CONSIDERATIONS

It goes without saying that high-stakes testing dominates in school settings. Thus, tests and their results must be used with caution, and educators who develop, administer, score, interpret, or use assessment instruments must do so when it is useful for improving the student's educational outcomes. We must be familiar with the reliability and validity of instruments used with minority students. This also requires recognizing the limits of tests for making judgments or predictions about racially and culturally diverse students. Specifically, school personnel must identify situations in which certain instruments and norms may not be applicable, or when they may require adjustment in administration or interpretation because of such factors as the student's race, ethnicity, gender, language, SES, or other socio-demographic variables.

We recognize that making adjustments to increase the representation of minority students in gifted programs has been controversial (e.g., lowering test cutoff scores). On the one hand, proponents of adjustments argue that the heavy or exclusive reliance on standardized tests inhibits the representation of minority students in gifted programs; on the other hand, opponents argue that making adjustments comprises standards and is unfair to students who meet traditional criteria. Several options regarding test outcomes have been recommended, however, to increase the representation of minority students in gifted education. The following must be considered: (a) re-norming tests and instruments based on local needs; (b) using the subgroup norms established by test developers for each minority group—in many cases, this means lowering the predesignated cutoff test scores; (c) using a range of scores; (d) using alternative or nontraditional instruments believed to measure the same construct (e.g., replace the Weschler intelligence tests with the Raven's Matrices); and (e) basing placement decisions and gifted services on multiple assessment criteria and sources of information (e.g., matrices). Many efforts are underway in gifted education, primarily through Javits programs, to locate valid and reliable instruments for identifying talent and potential among minority students (U.S. Department of Education, 1993).

As this chapter suggests, assessment is a complex enterprise and its results have a significant impact on the lives of students. Educators involved in assessment have a responsibility to adhere to ethical guidelines, which helps to ensure equity on behalf of all students, regardless of socio-economic status, and racial, cultural, and linguistic backgrounds.

IMPLICATIONS FOR GIFTED EDUCATION

Nationally, school districts rely heavily or solely on norm-referenced intelligence or achievement tests as their primary assessment instruments. Testing is also big business in gifted education. Data indicate that the majority of schools rely extensively on standardized intelligence and achievement tests in the identification of gifted students. Specifically, Archambault et al. (1993) surveyed over 3000 third- and fourth-grade teachers regarding identification practices. Results indicated that most of the public school teachers used achievement tests (79%), followed closely by IQ tests (72%). Similarly, a study by VanTassel-Baska, Patton, and Prillaman (1989) revealed that almost 90% of states rely primarily on standardized, norm-referenced tests to identify gifted students. In fact, the study found that few states make accommodations for students from economically and racially diverse groups. That is, schools seldom use multidimensional, multimodal assessment strategies, even though numerous researchers have emphasized the importance of this identification strategy. VanTassel-Baska and colleagues reported that only 12 districts have adopted definitions of "disadvantaged" gifted students. Of those, nine districts reported a definitional construct, and four included culturally different, minority, and low SES students. One definition reported by the researchers follows:

> . . . those children regardless of race or ethnic group who may have language patterns and experiences, cultural backgrounds, economic disadvantages, educational disadvantages, or differences that make it difficult for them to demonstrate their potential using traditional identification procedures. (p. 10)

Albeit long overdue, Coleman and Gallagher (1992) and Coleman, Gallagher, and Foster (1994) noted that some, but not all, states have begun to screen all student files for indications of giftedness, to require a plan for staff development of regular education staff to increase their ability to recognize nontraditional students who may be gifted, to use checklists in identifying underachieving gifted students, to use autobiographies for additional assistance, and to refer students for further assessment if they obtain scores at the 85th percentile or above on standardized tests. Nonetheless, we too often continue to attach a cutoff number, IQ score, or percentile in our identification practices. Holistic assessment strategies, culturally sensitive tests, parent and peer nominations, portfolio and performance-based assessments, and creativity checklists, for example, along with learning style assessments, represent promising strategies for identifying underrepresented students for gifted programs (Ford, 1996).

The perceptions and recommendations of teachers are also given extensive weight in the identification of gifted students. Tuttle, Becker, and Sousa (1988) and Cox, Daniel, and Boston (1985) noted that the most prevalent method of identifying gifted learners is teacher recommendations, a method they and others have found to be inadequate. Archambault et al. (1993) also reported that teachers are among the most highly used sources of referral and identification — 70% of school districts rely on teacher nominations. Yet teachers are not necessarily effective at identifying gifted students.

Specifically, Pegnato and Birch (1959) found that junior high school teachers not only failed to nominate over 50% of the gifted students in their school, but they also identified many average students as gifted. Jacobs (1971) found that primary teachers surveyed could identify only 10% of the students who had scored high on individual IQ tests. Cox, Daniel, and Boston (1985) found that almost 38% of the third- and fourth-grade teachers in their study reported unidentified gifted students in their classrooms; yet 90% of school districts used teacher nominations for identification purposes. Further, teachers are less likely to refer or nominate minority students for gifted services than White students (High & Udall, 1983).

The inability of teachers to reliably identify gifted and gifted minority students has important implications for their assessment competence. The concern over teachers' inadequacy in assessing students for educational programs prompted a report by the American Federation of Teachers, National Council on Measurement in Education, and National Educational Association (1990). The report recognized the critical role of teachers in student outcomes, and recommended that teachers demonstrate competence in student assessment, including

1. understanding students' cultural backgrounds, interests, skills, and abilities as they apply across a range of learning domains and subject areas;

2. understanding students' motivations and interests in specific subject areas, as well as interest and motivation regarding class content;
3. clarifying and articulating the performance outcomes expected of students;
4. judging the extent of student attainment of instructional outcomes;
5. communicating strengths and weaknesses to students based on assessment results;
6. recording and reporting assessment results for decision-making purposes;
7. evaluating the effectiveness of curriculum and instruction, and making appropriate adjustments;
8. working with school personnel and decisionmakers to develop and select assessment methods for building or school purposes;
9. participating in reviews regarding the effectiveness of assessment instruments and methods; and
10. interpreting the results of state and national student assessment programs.

These activities require that teachers be skilled in: *choosing and developing* assessment methods appropriate for instruction decisions; *administering, scoring, and interpreting* the results of both externally produced and teacher-produced assessment methods; *using* assessment results when making decisions about individual students, planning teaching, and developing curriculum; *communicating* assessment results to students and parents; and *recognizing* unethical, illegal, and otherwise inappropriate assessment methods and uses of assessment instruments. In essence, like psychologists, teachers and other educators must take professional responsibility for how assessment results are used and the impact of assessments on gifted minority student outcomes.

In gifted education, an important outcome of testing relates to placement in gifted programs. Too often, minority students are excluded based on poor test score performance and lack of teacher referral or nomination. This raises a number of important questions: How can teachers, a major variable in the assessment process, use assessment results to help identify gifted and potentially gifted minority students? Are teachers able to address the extent to which they believe the results are invalid and otherwise limited for individual minority students? What suggestions might teachers make, based on their interactions with students, about the most appropriate method(s) and instruments for assessing minority students' abilities, strengths, and potential? How might teachers, based on assessment results, develop the most appropriate gifted education services for minority students? In essence, how can teachers, the school professionals who work most closely with students, become more qualified and skilled in the assessment of gifted students, particularly culturally, racially, and linguistically diverse students?

Admittance to gifted programs is based on high-stakes testing—those who meet the designated cutoff test score receive services; those who fail to meet the criteria do not receive services. Certainly, educators must be concerned with programming and services offered to those who pass high-stakes tests; however, we must not forget about the needs of students who have failed these tests and subsequently been denied gifted education services—too often, those denied gifted education services are racially, culturally, and linguistically diverse students. Below, we use a case study with one student, Dewayne, to illustrate the important role of assessment instruments, personnel, and practices in recognizing the needs and abilities of gifted students.

ASSESSMENT OF MINORITY STUDENTS: THE CASE OF DEWAYNE

School Setting and Background Information

This case takes place in an urban school district of 25,000 students. Black students represent 67% of district, Hispanic Americans are 20%, and the remaining students are White (13%). Conversely, 65% of the gifted program is White, 25% are Black, and 10% are Hispanic Americans. Students are screened in grade 2 and identified in grade 3. They are served in a pullout program (a resource room each Wednesday). Initial screening is based exclusively on teacher referral, with admission based on performance at the 95th percentile on the WISC-III or 95th percentile in reading and math on the Iowa Test of Basic Skills (ITBS).

The district is aware that minority students are underrepresented in its gifted programs, particularly at the middle and high school levels. Likewise, they know that minority students are not performing well on the two tests and are not being referred at high rates for screening. Recently, teachers have been requested to refer more students of color for screening. Informally, school personnel have been informed that the Office for Civil Rights might investigate the district.

Case Overview

Dewayne, a 10-year-old Black male, sat in the waiting area of the psychologist's office waiting to be assessed for the second time in two years. Dewayne's teacher had referred him for gifted education services. Dewayne sat patiently in the waiting room, thinking about his last visit. The last time there,

Dewayne did not do well on the test and he found the psychologist less than friendly, somewhat aloof, uninteresting, and abrupt. He kept referring to Dewayne as "Deon" and "Wayne".

Dewayne was patient, happy to miss class, but not happy to be there. "What is this test for anyway?" he wondered. His teacher said that it was for smart kids who might get to go to other classes once a week. Dewayne knew that a lot of the White students left his room on Wednesdays and went to a different school. Dewayne did not want to go, which meant leaving his friends.

As he waited, Dewayne saw the psychologist, a White male, come into a nearby room. Dewayne had to move slightly to see him clearly. The psychologist seemed to be hiding in the corner and was holding a cake. He had a sheepish grin on his face.

Three women, one of them Black, walked into the room. They did not see the psychologist. "Who's the Black lady"? Dewayne wondered. "Maybe she can test me," he thought. The psychologist jumped from his hiding place and all of them, except the Black woman, began to sing "Happy Birthday." It took a few seconds before Dewayne realized that they were singing to her.

Soon thereafter, the psychologist walked toward Dewayne and reintroduced himself as Dr. Davidson. He remembered Dewayne from the previous test administration—unfriendly, hard-to-reach students are hard to forget. Dewayne had been unwilling to sit next to him and was sarcastic and brief in his responses to the questions asked. He did not seem to care about the test or even being there for the test. He did not seem to care for the psychologist, either.

Bringing his attention back to Dewayne, Dr. Davidson saw something different. He was friendly, more relaxed, even smiling. Dewayne looked up and remarked on how pretty the cake was. He added, "The lady was so surprised!" When offered the chair across the table, Dewayne declined and sat by the psychologist. Looking up, he said, "My name is Dewayne, not Deon, not Wayne. The last time, you got it wrong. Call me 'D-e-w-a-y-n-e,'" he stressed, spelling his name. "I'm ready now."

Questions to Consider

1. What is the main problem in the case?
2. Why was there a change in Dewayne's demeanor and response to Dr. Davidson during the second meeting? Why was he more receptive to the psychologist?
3. How might the test outcomes have been affected by the climate during the first test administration? During the second administration?
4. How might Dr. Davidson's perceptions of Dewayne have influenced

his interpretation of the results during the first administration? During the second administration?

5. What factors in the case help to explain the underrepresentation of minority students in gifted programs in this district?
6. What would you do differently as a test examiner and interpreter?

As with any case study, readers often desire more information. What is Dewayne like as a student? How involved is his primary caregiver(s)? How have his siblings performed in school? What are his friends like? How did he score on the last test? What preparation have teachers had in gifted education and multicultural education? Why does the district rely exclusively on teacher referral for initial screening, and have they considered other methods of referral and other types of instruments?

In the real world, we often have to make decisions without a detailed case study of the child and surrounding circumstances. This case is no exception. However, we have provided enough information for readers to make inferences and to identify key issues. Specifically, it is clear that the first testing situation was not positive for either the examiner or the student. Test-taking conditions, including examiner effects, can influence test performance and outcomes. Although some school personnel administer standardized tests without formal training, it is safe to assume that since Dr. Davidson is a psychologist, he has been trained in testing and should be familiar with ethical standards. For example, giving the negative testing situation, Dr. Davidson should have attempted to promote a positive learning environment (i.e., try to get Dewayne to warm up, ask Dewayne about his interests and hobbies, ask Dewayne if he knew the reason for being in the office, etc.), postponed the test, or found another examiner. To clarify Dewayne's confusion or misperceptions about the test (as explained by his teacher), it is important that Dr. Davidson explain to Dewayne the reason for the assessment and how the results will be used. Of course, Dewayne's caregivers must also be given this information.

It seems reasonable to conclude that Dr. Davidson is aware that minority students are underrepresented in gifted programs. What alternative assessment instruments and procedures can he recommend? Figure 4.2 provides some options.

SUMMARY AND CONCLUSION

The best method of achieving equitable assessment is to adhere to ethical standards of testing, advanced by such authors as Sax (1989) and such professional organizations as the American Educational Research Association,

Figure 4.2 Sample Identification Instruments: A Multidimensional and Multimodal Framework

QUANTITATIVE

Traditional Measures

Weschler Intelligence Scale for Children-Revised (1)
Stanford-Binet Intelligence Test (1)
Otis-Lennon Mental Ability Test (2)
Iowa Tests of Basic Skills (2)
Comprehensive Test of Basic Skills (2)
Peabody Individual Achievement Test-Revised (2)

Nontraditional Measures

The Raven's Coloured, Standard, and Advanced Progressive Matrices (1)
The Kaufman Assessment Battery for Children (1, 2)
The Matrix Analogies Test-expanded and short forms (1)
Torrance Test of Creative Thinking (3)
Torrance Creativity Tests for Children (3)
Tests of Creativity in Movement and Action (3)
Vineland Social Maturity Scale (4)
California Preschool Competence Scale (4)
Basic Motor Ability Test (5)
Developmental Test of Visual and Motor Integration (5)
Purdue Perceptual Motor Survey (5)

QUALITATIVE

Portfolios and performance-based assessments (e.g., writing samples, artwork, audio
        or video taping of classroom discussions, journals, projects) (1–5)
Biographical inventories (1–5)
Nomination forms and checklists (completed by parents, teachers, peers, self) (1–7)
Transcripts (e.g., explore strengths in certain subjects and areas, look for inconsistent
performance) (1–5)
Learning styles inventories (6)
Motivational and attitudinal measures (7)

Promising Assessment Instruments for Developing Profiles

The Baldwin Identification Matrix
The Frasier Talent Assessment Profile
The Program of Assessment Diagnosis and Instruction
System of Multicultural Pluralistic Assessment

Note: 1=intellectual; 2=academic; 3=creative; 4=leadership; 5=visual and performing arts;
6=learning styles; 7=social and emotional (e.g., motivation, self-concept, self-esteem, attitudes
toward school, anxiety, peer relationships). Adapted from Ford (1996).

American Psychological Association, and National Council on Measurement in Education (1985), and the American Federation of Teachers, National Council on Measurement in Education, and the National Educational Association (1990). Teachers and other school personnel must be mindful that whatever the cause of poorer performance in school, the aim of intelligence testing is to identify needs in order to help and improve, not to label in order to limit. We must be wary of such testing becoming a theory of limits (Gould, 1981, pp. 152–153).

CHAPTER 5

Multicultural Curriculum and Instruction

It is not good for our children to eat and drink daily the sentiment that they are naturally inferior to Whites. . . . Cultural relevance empowers students intellectually, socially, emotionally, psychologically, and politically.

—Ladson-Billings (1994, p. 4)

INTRODUCTION AND OVERVIEW

Neither this book nor this chapter are designed to address curriculum development in detail. Instead, our objective is to demonstrate how existing curricula in both gifted education and multicultural education can be modified to accommodate diverse abilities and diverse cultures. Thus, we take several approaches to synthesizing curriculum in the two fields. First, we present barriers to implementing effective multicultural curriculum and instruction, namely biases in curriculum and instruction. Second, we modify lessons presented in several gifted education texts, illustrating ways to integrate multiculturalism into curriculum and instruction. Similarly, we modify lessons presented in multicultural education, demonstrating that these lessons can be modified to challenge students to think at higher levels. Finally, we present concept- or theme-based activities and lessons, a practice that is common in gifted education. While the lessons focus primarily on the four core content areas of math, science, social studies, and language arts, we recognize the importance of all subjects being taught from a multicultural perspective. We hope that these sample lessons help teachers to improve their knowledge, skills, and abilities relative to implementing effective multicultural gifted curricula and instruction.

LISTENING TO STUDENTS: WHY EDUCATION MUST
BE MULTICULTURAL

The most important and most effective way to determine the need for multicultural education is to listen to students. In 1993 and 1995a, Ford published the results of two studies that examined the nature and extent of underachievement among gifted Black students. Part of this examination included interviews with students regarding their perceptions of school curricula. The first study, conducted in one Ohio school district, consisted of 4th through 6th graders. The second study, conducted in five Virginia school districts, consisted of 6th through 9th graders.

When students in both studies offered comments on the curriculum, they were most likely to provide negative viewpoints, as reflected in Figure 5.1. In both studies, the students' comments reflect common themes worth noting. First, most students noted a lack of mirrors for minority groups in the curriculum; that is, most of their education focuses on the successes, contributions, accomplishments, and histories of White Americans. Students also noted that multicultural education, when addressed, was at the lowest levels of Banks's (1993, 1995, 1997) model—contributions and additive approaches. Students observed that their classes seldom focus on minority groups or other than African Americans. The Black students in both studies contend that classes consistently focus on the same minority heroes (e.g., Harriet Tubman, Martin Luther King Jr.), while also ignoring contemporary minority role models (e.g., Colin Powell, Barbara Clark, Nelson Mandela, Jesse Jackson) and controversial minority persons (e.g., Malcolm X, W. E. B. DuBois) and events (e.g., slave revolts). Students recognized that the superficial learning experiences also occurred primarily during February, Black History Month. Similarly, students recognize the focus on historical events at the expense of contemporary and pressing events in the present. These narrow discussions do not help students relate the past to the present. The students noted that school is more interesting, engaging, motivating, and relevant when they learn about their own culture and the culture of others. In essence, students' comments tell us that they *want* and *need* more multicultural education. Their overarching questions are: Why am I learning this? How does this relate to me? How will this information help me, now and in the future?

Students' comments provide important insights into what must be done to change curriculum and instruction. The students are telling us that they want their education to be relevant, meaningful, personal, and empowering. Students do not want to dwell on the past at the expense of the present and future. Ultimately, they want multiculturalism integrated throughout the curriculum in substantive ways and on a consistent basis. As one student questioned, "Is this too much to ask?" (See Ford, 1995a.)

Figure 5.1 Black Students' Perceptions of the Lack of Multiculturalism in the Curriculum

I get more interested in school when we learn about Black people. It's just more interesting. When I'm not paying attention and my teacher says something about Blacks, I drop everything and listen. I want to know what a White person has to say about Blacks. Is it good or bad? Most of what they say is in between, so I confront teachers . . . [goes on to tell how she gets into trouble for questioning teachers] (9th-grade female)

You get tired of learning about the same White people and the same things. We need to broaden our horizons and learn about other people and even other countries. The White people are just trying to advance other White people and leave us behind and ignorant! (8th-grade male)

I get tired of learning about White people in class. They [teachers] always talk about George Washington or Abe Lincoln. We never learn about Malcolm X or Martin Luther King Jr. We always learn about what White people have done. Black History Month should be more than one month. . . . It's important to learn about your culture and heritage, then you can understand yourself better. (8th-grade female)

It just excites me and I like to learn about our accomplishments. I like to watch the expressions of White students when they hear that Black people are successful. I love seeing their faces because they are shocked! They need to be educated about us—we are not bad people! (8th-grade female)

It gets so boring when you learn about White people all the time. You want and need to learn about other cultures and your heritage. . . . We learn about the same people all the time. My mom tells me about Black people, which is more interesting. I want to learn more about my own heritage. (8th-grade female)

It seems like every day we learn about White people in school. Black History Month is only one month. And even then, we don't learn a lot about Black people. Teachers leave out a lot. (7th-grade female)

Seriously, there are 12 months in a year. They choose February—the shortest month to teach Blacks about themselves. Black people get one month! White people get 11 months! . . . One month is ridiculous. You cannot fit our history into 28 days! It's not possible. White kids get 200 days! (8th-grade male)

It's more interesting to learn about Black people than to learn about Presidents who are all White. We always learn about White people; when we learn about Blacks, they are slaves. (7th-grade female)

I think we should learn more about Black people. We learn about Black people for a month. Today [Feb 28] is the last day to learn about Blacks this year. (8th-grade female)

Figure 5.1 (Con'd)

There should be an equal amount of attention given to all groups—Black, White, Hispanic, and others should be in the curriculum. . . . Blacks have contributed as much to society as White people. Blacks have come up with new theories and inventions just like White people. Blacks need to know what other Blacks have done. (7th-grade male)
I get tired of hearing about how bad Black people are doing. It would be nice to hear some good things about Black people. (8th-grade male)
Since kindergarten, all you learn is about Whites and George Washington. I haven't learned much about Black people and our history. . . . There is only one month that schools do anything for Black folks. . . . Throughout history, we have been treated like dirt . . . like during slavery; fights against integration; putting us in lower level classes . . . (9th-grade male)

Note: More detailed comments appear in Ford (1995a)

RECOGNIZING AND ELIMINATING BIAS IN THE CURRICULUM

It is impossible to have an education that is multicultural when biases exist in curriculum and instruction. Curricular biases come in many forms; some are direct and overt, others are indirect and covert. Multicultural education attempts to eliminate these biases, providing mirrors and windows that are not distorted or broken. School personnel must carefully and consistently examine the materials and resources used in curriculum and instruction. Key biases to look for are:

1. *Negative representations* — Representing certain groups in an unflattering or demeaning manner (e.g., Jews are money-hungry and stingy; American Indians are savages; Mexican Americans are lazy; African Americans are on welfare; gang members are Black or Hispanic);
2. *Overgeneralizations* — Black families are always headed by females and/or Hispanic families have many children; drugs, violence/crime, poverty, and homelessness are presented as primarily restricted to minority groups;
3. *Stereotyping* — This occurs when minorities are presented in stereotypical roles and assignments (e.g., Asians are studious; Blacks are athletic; Hispanics are lazy);
4. *Omissions* — The materials omit minority groups altogether or underrepresent them;
5. *Superficial and insignificant changes* — To diversify materials, some au-

thors and publishers simply darken pictures of Whites without changing content, etc.; thus, pictures of diverse groups may be unrealistic;

6. *Superior–inferior positions* — Materials place minority groups in low-level or subservient roles/jobs; Whites are in supervisory, prestigious, professional positions;

7. *Ethnocentrism* — materials present the White perspective solely or exclusively;

8. *Minimization* — Materials gloss over, ignore, or trivialize the contributions, histories, and strengths of minority groups, glossing over, ignoring, or trivializing such troublesome issues as slavery discrimination, oppression, and other injustices; and

9. *Classism* — Materials present and show preference for middle-class standards and values (e.g., success means having a college degree, the ideal family is nuclear) (see Ford, 1996).

Students in the studies just described noted many of these biases — superior–inferior roles, with Blacks portrayed as defenseless and weak, particularly during slavery; they noted negative portrayals of Blacks (e.g., lack of power as slaves); and they noted minimization with little emphasis on the major contributions of minority groups to society. If children notice these biases, surely adults notice them.

QUESTIONS TO CONSIDER REGARDING CURRICULUM AND INSTRUCTION

As Davidman and Davidman (1994) noted, teachers must ask at least four questions when assessing curriculum and instruction (i.e., lessons, materials, and strategies) for biases. These questions help guide changes in curriculum and instruction.

1. Do materials, lessons, and strategies promote educational equity? For instance, does the lesson help to create a curriculum where all students participate and contribute in substantive ways?

2. Do curriculum and instruction promote cultural pluralism or intergroup harmony in the classroom? Are students treated as equal members of the classroom community? Are cooperative strategies and groupings used to teach lessons and to promote positive, affirming student relationships?

3. Do curriculum and instruction help increase students' knowledge regarding various cultural groups, including their own? Are mirrors (focus on self and own cultural group) and windows (focus on others

and other cultural groups) provided: (a) so that learning is relevant, motivating, engaging, interesting, and empowering? (b) so that different perspectives are heard and seen?

4. Do curriculum and instruction help to correct distortions about minority groups? (e.g., are distortions discussed?)

Suggestions for Reducing or Eliminating Biases

Educators can adopt many strategies to eliminate biases in curriculum and instruction, as well as biases in the classroom. The suggestions below help empower students to live in and contribute positively to our multicultural schools and society.

Dealing with Prejudice. Make discussions of injustices an explicit aspect of the curriculum — do not allow these problems to be ignored; introduce pertinent incidents of prejudice and discrimination in the news or their particular field of study into the curriculum on a regular and timely basis; have students examine TV programs, movies, magazines, and textbooks for prejudice, bias, and stereotyping. For example, students might read *Everybody Knows What a Dragon Looks Like* by Williams (1976). In this Chinese tale, children learn about the consequences of presumptions and prejudices.

Dealing with Stereotypes. Eliminate stereotypes by demonstrating to students that whatever the stereotype, there are exceptions; invite guest speakers to talk with students about how to counteract stereotypes; replace teaching about tepees, igloos, and other out-of-date stereotypes with discussions of real, current problems and issues in the lives of different groups; adopt a schoolwide philosophy that communicates that to treat some students negatively is discriminatory; hold ongoing and serious discussions with school administrators about shortcomings (biases, stereotypes, etc.) in textbooks and curricular materials. For example, *The Five Chinese Brothers* (Bishop, 1938/1996) is a very stereotypical book; however, the same story is told without the stereotypes in *The Seven Chinese Brothers* (Mahy, 1990).

Building a Sense of Community. Provide class time for students to get acquainted at the beginning of the school year; provide opportunities to maintain student dialogue; provide each student with a partner (buddy, liaison, tutor, interpreter) to facilitate learning both within and outside the classroom; hold meetings to develop and refine classroom and school rules and justice systems. (Those who help develop rules are more likely to follow them.)

Increasing Self-Understanding. Work to increase students' cultural pride and belief that their education can lead to attainable and interesting goals; incorporate self-esteem, self-concept, and racial/cultural identity-building as part of the affective curriculum.

Increasing Empathy. Help students to see history and current events through the eyes of the "oppressed"; create opportunities for students to articulate and consider the various perspectives surrounding culturally laden issues.

Instructional Considerations

Multicultural education will be difficult to implement when efforts center primarily or exclusively on curriculum. We recognize the role of questioning techniques in promoting higher levels of thinking. When teaching students, educators must consider their styles of learning. One of the most concrete recommendations for addressing learning styles comes from a Chinese proverb: "I hear and I forget; I see and I remember; I do and I understand." More specifically, teachers must take into account minority students' learning styles, as discussed in Chapter 1 and further summarized in Figure 5.2. Specifically, a considerable amount of research indicates that minority students tend to be: (a) field-dependent or contextual learners who seek meaning and personal relevance when learning; (b) concrete learners who prefer practical learning experiences; (c) social learners who value interdependence; (d) visual learners; and (e) tactile and kinesthetic learners who prefer active and experiential learning opportunities (e.g., Boykin, 1994; Irvine & York, 1995; Saracho & Gerstl, 1992; Shade, Kelly, & Oberg, 1997). These characteristics, of course, are *guidelines* and frameworks. To reach all students, to stimulate and engage all students, teachers must adapt their teaching styles to students' learning styles, particularly when students are struggling, frustrated, and/or confused. Such adaptations help to accommodate cultural differences in how children learn and make sense of what is taught. Thus, teachers might use discussions, social learning, independent projects, simulations, role-plays, drama, music, dance, and other instructional techniques to meet students' learning preferences and needs.

At minimum, high-quality instruction includes questioning strategies, grouping practices, and teaching and learning styles. The lessons below depend heavily on questioning strategies. In many respects, the questions teachers ask are the most important aspect of classroom learning. The questions asked by teachers help determine what students learn and what they think about. For instance, "Why did slavery end?" is quite different from "How could slavery have been prevented?" The question "What have you learned

Figure 5.2 Comparative Framework of the Preferred Learning Styles of Minority and White Students

White Students	Minority Students
Abstract thinkers	Concrete thinkers
Deductive thinkers	Inductive thinkers
Field-independent learners	Field-independent learners, contextual and situational learners
Individualistic, independent learner	Interdependent, social, cooperative learners
Require/prefer less structure, direction	Require/prefer more structure, direction, specificity
Seek academic meaning	Seek relevance—personal meaning and significance
Kinesthetic learners	Kinesthetic & tactile learners
Verbal, auditory	Visual, spatial

Sources: Boykin (1994); Irvine & York (1995); Saracho & Gerstl (1992); Shade (1994); Shade, Kelly, & Oberg (1997)

Note: These characteristics are to be used as a "framework" or guideline for understanding diverse cultural groups and targeting their needs and strengths.

about slavery" is quite different from "How have you grown from learning about slavery?" Further, "What is the meaning of democracy?" is not the same as "How does the U.S. demonstrate its commitment to the ideals of a democratic society?" Finally, "Who was Malcolm X?" is less cognitively stimulating than, "How did Malcolm X improve the lives of African Americans?" and "How did Malcolm X's efforts affect your life?" Our point, as noted by Taba, Levine, and Elzey (1964),

> The role of questions becomes crucial and the way of asking questions is by far the most influential single teaching act. . . . Questions can be arranged to create stepping stones for transitions from one mode of thinking to another or for the formation of new conceptual schemes. (pp. 53–55)

Thus, effective questioning focuses on depth rather than breadth; effective questioning is explicit and precise; effective questioning promotes critical thinking, creative thinking and problem-solving; and effective questioning is cohesive. Many types of questions can be asked—clarification questions, prompting questions, and critical awareness questions. In essence, effective questioning cues and directs the thought processes of students and facilitates classroom discourse. In the lessons below, we focus primarily on critical awareness questions; most questions are divergent, inferential, predictive, interpretive, analytical, and evaluative, and they are active rather than passive. Similarly, students are asked to generate questions, not just to answer them. Thus, students are asked to compare and contrast, to think about cause–effect relationships, to predict consequences, and to draw sound conclusions. They ask and answer basic questions (who, what, when, where, why, and how), as well as "what if," "why not," and "in what ways" questions. In generating questions, students can brainstorm, create questioning webs, and use SCAMPER[9] techniques. The possibilities are numerous.

Essentially, many of the questions and activities in this chapter ask students to compare, identify, create, explain, compose, defend, justify, and support. Thus, as presented in Table 5.1 and Figure 5.3, educators can and must create a climate that nurtures critical and creative thinking. A culture of thinking helps to raise the level of instruction, and increase students' engagement. A more extensive vocabulary (e.g., substituting "guess" for "hypothesis," "tell me" for "explain," etc.) prepares students for higher-level thinking.

Grouping practices represent another instructional strategy that facilitates students' learning. While assignments can be completed individually and independently, we advocate for more peer collaboration and small-group work. In particular, as stated in Chapter 1, much research indicates that minority students thrive in social learning situations, particularly cooperative learning and small-group work. Teachers must vary grouping practices so that all students have an opportunity to work in situations that facilitate their learning, increase their motivation, and improve their achievement. In this regard, cooperative learning and group work offer much promise.

While the lessons presented in this chapter focus primarily on literature, it goes without saying that films, TV shows, newspapers, and other media are essential elements of teaching and learning. Similarly, students' products should vary. Students can write reports, essays, stories, and poems. They can create documentaries, plays, and songs. Finally, evaluation or assessments must vary. Students should have every opportunity to put their best foot forward, namely, through authentic assessments (e.g., portfolios, projects, and performances).

Selecting High-Quality Literature

Several alarming reports describe factors impacting literacy rates nationally. It has been noted that not one book was purchased in 35% of U.S. homes in 1992. And although Americans purchased 7% more books in 1992 than in 1991, book purchases by those under 25 dropped 27%. Further, 80% of

Table 5.1 Description of Bloom's Taxonomy of Educational Objectives

Category	Definition	Action Verbs	Sample Products
Knowledge	Ability to remember information that has been taught	Define, describe, identify, label, list, match, name, outline, select, state	Exams/tests, reports of facts
Comprehension	Demonstrates basic understanding of concepts and curriculum; can translate to other words	Convert, estimate, explain, extend, generalize, give examples, infer, paraphrase, rewrite, summarize	Diagrams, drawings, outlines
Application	Applies and transfers knowledge learned in one situation to another	Change, classify, compute, demonstrate, discover, manipulate, modify, operate, organize, predict, prepare, produce, relate, show, solve, use	Demonstration, model, report, recipe
Analysis	Understands how parts relate to the whole; understands structure and motive	Break down, compare/contrast, diagram, differentiate, discriminate, distinguish, examine, identify, illustrate, infer, outline, point out, relate, select, separate, subdivide	Plan or prospectus, questionnaire, reviews
Synthesis	Changes, (re)forms, remakes, rebuilds parts to make a new whole	Combine, compile, compose, create, design, develop, devise, plan, produce, revise	Creation, invention, poem, song, story
Evaluation	Judges value of something using certain criteria; supports belief, judgment, opinion, perspective, point of view	Assess, appraise, compare, conclude, contrast, criticize, defend, describe, discriminate, explain, justify, interpret, persuade, relate, summarize, support	Critiques, makes decision, debates, writes editorial, takes a position, makes judgments

Figure 5.3 Promoting a Culture of Thinking: The Language of Thinking

Analyze	Contradict	Dispute	Defend	Presume	Review
Ascertain	Convince	Dissect	Hypothesize	Probe	Resolve
Assess	Criticize	Doubt	Infer	Propose	Ruminate
Assume	Deduce	Elucidate	Inquire	Prove	Scrutinize
Comprehend	Deliberate	Entertain	Interpret	Question	Solve
Conclude	Demonstrate	Establish	Investigate	Rate	Speculate
Confirm	Derive	Estimate	Judge	Reason	Study
Conjecture	Detect	Evidence	Justify	Rebut	Suggest
Consider	Determine	Examine	Ponder	Recognize	Suppose
Contemplate	Discern	Explain	Posit	Reflect	Theorize
Contend	Discover	Explore	Postulate	Research	Think

book purchases were made by 10% of the population (*Wall Street Journal,* 1993).

The majority of multicultural education as discussed in this chapter uses literature to integrate curriculum and instruction. Our rationale is simple — language, and hence literature, is the communication currency of the world. All school subjects rely extensively on language; it is the primary instrument for the reception of expression or thought (Johnson, VanTassel-Baska, Boyce, & Hall, 1995).

Additionally, many minority students are performing poorly on standardized measures of language (e.g., vocabulary, writing, reading, comprehension, etc.). We believe that multicultural literature — literature that is personally meaningful and culturally relevant — can increase minority students' literacy, achievement, and motivation, and enhance self-perception and self-understanding. Appendix A contains a list of multicultural literature and gifted education resources.

Few books have been written by people of color. According to Muse (1997), less than 7% of books have been written by African Americans, calling into questions issues of authenticity. Halsted (1994) and Baskin and Harris (1980) summarized criteria for selecting literature for gifted students. We have added to these criteria in order to add a multicultural perspective. Specifically, literature should be rich, varied (folk tales to biographies, fiction to nonfiction), complex, relevant, and inspirational. Literature should be chosen with openness in mind, and foster and nurture interpretive and evaluative behaviors. Literature should build problem-solving skills and develop critical and productive thinking. Literature should provide positive role models from all cultural groups, including race, gender, age, and socio-economic level. Finally, this literature must adhere to the multicultural guidelines listed in the previous section (avoid stereotypes, etc.).

A SYNTHESIS: MULTICULTURAL GIFTED EDUCATION

Each lesson in the chapter is based on the model presented in Tables 5.2 and 5.3. This synthesized model (hereafter referred to as the Ford-Harris matrix) combines the works of Banks (1993, 1995, 1997) (see Table 3.1) and Bloom (1956) (see Table 3.4). We contend that, at its best, multicultural gifted education focuses on Banks's transformation and social activism levels, and on Bloom's analysis, synthesis, and evaluation levels. In all instances, as depicted in Table 5.3, it is assumed that products, content, and processes reflect the goals, objectives, and perspectives of both gifted education and multicultural education, as described in Chapter 3. We use Table 5.2 to guide the development of questions, activities, and products. The Ford-Harris ma-

Table 5.2 Ford-Harris Matrix of Multicultural Gifted Education: Definition of Categories

	Knowledge	Comprehension	Application	Analysis	Synthesis	Evaluation
Contri-butions	Students are taught and know facts about cultural artifacts, events, groups, and other cultural elements.	Students show an understanding of information about cultural artifacts, groups, etc.	Students are asked to and can apply information learned on cultural artifacts, events, etc.	Students are taught to and can analyze (e.g., compare and contrast) information about cultural artifacts, groups, etc.	Students are required to and can create a new product from the information on cultural artifacts, groups, etc.	Students are taught to and can evaluate facts and information based on cultural artifacts, groups, etc.
Additive	Students are taught and know concepts and themes about cultural groups.	Students are taught and can understand cultural concepts and themes.	Students are required to and can apply information learned about cultural concepts and themes.	Students are taught to and can analyze important cultural concepts and themes.	Students are asked to and can synthesize important information on cultural concepts and themes.	Students are taught to and can critique cultural concepts and themes.
Trans-formation	Students are given information on important cultural elements, groups, etc., and can understand this information from different perspectives.	Students are taught to understand and can demonstrate an understanding of important cultural concepts and themes from different perspectives.	Students are asked to and can apply their understanding of important concepts and themes from different perspectives.	Students are taught to and can examine important cultural concepts and themes from more than one perspective.	Students are required to and can create a product based on their new perspective or the perspective of another group.	Students are taught to and can evaluate or judge important cultural concepts and themes from different viewpoints (e.g., minority group).
Social Action	Based on information on cultural artifacts, etc., students make recommendations for social action.	Based on their understanding of important concepts and themes, students make recommendations for social action.	Students are asked to can apply their understanding of important social and cultural issues; they make recommendations for and take action on these issues.	Students are required to and can analyze social and cultural issues from different perspectives; they take action on these issues.	Students create a plan of action to address a social and cultural issue(s); they seek important social change.	Students critique important social and cultural issues, and seek to make national and/or international change.

Note: Based on the models of Banks (multicultural) and Bloom (thinking skills). Actions taken on the social action level can range from immediate and small-scale (e.g., classroom and school level) to moderate (e.g., community or regional level) to large-scale (state, national, and international levels). Likewise, students can make recommendations for action or actually take social action.

Table 5.3 Applying the Ford-Harris Matrix to the Concept of Social Injustice (Stereotypes and Prejudice)

	Knowledge	Comprehension	Application	Analysis	Synthesis	Evaluation
Contributions	Name three songs that were popular among slaves.	Make an outline of events leading to the Civil War.	Create a model of the Underground Railroad.	Examine how stereotypes about minority groups contribute to slavery.	Write a story about the contribution of Hispanic Americans to the music industry.	Critique the work of a famous American Indian artist.
Additive	List three factors that contribute to prejudiced beliefs.	After reading a biography about a famous person of color, summarize the racial barriers that the person faced.	Find a book or song that discusses the problems of racial prejudice in society.	Compare and contrast the writings of W. E. B. DuBois and Booker T. Washington on issues of racial discrimination.	Write a play about the Spanish Inquisition.	Write a paper explaining why you think it is important (or not important) to learn about prejudice.
Transformation	Describe how slaves might have felt being held in captivity.	Explain why American Indians use folk tales and storytelling as a means of coping with oppression.	Read the essay "What America Means to Me." Write a paper showing how members of a minority group might respond to this essay.	Predict how our nation would have prospered without slave labor. What other forms of labor could have been used?	Develop a survey regarding students' experiences with prejudice in their school or their community.	Assume the identity of a plantation owner or a slave. From that perspective, write a story outlining the differences between your life and the ideal of liberty and justice for all.
Social Action	What would you have done during the 17th century to end slavery?	List some ways that the media contribute to our perceptions of minority groups. What can be done to improve how the media portray minorities?	Review 3 to 5 sources on affirmative action; then write and submit an editorial to a newspaper describing your views on this topic.	Spend a day (week, etc.) observing and analyzing how minority groups are treated at the mall. Share the results with storeowners.	Form a school club whose goal is to create a sense of community and respect in the school building.	Examine school policies to see if democratic ideals are present. Write a new school policy and share the findings and recommendations with administration.

trix in Table 5.2 can be used as a checklist in which curriculum and instruction (questions, activities, and products) are examined for their level of cognitive complexity and multiculturalism. For example, at the Knowledge-Contributions level, students are taught and know facts about cultural artifacts, events, groups, and other cultural elements. At the Application-Additive level, teachers teach about cultural concepts and themes, and students can apply this information. As discussed in chapter 3, the additive level goes beyond a discussion of cultural elements and artifacts (e.g., tepee, kente cloth, pottery, and Black History month) to a discussion of cultural concepts and themes (e.g., discrimination, power, etc.). At the Comprehension-Transformation level, teachers help students to understand cultural concepts and themes from the minority group's perspective. Without this empathy, students are working at the additive level. Likewise, when teachers help students to evaluate or critique important cultural concepts and themes from diverse perspectives, they are teaching at the Evaluation-Transformation level. When targeting the Synthesis-Social level, teachers encourage or require students to create a plan of action, for example, to address social and cultural issues. As noted in Table 5.2, social action activities exist on a continuum. Specifically, action can target immediate and small-scale audiences (such as a classroom or school) or increase to larger audiences, such as the community, region, and state. The most far-reaching, large-scale audiences are national and international. Further, students can be asked to make recommendations for action or to actually take action.

Concept-Based or Theme-Based Lessons Using Multicultural Literature and Perspectives

To teach about cultural diverse groups in substantive and meaningful ways, Banks (1997) recommends that schools focus on such critical topics as acculturation, perception, prejudice, power, and immigration-migration. We must also teach about empowerment, namely, faith, hope, and optimism, as described later.

In teaching about prejudice, students should be introduced to Allport's (1979) or Merton's (1949) model of prejudice. Allport placed levels or expressions of prejudice on a 5-point continuum, from antilocution to extermination:

1. *Antilocution* — this is the mildest form of prejudice, which is characterized by prejudicial talk.
2. *Avoidance* — the individual moves beyond talking to conscious efforts to avoid certain groups.

3. *Discrimination* — the person takes active steps to exclude or deny members of another group entrance or participation in a desired activity.
4. *Physical attack* — a physical confrontation against another group.
5. *Extermination* — the systematic and planned destruction of a group of people based on their membership.

Using a historical perspective, students can analyze wars and other events for different types of prejudice; they can examine historical documents for viewpoints on minority groups; they can view and analyze media to see if prejudices are evident.

Merton's model has four types of prejudice that clarify the extent to which discrimination is contextual, situational, and related to the social setting in which people function:

1. *Type I* — The unprejudiced nondiscriminator or all-weather liberal. This person believes in racial equality and acts on his/her beliefs.
2. *Type II* — The prejudiced discriminators or fair-weather liberal. This is a person of expediency. He/she does not have personal prejudices, but will discriminate when it is easier or more profitable to do so.
3. *Type III* — The prejudiced nondiscriminator or fair-weather illiberal. This person neither believes in racial equality nor discriminates because of factors (e.g., laws) that negatively sanction racial discrimination.
4. *Type IV* — The prejudiced discriminator or the all-weather illiberal. This person is a bigot who is not ashamed of his/her attitudes and who acts on his/her beliefs and prejudices.

Using Bloom's Taxonomy, teachers can incorporate the topic of prejudice at all levels into their curriculum (see Table 5.3 and Figure 5.4):

Knowledge — Ask students to define the term "prejudice" and identify related words; to list components of the Merton and Allport models; to list factors that contribute to prejudiced beliefs; and/or to identify groups who face discrimination in our society (and/or other societies).

Comprehension — Ask students to explain the levels of each model; to summarize the main points of each model; to determine which type or level of prejudice is most evident in a case or scenario that focuses on prejudice; and/or to list ways in which the media contribute to negative perceptions of minority groups.

Application — At this level, students are asked to and can apply the concept of racial prejudice to other types of prejudice (e.g., Jews, females, etc). Students can interview a person of color about the impact of prejudice on his/her life; conduct an interview with a famous Civil Rights leader in the

Figure 5.4 A Multicultural Gifted Education Model

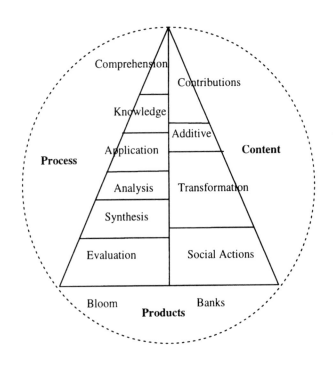

present or past; develop a timeline of events leading to the passage of the Civil Rights Act; and/or apply one or both of theories of prejudice to slavery, the Holocaust, or some other past or contemporary social injustice.

Analysis—Students taught at this level can analyze how Merton's and Allport's theories of prejudice are similar and different; they can examine the effects of prejudice on one's self-perception or self-esteem; they can examine how prejudice impacts a person's life at home, school, and work; they can research when and how prejudiced attitudes develop; or they can speculate about the level of prejudice of slave owners. Students can explain the advantages and disadvantages of prejudice from the point of view of the perpetrator (or victim); hypothesize about what life would be like for people of color without the passage of the various Civil Rights acts; read King's "I Have a

Dream" speech and relate it to Langston Hughes' "I Dream a World"; and/ or analyze folk tales to determine how they address issues of prejudice.

Synthesis—At the synthesis level, students can develop school or classroom rules that address reducing or eliminating prejudice; they can write a song about the influence of Thurgood Marshall on improving the quality of life for people of color; and/or write and present a poem, song, play, story, or skit about preventing (or overcoming) prejudice.

Evaluation—Students can evaluate the effectiveness of those laws aimed at eliminating prejudices based on race; write a position paper on how prejudice might have played a role in creating affirmative action laws; make a case for or against affirmative action; evaluate television shows, newspapers, magazines, or books for examples of prejudice, and contact these media with their results and recommendations; survey their friends (and/or adults in their community) regarding instances of prejudice in their lives and prepare a report and/or presentation on the results; using this same activity, students might evaluate the response patterns or themes of friends versus adults; they can also judge whether one type of prejudice seems to be more harmful than another.

Additional Considerations

The goals and objectives of the lessons on prejudice will vary by the levels in the Ford-Harris framework targeted or selected. At the lower levels, a teacher's primary goal might be to increase students' knowledge base about different types of social injustices. At higher levels, the major goal might be to promote a stronger sense of justice and social responsibility in students. At the synthesis level, a few of the activities just listed require students to write a skit or play. If students choose to submit the work for publication or dissemination, then their efforts would be at the highest level of social action in Banks's model. Students' work is designed to have an impact socially.

In each of the activities just recommended, teachers must check to see that students know and understand the issue of prejudice before moving to higher levels of the matrix we have proposed. For example, at the highest levels, students will be able to critique, form an opinion, and defend a position, according to evaluation in the Bloom model; likewise, students will be able to do something with this information so that it has an impact socially, according Banks's social action level. The following two examples are at the highest levels in both models (evaluation-social action level): (1) have students evaluate television shows, newspapers, magazines, or books for examples of prejudice, and contact these media with their results; and (2) have students survey their friends (and/or adults in their community) regarding instances of prejudice in their lives and prepare a report and/or presentation on the results for school administration. Thus, the goals, objectives, outcomes, and products of students' work play a major role in determining its level within the Ford-Harris framework we have created. In some instances, it may be difficult to distinguish application from synthesis, depending on the level of creativity or innovativeness of teachers' assignments and students' products.

Teachers must adapt the content of the Ford-Harris matrix in Tables 5.2 and 5.3 so that learning is appropriate and optimal for their particular classroom and context. Clearly, some of the suggestions or terminology are not appropriate for very young children. However, teachers are encouraged to strive for the highest levels in the matrix with developmental theories in mind. Three examples follow.

1. Have students read the essay "What America Means to Me" and:
   a. Write a paper on how a member of a minority group might respond to this essay (application-transformation);
   b. Summarize the major idea of the essay and explain why they like or dislike it (comprehension-additive); and
   c. Write a new essay entitled "What America Means to Me as an Asian American" (synthesis-transformation) and submit it for publication (synthesis-social action)

Teachers must also incorporate multicultural literature into the lessons to reinforce concepts and themes. For instance, young children might read *Black Is Brown Is Tan* (Adoff, 1973), *All the Colors of the Race* (Adoff, 1982), or *We Are a Rainbow* (Tabor, 1997) to gain an appreciation for the richness of different skin colors and shades, and to gain an appreciation for commonalties despite these differences. (See Appendix A for additional sources that contain annotated multicultural literature and Appendix B for multicultural activities). Using a theme or concept from music, students can discuss the importance of different notes in creating melody—without different notes, there would be no melody. This notion can be related to cultural and racial diversity.

We also believe that multicultural education can be taught with literature that is not multicultural. For example, *It's Nice to Have a Wolf Around the House* (Allard, 1977), *Cuckoo/Cucu* (Ehlert, 1997), *Swimmy* (Lionni, 1963), *A Color of His Own* (Lionni, 1975), *The Mixed-Up Chameleon* (Carle, 1975), and *Eggbert: The Slightly Cracked Egg* (Ross & Barron, 1994) all provide powerful messages that are consistent with multicultural teaching. As with multicultural literature, these books focus on enhancing identity, increasing self-empowerment, instilling faith, and decreasing stereotypes. For teachers who are just beginning to teach from a multicultural perspective and those who are not yet comfortable doing so, these books offer solid guidance and assistance.

Equally important, every effort should be made to use lessons in an inter-disciplinary way. For instance, multicultural activities and lessons are used most often in language arts, music, art, and social studies curricula, but virtu-ally ignored in math and science. Likewise, lessons should incorporate key concepts, objectives, and goals from various disciplines.

LITERATURE-BASED ACTIVITIES AND LESSONS[10]

I. Theme/Topic: Different Fairytales (Little Red Riding Hood)

Main goal: Students will understand the purpose of fairytales. They will understand that fairytales (and/or folk tales and legends) differ from culture to culture, and that these fairytales share similarities and differences.

Specific objectives: (1) Students will increase their awareness of folk tales, fairytales, and legends from other cultures; (2) students will be aware of simi-larities and differences between fairytales from other cultures; (3) students will be able to compare and contrast at least two fairytales in terms of signifi-cant differences and similarities; and (4) students will understand the reasons for different versions of the fairytale.

Grade levels: 3–5

Disciplines: Language arts, social studies

Key questions: (1) What is the purpose of fairytales? (2) What is the main idea of each version? (3) How are fairytales from various cultures different and similar? (4) Where are the cultural groups located (e.g., Where is China and what are some of the significant different cultural values of Chinese Americans)? (5) What themes underlie fairytales from the different cultures (e.g., nature, trees, animals, unity, peace, etc.)? (6) Do certain cultures seem to write about one theme more than other cultures (e.g., trees, wolves, wind, moons, etc.), and why? Why are there different versions of the same fairytale?

Activities: Pre-instruction activities should introduce students to other cultures, in this case Asian cultures. Such activities might include having a Chinese American visit the classroom and talk about their culture, values, and traditions; students should locate China on the map, bring in books (poems, songs, etc.) from Asian countries and cultures, and so forth. (Of course, the lesson below can be used with other fairytales. For example, students should also be informed that there are almost 350 versions of Cinderella. Cinderella fairytales from different cultures include: *Sootface: An Ojibwa Cinderella Story; The Algonquin Cinderella; Yeh-Shen: Chinese Cinderella; The Korean Cinderella;*

The Scar-Faced Girl; Chinye: A West African Folk Tale; and *The Egyptian Cin-derella*).

Have children read two versions of Little Red Riding Hood—the tradi-tional version and the Chinese version (*Lon Po Po*, Young, 1989)[11]. Students will respond to various questions and statements about the fairytales, as well as produce different products. The questions are categorized by Bloom's lev-els. Within each of the Bloom categories, questions fit various levels of Banks's model. Not every question fits into the Ford-Harris matrix presented in Table 5.2. For example, "Who was Little Red Riding Hood?" is a knowledge ques-tion that does not have a multicultural focus. Neither does "Why did the wolf blow out the candle in *Lon Po Po*?" On the other hand, "Justify the need for more than one version of fairytales and explain why you think schools should have students read them" clearly has a multicultural focus. Ideally, all ques-tions and projects should fit neatly into the Ford-Harris framework. Realisti-cally, this is not possible. We hope that educators will strive for the ideal, while understanding that reaching the evaluation-social action level is not al-ways possible.

1. *Knowledge*—Who was Little Red Riding Hood? Why was she visiting her grandmother? What was she taking to her grandmother's house? Where was the house located? Who was Lon Po Po? How many children were in this fairytale? Why did the mother visit Lon Po Po? How was the wolf disguised? What directions were given to the children in both stories?
2. *Comprehension*—Explain the main idea of both fairytales. Explain how the wolf was able to trick both Little Red Riding Hood and the daughters in *Lon Po Po*. Why did the wolf blow out the candle in *Lon Po Po*? How did Little Red Riding Hood and the daughters in *Lon Po Po* fail to follow their mothers' directions?
3. *Application*—Rename both books based on the most important ideas in each. Write a newspaper report on either story. Find and share another fairytale about wolves or another version of little Red Riding Hood. Re-write either of the fairytales from the wolf's point of view. Make a poster that orders the events in either or both fairytales. Using the themes from either version, develop a news story warning other students about a wolf on the loose. Prepare a list of rules for the girls about following directions when adults are not around.
4. *Analysis*—What is the morale of the two fairytales? How would events in both books be different if Little Red Riding Hood and the three daughters had been boys? Why do you think the authors made the children girls rather than boys? What other ways might the wolf have tricked the girls in both books? Predict what might have happened if Shang had not turned on the light and seen the wolf. In what other ways might the daughters

have gotten out their predicament? Compare the two versions of Little Red Riding Hood to each other; how are they similar and different? Which do you think was the original fairytale and why was the other version written? Why are there different versions of many fairytales? What other versions of this fairytale can you find and how do they resemble these two versions? What role do fairytales serve in the lives of people from different cultures? Why might some cultures rely more on fairytales than other cultures? How are wolves in traditional books depicted compared to wolves in other cultures?

5. *Synthesis* — Create a new version of one of the stories (or both) with boys rather than girls. Create a new story with a different location (e.g., in the city). Rewrite the fairytale with a grandfather or father. Write a story of Little Red Riding Hood or Lon Po Po and a "good" wolf. Write another version of Little Red Riding Hood that includes all of the children from the two versions read in class. Rewrite the story from the perspective of another cultural group (e.g., American Indian, Hispanic American, and/or African American). Create a play based on one of the versions of the fairytale. Write a sequel to either version. Assume that Little Red Riding Hood's grandmother decided to press charges against the wolf and you are her lawyer, write your opening statements.

6. *Evaluation* — Which version of the two fairytales do you prefer and why? Which character (e.g., Shang or Little Red Riding Hood) would you like to be and why? Evaluate the daughters' plan to trick the wolf in *Lon Po Po*, and explain what might you have done differently to solve the problem. Justify the need for more than one version of a fairytale and explain why you think schools should have students read them. If you were invited to make a speech on how authors depict wolves in books, what would you say? Evaluate the way females are depicted in fairytales; share your critique with the author or publisher of the works.

For related lessons, introduce students to different versions of Henny Penny. That is, students can read *Henny Penny, The Sky Is Falling*, and *The Rabbit's Foolish Wish*, a Jakata tale thought to be the original version of *Henny Penny*. Similarly, very young students might enjoy reading *The Ugly Duckling* and *The Ebony Duckling*, where initial discussions about race can begin.

II. Theme/Topic: Different Perspectives

Main Goals: To introduce students to the concept of "perspective" or "point of view." To introduce students to nature and the process of change.

Specific Objectives: To increase students' self-awareness (insight) and other-awareness (empathy). To use nature to increase students' ability to view concepts, themes, and events from a different perspective.

Grade Levels: 2–6

Disciplines: Language arts, science, social studies, and mathematics.

Activities: One goal of multicultural education is to have students see the world and situations from the perspective of minority groups (i.e., Transformation Level). Likewise, gifted education seeks to increase students' perceptiveness and insight by providing them with opportunities to see things from different angles. Hence, mirrors and windows are provided to increase gifted students' self-understanding and empathy. *A Place to Bloom* (Siomades, 1997) is a powerful beginning for helping students to acquire this skill. Siomades illustrates how the things we take for granted may be precious to someone else, be it food on the table or trees in the park. The book encourages children to think about the world around them and where others fit into this world.

Similarly, *A Ruined House* (Manning, 1994) tells the story of a deserted farmhouse that has become a haven for animals and plants over the years. Students will better understand that "a home is never truly abandoned" because it is always occupied by something. Manning also provides students with an initial understanding of ecosystems as he describes seasons and weather, along with animals and plants that inhabit places affected by rain and snow. Students are introduced to flowers that grow in wild gardens (e.g., foxglove, lichens), plants that grow in compost (e.g., nettles), insects that thrive in damp places (e.g., wasp, mites, earwigs, wood lice), and animals that grow on nettles (e.g., aphids, ladybugs, caterpillars).

Further, students can read *The Great Kapok Tree* (Cherry, 1990), which is often used in science curricula because of its focus on nature. The book also teaches students about different perspectives. The story tells of a man who falls asleep after taking the initial steps of chopping down a Kapok tree in the Amazon. The animals who live there (e.g., butterflies, monkeys, porcupines, frogs, jaguars, anteaters, birds, and sloth) and a child whisper in the man's ear, asking him not to destroy their home. The child and each animal tell the man how important every tree is in the rain forest. For instance, the bee whispers, "my hive is in the Kapok tree, and I fly from tree to tree and flower to flower collecting pollen. In this way, I pollinate the trees and flowers throughout the rain forest. You see, all living things depend on one another." The book jacket also contains important reference-type information about rain forests, including a map of current rain forests, original rain forests, and their inhabitants.

Students should be given ample opportunity to discuss their reactions to the readings. A few suggestions for questions and activities follow. Students and teachers should generate additional questions and activities, and target them at higher levels in the matrix. For instance, how might we relate the readings and concept (perspective) to social issues? (e.g., How could "old" homes be made into homeless shelters, etc.? Why do we destroy homes when so many people have no place to live? How can we take better care of our homes?)

Students can research and write a report on methods for preserving items (application). They can search their homes and neighborhoods for the plants and animals mentioned in the books, and bring in photos of samples of these items (e.g., make a collage) (application). They might write a report on one or more of the animals discussed in the books (application). If interested, students can create a conservation club in the classroom (synthesis). They can interview scientists, conservationists, botanists, or other professionals regarding their work (application). Similarly, students can visit older communities, particularly those with homes being demolished, and interview decisionmakers, community leaders, and/or community members regarding decisions to demolish the homes (What factors should be considered when making such a decision? What is done to preserve the lives of plants and animals in the homes, etc.?) (analysis). After gathering this information, students can write a book, poem, or song to share the information they gathered (application, synthesis). They might also evaluate the reasons given by the community members, community leaders, or decisionmakers regarding the decision (e.g., Do the reasons seem valid or justified? How might losing the home affect the community? How do the three groups differ from or resemble each other on the decision?) (analysis and evaluation). Based on the information gathered during interviews, what can students do to help save the home, if this is their preference (application-social action)? If the home is demolished, have students find ways to use or donate the materials (e.g., wood, banisters, etc.) (application and synthesis). If the home is not demolished, what can it be used for (application and synthesis)? Finally, students might calculate the cost of maintaining versus demolishing the home, and submit a report with findings and recommendations to decisionmakers (analysis and application).

III. Theme/Topic: Empowerment (Faith, Hope, and Optimism)

Main goal: The goal of this lesson is to teach students to have faith in difficult times, to develop problem-solving skills, and to use multicultural literature to help achieve this goal.

Specific goals: (1) To increase students' sense of self-efficacy; (2) to increase students' understanding of delayed gratification and persistence; (3) to help students better understand the importance of collaboration; (4) to develop and increase students' problem-solving skills; and (5) to introduce students to multicultural literature.

Grade levels: 4–6

Disciplines: Language arts, science, and social studies

Activities: The Story of Jumping Mouse, by Steptoe (1984), is a Native

American[12] legend. This book traces the adventures of a young mouse who takes a long and perilous journey to the Land of Legend in search of a goal. The mouse faces numerous obstacles on his journey and sacrifices much to help others. For example, Jumping Mouse comes upon a wolf who has lost his sense of smell and thus cannot survive in the wilderness. Using his magic, Jumping Mouse returns the wolf's sense of smell. He also helps a boulder who has lost his sight and thus will die in the wilderness. At the story's end, Jumping Mouse is rewarded for his deeds by a Magic Frog. Jumping Frog becomes an eagle, an important symbol among Native Americans.

Imani in the Belly (Chocolate, 1994) is an African folk tale in which Imani's faith is tested when her children are swallowed by Simba, King of Beasts. Armed with courage, Imani sets out to find her children. In the process of saving her children, Imani saves a nation. At one point in the book, Imani deliberately allows herself to be swallowed by the beast. There, she finds her children and most of the villagers. Using a rope tied to the beast's tonsil, Imani and the villagers pull each other out of the beast. Essentially, the legend emphasizes how an individual who is armed with faith and courage can succeed. The legend also communicates the importance and power of teamwork and collaboration.

The People Shall Continue (Ortiz, 1988) presents an honest appraisal and overview of American Indian history for young children. Students learn about life on reservations, as well as life before and after the American and Spanish invasions. Despite severe hardships, many of which were imposed externally, American Indians continued to have faith and to work as one.

Willams's (1986) *A Chair for My Mother* tells the story of Rosa, a Hispanic American child who works in a restaurant after school with her mother. The family is poor and saves extra money in a jar to buy a chair. The house gets destroyed by a fire and all of their possessions are destroyed. With the help of friends and family, Rosa's family is able to replace some of their possessions. However, they cannot afford the chair that her mother wants, a chair upon which to rest her feet. Through hard work, persistence, and faith, Rosa, her mother, and grandmother save money until they can afford to buy one big chair that all three of them can enjoy.

Whether one uses one, two, or all four of these books, certain issues are worthy of discussion. Students should be introduced to the concept of persistence, and share situations in which they were persistent (e.g., doing homework, studying, walking home in bad weather, making a friend, etc.). Students should have an opportunity to talk about feelings associated with putting forth effort and not giving up. Let students share their strategies for maintaining motivation, and provide students with additional supportive strategies (e.g., set short-term goals, prioritize, seek the help of others, try to learn from mistakes, try to keep focused, try to keep a positive attitude, read inspirational quotes, etc.).

Students can: (1) relate the works to each other, discussing themes and concepts (analysis); (2) examine the works for similarities and differences (analysis); (3) analyze how characters demonstrated resilience, persistence, hope, and faith (analysis); and (4) share newly learned strategies for persistence with classmates (application).

Any lesson using these books would be incomplete without substantive discussions of the different racial and cultural groups represented. These cultures must be discussed in depth. For example, "Who are Native Americans? What is their history in the United States? What are their cultural beliefs, values, and traditions?" Students can also complete projects that further promote cultural understanding and respect.

In terms of application, analysis, synthesis, and evaluation, students might be assigned projects that take the form of finding other works about optimism and sharing them with classmates (e.g., *You Can Do It Little Rabbit* and *The Little Engine That Could*). They can write a poem or song about optimism and persistence; create strategies for self-motivation; survey other students and family members about strategies for persisting and coping with difficulties and analyze the survey by age, gender, or age (e.g., Were older or younger more persistent? In what ways do the self-motivating strategies of males and females differ?). Further, students can create a classroom motto about motivation, optimism, and faith.

Ultimately, transference is desired—students must be able to relate the above concepts and themes to social issues, including central issues facing people of color. Equally important, students must be able to transfer this understanding, that is, to critically analyze other injustices, such as the Holocaust, the Trail of Tears, and the Japanese relocation camps (analysis-comprehension; evaluation-comprehension). For example, during a unit on slavery, students can discuss the strengths of slaves and their efforts to survive in the face of harsh circumstances (analysis-transformation). Specifically, strengths include survival on slave ships, survival after families were broken, and survival working unreasonable hours and under harsh conditions. Unlike many discussions of slavery, students are able to see African Americans from another perspective, a perspective of Black empowerment. The Ford-Harris matrix can help to guide or generate questions, discussion, activities, and projects.

IV. Theme/Topic: Art Appreciation

Major goal: To increase students' interest in and attitudes about the arts; to increase students' knowledge and awareness of the arts from the perspective of other cultures.

Specific objectives: (1) To increase students' interest in painting and puzzles as a form of art; (2) to increase students' awareness of and appreciation for art from China and Japan; (3) to use affective techniques as a basis for inspiring students; and (4) to promote multicultural awareness and understanding.

Disciplines: Language arts, art, and social studies

Grade level: 4–6

Mieko and the Fifth Treasure (Coerr, 1993) is the story of a Japanese student who goes to live with her grandmother. Mieko has five treasures, four of which are a fine sable brush, an inkstone shaped like a lily pond, an inkstick, and a role of rice paper. According to a former teacher, Mieko's fifth treasure is the beauty in her heart. Combined with practice, these five treasures are the ingredients to a great artist. However, having grown bitter from her recent move, Mieko does not recognize this fifth treasure. She hates her school, is teased about her scarred hand, and can barely hold the paintbrush. Although Mieko longs to paint, beliefs about her scarred hand and bitter heart keep the brush from dancing across the paper. Eventually, time and friendship heal Mieko and she is able to paint.

Grandfather Tang's Story (Tompert, 1990) is a tale told with tangrams. The grandfather creates several stories and tangrams for his granddaughter. For instance, he tells the story of a rabbit and makes a tangram of one. Other stories and tangrams include a dog, hawk, squirrel, turtle, crocodile, goldfish, lion, and goose. Messages regarding strong family relations (across generations) are powerful.

As part of an art lesson or unit on other cultures, students should be taught the history of tangrams[13] (knowledge-contributions; comprehension-contributions). Students should also be taught that fox fairies are an integral part of Chinese folklore because they are believed to be endowed with supernatural powers (knowledge-additive).

As part of the teaching and learning process, teachers can have students research the history of art from diverse cultures (analysis-contributions). Students can trace the various art eras of China and Japan (application-additive). These eras can be compared with those in the U.S. For instance, students might compare art in Japan and/or China with art in the U.S. that is made by Japanese Americans and Chinese Americans (analysis-additive). In other words, how has the U.S. influenced the work of immigrants? Students can also write biographies of famous artists from other cultures (application-additive). Students can discuss how one's cultural beliefs and values influence art (application-transformation). Teachers might wish to invite artists from different cultures to visit the classroom to teach various art forms to students (knowledge-additive).

As with core subject areas, students must be taught to think critically and creatively about art. Studying other cultures provides this opportunity and exposure. Both of the Asian stories provide insightful and inspiring opportunities for students to understand and appreciate the value many cultures place on the arts. As with many of the lessons we have discussed, students living in a multicultural society need exposure to higher-level thinking and problem-solving in all school subjects. Books such as these are directed toward students' affective development, namely, their attitudes. For example, Mieko reinforces the belief among many artists that the heart is an essential part of creative productivity (e.g., inspiration, direction, and vision).

APPROACH I: INTEGRATING MULTICULTURAL EDUCATION INTO GIFTED EDUCATION

In this section, we adapt gifted education lessons[14] so that they have a multicultural perspective. Albeit a slight play on words, this approach might best be called "Multicultural Gifted Education." Our primary goal in writing this book is to inspire educators of gifted students to adopt a multicultural approach to curriculum and instruction, hence the title of this book. In 1994, the National Association for Gifted Children (NAGC, 1994b) adopted a position statement on curriculum for gifted students. The paper contends that:

> Differentiation for gifted students consists primarily of carefully planned, coordinated learning experiences that extend beyond the core curriculum to meet the specific learning needs evidenced by the student . . . Appropriate differentiation allows for increasing levels of advanced, abstract, and complex curriculum that are substantive and that respond to the learner's needs . . . the use of such differentiation is essential to maximize the educational experience for gifted and talented students.

The position paper also noted that curricula for gifted students must focus on affective needs and development. The modified lessons in this section, based on Table 5.2, show how teachers can teach at higher levels *and* teach from a multicultural perspective. In our analyses of the lessons, we plot questions on the Ford-Harris matrix. Doing so helps to ensure that questions and activities are at various levels, particularly the higher levels. The lessons must meet the academic, cognitive, and affective needs of gifted and minority students.

LESSON 1 *(Adapted from VanTassel-Baska, 1992)*

Topic: Archeology—Culture and Artifacts
Goals and outcomes: For the unit, students will understand the concept of systems; engage in scientific research; and understand the principle of archeology.

Specific unit outcomes: (1) Students will be able to use appropriate systems language to identify boundaries, important elements, input, and output; (2) students will be able to analyze the interactions of various system components with each other and with input into the system; (3) students will be able to transfer their knowledge about systems in general to a newly encountered system; (4) students will be able to explore a new scientific area; and (5) students will model the scientific process through problem-solving.

In *What a Find! A Problem-Based Unit,* VanTassel-Baska (1997) presents 17 lessons on archeology. The unit is designed for 2nd through 4th graders. Students are introduced to the field and study of archeology in many ways. For instance, they take field trips to a dig site and museum; they spend time defining archeology and familiarizing themselves with excavation tools; they must solve a problem; and they spend lesson 8 (6 sessions) on cultures and artifacts. It is this lesson that we will adapt from a multicultural perspective. In session 1 of lesson 8, VanTassel-Baska (1997) asked students: (a) to pick a culture that they are already studying (e.g., American Indians, Egyptians, etc.); (b) to define its boundaries (location and space occupied) and elements (subsystems such as transportation, food production, political system, economic system, and religious beliefs); (c) to list input (e.g., import of trade, art, ideas, culture); and (d) to list output (e.g., exports of trade, art, ideas, and culture).

Students are asked such questions as, How is a culture like a dig? List the things they have in common. How is a cultural system like a dig system? How might a dig reveal the system of a culture? How do artifacts help us to understand the system of the culture? (These are all analysis-level questions.)

In sessions 2 and 3, students are required to research the cultural system elements that they find in the dig (analysis-contributions), to make a bulletin board with index cards representing each researched elements (application-contributions), to summarize and share information about the element with other students (application-contributions), and to link their elements to other elements to show that no element in the system can function by itself (application-contributions). Students are asked to discuss the different artifacts, to tell what they do, and to determine whether the elements affect each other (analysis-contributions). They identify whether each artifact adds to their understanding of culture, and what makes elements change (analysis-contributions). In sessions 4–5, students discuss an interaction that affects the elements of the system and to summarize these interactions and the final shape of their culture (comprehension-additive). Questions include: What might a dig system reveal about a culture system (comprehension-additive)? What doesn't it reveal (comprehension-additive)?

Suggestions for Integrating Multiculturalism

In integrating multiculturalism into this lesson, we recommend more in-depth discussions and readings of cultures, including values, beliefs, traditions, and ways of living. Specifically, it is almost impossible to discuss archeology without a substantive introduction to American Indian cultures; thus, we will use American Indians as a case in point. Thus, students might read *The Sacred Tree* (Bopp, Bopp, Brown, & Lane, 1989) to better understand the concept of "culture," in particular, American Indian cultures (knowledge-transformation; comprehension-transformation). Students can also read *When Clay Sings* (Baylor, 1972), which traces the daily life and customs of prehistoric Indian tribes from the southwest (Anasaki, Hohokam, Mimbres, and Mogollon) based on the designs that remain on their pottery. The book encourages students to respect artifacts, and to remember that "every piece of clay is a piece of someone's life. . . that everything has its own spirit — even a broken pot" (knowledge-transformation). Students learn that "the molding of the lump of clay has always been a slow and gentle work" because of the meaning American Indians attach to their work. In essence, students are encouraged to dream and imagine life for these particular American Indians, and they gain a better understanding of the significance of pottery in the lives of others (knowledge-transformation; comprehension-transformation). *When Clay Sings* was written for 6-to-9-year-olds, but its simple yet powerful messages are appropriate for all ages. Other books can be used to teach archeology and culture (e.g., *The Desert is Theirs,* Baylor, 1975; *If You Are a Hunter of Fossils,* Baylor & Parnall, 1980).

In terms of the Ford-Harris matrix, teachers must spend time discussing the impact of the book on students. Students can share reactions to the metaphors, similes, pictures, and so forth, presented in the book(s). The following questions are categorized relative to Bank's multicultural levels.

Contributions: What can we learn about the traditions and beliefs of other cultures based on artifacts (knowledge-contributions)? What cultural artifacts might the U.S. be remembered by 100 years from now (analysis-contributions)? Compare and contrast pottery (or other artifacts) from another culture with pottery by European American artists (analysis-contributions). Based on these analyses, how have your beliefs about other cultures changed (evaluation-contributions)? What cultural artifacts do you want to be remembered by and why (evaluation-contributions)?

Additive: What other American Indian artifacts do you want to learn about (knowledge-addictive)? While clay is used to make pottery and other artifacts, what role does clay play in preserving artifacts (analysis-additive)? Find and share a piece of work that describes the cultural values and beliefs of American Indians (application-additive). Write a paper (story, poem, song,

etc.) that describes the cultural values and beliefs of Native Americans (synthesis-additive). How important is it to study other cultures, and what can we
learn from doing this (evaluation-additive)?

Transformation: How is disrespecting cultural artifacts a form of disrespecting other cultures (analysis-transformation)? What might other cultures
think of cultural artifacts of the U.S. (analysis-transformation)? Interview a
minority family or community member about their cultural beliefs, values,
traditions, and artifacts (application-transformation). When students share
this information and artifacts with classmates (application-transformation),
classmates can look for commonalities, themes, etc. (analysis-transformation).
How do students think other cultures feel about their cultural artifacts being
unearthed, or about their land being destroyed (analysis-transformation)?
From the perspective of American Indians, students can justify the need to
maintain the land rather than unearth cultural artifacts (evaluation-transformation).

Social Action: What can students (or the class) do to respect, protect and
preserve the cultural heritage of others (analysis-social action)? Students can
join an organization dedicated to preserving natural resources, etc. (application-social action). They can create guidelines on caring for artifacts removed
from sites (synthesis-contributions) and share them with persons working at
a nearby site (synthesis-contributions, synthesis-social action). Have students
critique a movie or book on American Indians (evaluation-additive) and send
the review to the author (evaluation-social action). They can evaluate five
books on Hispanic Americans (evaluation-additive) and submit their recommendations to a bookstore regarding the need to purchase them (evaluation-
social action). Finally, students can evaluate and submit a list of recommended
multicultural books to their school or community library (evaluation-additive, evaluation-social action).

In summary, the application of Banks's multicultural model significantly
increases students' opportunities to understand other cultures, as well as
multicultural topics, themes, and concepts. Questions and activities facilitate
depth as they target higher levels of thinking and multicultural education.

LESSON 2 *(Adapted from VanTassel-Baska, 1992)*

Topic: Weather Folklore
Goals: (1) students will understand the causes of weather change; (2)
students will develop a knowledge of basic weather instruments and how they
help measure and predict weather; (3) students will become familiar with
weather-predicting technology in use today; (4) students will attempt to
prove or disprove the accuracy of selected weather folklore through observation and discussion, projects, and experiments.

Grade level: 4

Activities: In *Planning Effective Curriculum for Gifted Learners,* VanTassel-Baska (1992) shares several sample curriculum units. One unit, "Investigating Weather Folklore," by William Chapman, targets 4th graders. The unit helps students to predict weather accurately, to understand the causes and indicators of weather change, and to understand the world. Students study and evaluate the accuracy of selected folklore by learning the causes and physics of weather, and by understanding measurement and prediction tools. Higher-level thinking skills and problem-solving are addressed, including the ability to analyze, predict, infer, judge, draw conclusions, identify problems, and solve them.

Major content topics are temperature, wind, water in the air, air pressure, and air masses and fronts. Students also explore the history of the Weather Bureau, weather instruments, and weather maps (knowledge and comprehension). Likewise, a meteorologist visits the classroom and students take a field trip to view a meteorologist in action. Finally, students study and judge the validity of weather folklore (analysis and evaluation). For instance, students are provided a collection of weather folklores and discuss their reasons for categorizing each folklore as valid or invalid (analysis). Sample folklores include: "If the woolen fleece spread the heavenly ways, be sure no rain disturbs the summer" (a valid folklore) and "If the cat washes her face over her ear, 'tis a sign the weather will be fine and clear" (an invalid folklore).

In the lesson, students read several books on weather and get information from various types of media (knowledge and application). Activities are varied. Students can choose to form a team to interview residents of nearby retirement homes, farmers, and meteorologists in order to develop and publish an article on weather folklore for the local newspaper (application and synthesis). They may choose to form a cooperative learning team to prove or disprove the accuracy of selected weather folklore (e.g., hold a debate, present a research report) (analysis and synthesis). Pre- and post-assessments target knowledge (e.g., define the term "relative humidity"), comprehension ("What causes wind to blow?"), analysis ("Which weather instruments are most helpful in predicting weather?"), and evaluation ("How has modern technology made weather prediction more accurate?").

Suggestions for Integrating Multiculturalism

In modifying this gifted education lesson/unit from a multicultural perspective, we recommend that teachers provide a context for each of the weather folklores. For instance, what are the origins of "If the woolen fleece spread the heavenly ways, be sure no rain disturbs the summer" and "If the cat washes her face over her ear, 'tis a sign the weather will be fine and clear"?

That is, are these American Indian or African American weather folklores (knowledge-contributions)? Students should also examine factors that affect how different groups use their environment to survive (analysis-additive).

Students can examine the content of folklores from different cultures and generate themes (analysis-additive). They can examine the ways American Indians view nature (comprehension-additive). How does this view differ from students' views (analysis-transformation)? How does it differ from views presented in books that students have read (analysis-transformation)? In books on weather, do American Indians tend to focus on one topic (e.g., wind) compared to another culture (analysis-additive)? Essentially, students must read some of the numerous multicultural books on multicultural weather folklore, such as *Bringing the Rain to Kapiti Plain* (Aardema, 1981), *When the Wind Stops* (Zolotow, 1995), *October Smiled Back* (Peters, 1995), and *Housekeeper of the Wind* (Widman, 1990). These books provide another perspective, additional insight, into weather, seasons, and nature, particularly from other viewpoints. They help students understand how different cultures hold different views of weather and its elements. Similarly, inviting a culturally diverse presenter(s) to the classroom would reinforce readings (knowledge-transformation).

Student projects can focus on compiling and researching weather folklore from a specific culture or conducting interviews with persons from different cultures about their views on weather folklores (application-transformation). If students live near a reservation, they might get permission/approval to view a rain dance, and to present a report on this event (application-additive). The presentation should focus on the meaning and significance of rain dances to American Indians, as well as other information (e.g., length and frequency of rain dance, participants, etc.). If permission is not granted, students can research this topic and present a report or develop some other project of interest.

In summary, the topic of weather is common in school curricula. However, concepts can be broadened and enriched when a multicultural approach is adopted. Students have additional opportunities to analyze and evaluate important issues and concepts. Likewise, they have more opportunities to apply and synthesize this learning. At its highest level, this means that students take social action.

LESSON 3 *(Adapted from Beecher, 1995)*

Topic: Construction of a tepee
Instructional objectives: The class will discuss how to construct a life-size teepee in the classroom, which will remain for the duration of the study.
Instructional strategies: Discussion, large-group planning

Description: The class will discuss their desire to construct a life-size tepee in the classroom. The teacher will explain that in order to do this, they need to plan how to proceed. The children will be introduced to the Process/Sequencing chart and learn how it will help them to determine the steps needed to complete their task. As a whole group, the teacher and class will complete the Sequencing chart.

Disciplines: Language arts, social studies, art, mathematics, and other (critical thinking analysis)

Grade level: 4

Activities: As stated in chapter 3, one of the most common programs for serving gifted students is the Enrichment Triad (Renzulli & Reis, 1977, 1997). In *Developing the Gifts and Talents of All Students in the Regular Classroom,* Beecher (1995) presents planning guides for an interdisciplinary unit on Native Americans of the Plains. The planning guide for lesson 13 of that unit is titled "Sequencing/task analysis: Construction of a Tepee." Students create a life-size tepee in the classroom, and evaluate themselves on their success in building a tepee (evaluation-contributions). Students also consider whether they should have done something differently and how to improve the tepee (analysis-contributions). Other details on this lesson are not provided by Beecher (1995).

Suggestions for Integrating Multiculturalism

Focusing on tepees when studying American Indians is common in many schools. Lessons regarding cultural "artifacts" must not stop at the contributions level. Thus, in integrating multiculturalism at higher levels, students must understand not just *how* tepees were constructed, but also why. Specifically, what role did weather and resources (e.g., cement, transportation, machinery, etc.) play in the decision of American Indians to build tepees rather than other types of homes (analysis-contributions, analysis-additive)? Why might homes such as those built in most parts of the United States be unsuitable for American Indians in the plains (analysis-contributions)? Students can research whether tepees would be suitable in such states as Michigan, Ohio, Florida, Kentucky, or Maine (or some other state) (analysis-contributions). Students might also examine the rationale for igloos, longhouses, wigwams, and other types of homes based on environmental and economic factors (analysis-contributions).

Further, as stated in previous lessons, students must be given the opportunity to explore American Indian culture in order to appreciate and respect their values, beliefs, and traditions. Without studying the culture of diverse groups, students are likely to acquire a superficial understanding of the artifacts. Building tepees, therefore, becomes just another art project.

LESSON 4 *(Adapted from Beecher, 1995)*

Topic: Native Americans of the Plains

Instructional objectives: Students will work cooperatively in groups of two to compare and contrast four characteristics of three Native American cultures (Northwestern, Plains, and Desert).

Instructional strategies: Discussion, lecture, and cooperative learning.

Disciplines: Language arts, social studies, and other (critical thinking)

Grade level: 4

Description: Before beginning this lesson, students will have obtained background knowledge of three tribes. This information makes it possible for students to successfully complete the assignment. Students are introduced to the Concept Map and shown how it can be used to compare and contrast information.

Activities: In this lesson planning guide, Beecher (1995) recommends that students use Concept Maps and notes from videos and speakers to understand group differences. It is recommended that students share their Concept Maps with each other and hold discussions.

Suggestions for Integrating Multiculturalism

As with the tepee lesson, teachers must take care to move the activities and questions to higher levels in the Ford-Harris matrix. For example, too often tepee lessons do not go beyond the contributions (Banks) and knowledge and comprehension levels (Bloom). We believe that comparisons must not focus only on dwellings and artifacts, but also on family structures, language, lifestyle, philosophy, and religious beliefs (knowledge-additive and knowledge-transformation). For example, a historical examination of migration patterns for each group might be informative (analysis-additive). Students can choose to focus on patterns attributed to wars, battles, and so forth. In essence, what role did White Americans play in American Indian migration for the different groups (knowledge-transformation)? This is an opportune time to discuss within-group differences relative to language, customs, and values.

LESSON 5 *(Adapted from Winebrenner, 1992)*

Topic: Civil War

Goals and objectives: Compacting

Grade level: 5

Activities: In chapter 4 of her book, Winebrenner (1992) presents strategies for compacting curriculum for gifted students in literature, science, and social studies. Beyond stating the goals and objectives for compacting, Winebrenner does not provide specific goals and objectives for the lesson. One lesson or activity focuses on the Civil War as an independent study project for students who performed well on the pretest. In the outline for a study guide, students are presented these seven items, all of which are knowledge- and comprehension-level questions, statements, or activities:

1. discuss the causes of the war (comprehension);
2. describe the basis of the economy for the North and South (knowledge);
3. know the meaning of the vocabulary words listed (comprehension);
4. complete a map of the states in 1861 to show which states seceded to the Confederacy and which stayed in the Union (application);
5. recite from memory Lincoln's "Gettysburg Address" (knowledge);
6. describe typical battle conditions that a soldier would be likely to encounter (knowledge); and
7. narrate a 3-minute biographical sketch of any Civil War personality (application).

For alternative topics, Winebrenner states that students can present a biography of someone who was important in the Civil War period (application-additive); research the music of both the Union and the Confederacy (application-contributions); demonstrate the action during a famous battle (application); prepare a first-person diary account of the time period from the point of view of a soldier, general, field hospital doctor, nurse, wife, or famous personality; or discuss the actual conditions of being a slave (e.g., daily life, food, shelter, family safety, religion, clothing, being a field slave vs. house slave, etc.) (analysis-transformation).

Suggestions for Integrating Multiculturalism

Clearly, any discussion of the Civil War will have a multicultural focus. However, the focus is often at the contributions and additive levels (Banks) and knowledge and comprehension levels (Bloom). This lesson is no exception—students are asked to "describe," "know," "recite," and "narrate." Few of the assignments and questions target analysis, synthesis, evaluation, transformation, and social action. Lessons for reaching higher levels in the matrix are discussed in detail below (see lessons 5a and 5b). However, a few recommendations are presented here.

In addition to listing or recalling the causes of the Civil War, students can discuss whether the war was justified or not (evaluation). They might also discuss alternatives to the Civil War or wars in general (analysis). Similarly, in addition to preparing their own first-person diaries, as recommended by Winebrenner, students can read, analyze, and critique the actual diaries of slaves, freedmen, soldiers, wives, and so forth (analysis-transformation and evaluation-transformation). If more than one diary is read, students can compare and contrast major issues and common themes (analysis-transformation). For example, what seem to be the major issues facing women versus men? Slaves versus owners? Northern soldiers versus Southern soldiers? Children versus adults? All of these are analysis- and transformation-level questions, some have more of a multicultural focus than others.

For additional understanding and insight, students might read *Working Cotton* (Williams, 1992), *John Brown: One Man Against Slavery* (Everett, 1993), and biographies of Benjamin Banneker, Harriet Tubman, and other slaves. Helpful resources include *If You Lived at the Time of the Civil War* (Moore, 1994) and *If You Traveled on the Underground Railroad* (Levine, 1988). These books provide invaluable information, as well as promote insight and awareness regarding the lives of slaves (knowledge-transformation, comprehension-transformation). Equally interesting might be to have students discuss the challenge of having a child fighting in the Civil War (analysis-transformation) or having a child sold away to be a slave (analysis-transformation).

Students can also summarize, critique, and compare important documents written before, during, and soon after the Civil War period (e.g., the Bill of Rights, Emancipation Proclamation, and the Constitution), thereby promoting analysis and evaluative skills. (As an 11th grader, our son was given the following assignment: "In your opinion, did Thomas Jefferson leave behind a negative or positive legacy regarding race relations in the United Stated?" Students were required to support their opinion.) Likewise, students can describe the roles of Ulysses S. Grant, William Sherman, Robert E. Lee, Jefferson Davis, Abraham Lincoln, and Thomas "Stonewall" Jackson in the Civil War (comprehension-additive).

Less often taught and perhaps more intriguing is that students examine the role women played in the war (analysis-transformation). Students might critique Lincoln's decision to sign the Emancipation Proclamation (evaluation-additive). Relatedly, they can compare the Civil War to the Civil Rights Movement (analysis-transformation). Students can predict and discuss what might have happened to Blacks if Lincoln had not been assassinated (analysis-transformation). Just as interesting might be a discussion on and examination of the lives of other minority groups in the Civil War (analysis-transformation).

Students can also write the headlines for an article announcing the end of the Civil War in a northern newspaper and southern newspaper (application and synthesis). Students can discuss what other countries might have written in their newspapers about the beginning and end of the war (analysis). Finally, students can compare and contrast different types of oppression (e.g., the Holocaust, concentration camps, and slavery) (analysis-transformation) and develop strategies for eliminating a particular form of social injustice (e.g., gender discrimination) in a school or social setting (synthesis-social action). Other suggestions regarding the Civil War and slavery are discussed in Lessons 10a and 10b. The various lessons (1–5) were adapted from resources targeting gifted students. Our recommendations integrate multicultural education into these lessons using Banks's model. We believe that depth, insight, awareness, and higher-order thinking skills are strengthened when a multicultural approach is adopted.

APPROACH II: INTEGRATING GIFTED EDUCATION INTO MULTICULTURAL EDUCATION

In this approach, we adapt several multicultural lessons so that they have a gifted education perspective, resulting in what might be called "Gifted Multicultural Education." Three of the lessons appear in Holmes and Guild (n.d.), and the remaining lessons appear in Grant and Sleeter (1989, 1998). This section ends with an interdisciplinary literature-based unit that we have developed on the topics of discrimination, segregation, and social action.

LESSON 6 *(Adapted from Holmes and Guild, n.d.)*

Topic: The Cultural Treasure Hunt[15]
Objectives: Students will understand the behavior, values, and way of life of persons of another culture through learning about the cultural significance of items used by those persons.
Setting: A community that represents a culture unfamiliar to the majority of students
Time: An afternoon or weekend
Procedures:

1. The teacher draws up short lists, each containing different items found within the unfamiliar community. These items might be certain kinds of local medicine, items related to religion, recreation, food, household supplies and decoration, literature, music, commerce — each of which defines, in some way, the people's behavior, values, and way of life.

2. Students should, under most circumstances, carry out their hunt alone. They are asked to learn as much as they can about how the item is used, so that they can describe and/or demonstrate its use to others in the class.
3. When the students are brought together again, they share the items and explain to each other what they have learned about their cultural importance. They also compare various experiences involved in carrying out the hunts—amusing incidents, hostile incidents, cultural differences, unexpected discoveries, etc.
4. It is useful if there are members of the group who come from the "unfamiliar" community who can assist in explaining to others about the culture of the treasures.

Suggestions for Promoting Higher-Level Thinking and Problem-Solving

Overall, we place this lesson at the knowledge and contributions levels, particularly procedures 2–3. Students at these levels are required to gather information. In procedure 4, students are asked to reflect upon their experiences, thereby increasing their self-awareness. Nonetheless, as students gather information and self-reflect, they can think at higher levels (i.e., think more critically about their experiences and act upon this information). For instance, ask students to make sure the items they select are meaningful or important to the minority community. That is, avoid selecting a superficial item. Ask students to compare and contrast the items in the minority community with items that are meaningful and important in their own community. Students can explore how it felt to be in another cultural setting—how did it feel to be a "minority" (analysis-transformation)? In terms of projects, students can write a report or make a video about their experiences to share with classmates (synthesis-social action). Once students have presented their projects, the class can discuss common themes and findings, and make a documentary on their findings (synthesis-social action). Finally, students or the teacher can invite a representative from the minority communities to speak with the class about substantive cultural values and customs (knowledge-transformation).

LESSON 7 (Adapted from Holmes and Guild, n.d.)

Topic: Community Exposure
Objective: To help students develop an initial awareness of another culture by introducing them to a few fundamental cultural differences, and to generate motivation to learn more about the unfamiliar culture and about themselves.

Setting: A community that represents a culture different from the students' culture

Time: 1 to 3 days

Procedures:

1. The teacher makes initial contact with the host communities by visiting with the leaders and explaining the purposes of the students' visit.
2. Require students to keep a journal of their experiences, especially taking note of any cultural differences they observe (analysis-additive).
3. As soon as possible, the students should convene to discuss their experiences. The following questions may be helpful to facilitate discussions:
   a. have students share observations about the physical features of the community (houses, etc.) (knowledge-contributions);
   b. have students describe cultural differences between members of the community and self (analysis-additive);
   c. have students share instances in which they felt "at home" during the visit (comprehension-transformation);
   d. ask students to share instances in which they felt uncomfortable (comprehension-transformation);
   e. have students provide suggestions for others who wish to visit or live in the community (application-social action); and/or
   f. ask students to share changes/adaptations needed to live effectively in the community (application-transformation, application-social action).

Suggestions for Promoting Higher-Level Thinking and Problem-Solving

In general, this lesson is at the comprehension and transformation levels. To move up the levels in the Ford-Harris matrix, students must engage more in exploring the experiences personally, placing themselves in the position of community members and evaluating these experiences. For example, how might community members have felt about an "outsider" coming into their community and why might they feel this way (evaluation-transformation)? Students can conduct a historical analysis of the community/organization, including significant events, milestones, and trials and tribulations, and examine how members coped with these events (analysis-transformation). If relevant, students can develop a plan or proposal for improving the quality of life for that community (e.g., improving housing, increasing access to higher education, decreasing drug use among teens, etc.) (synthesis-social action). Students can also write about the strengths of the communities (e.g., strong extended families, strong social networks, resilience in the face of obstacles, strong spirituality, etc.) (analysis-transformation).

LESSON 8 *(Adapted from Holmes and Guild, n.d.)*

Topic: Community Involvement and Social Service

Objective: To consider a community from the perspective of social and economic change; and to understand one's own problems/difficulties in introducing change an outsider who offers some social service to another society

Setting: A community that represents a culture different from the students' culture.

Procedures:

1. Arrangements should be made by the teacher or student to provide some voluntary service to the host community in return for the field experiences.
2. Each student keeps a journal of his/her experiences, which addresses the following topics:
   a. examples of how the community initiates or responds to social change (knowledge-additive);
   b. experiences and problems related to giving and receiving assistance (comprehension);
   c. areas where the student's values, living style, and behaviors differ from those in the community (analysis-additive);
   d. examples of comfortable situations and uncomfortable ones (analysis);
   e. changes the student has experienced in his/her attitude (analysis-transformation);
   f. methods of developing rapport with community members (application-transformation);
   g. ways of initiating and gaining approval for the service project by the community or representative (application-social action);
   h. perceived impact of the student on the community and how it was gauged (evaluation); and/or
   i. how the student concluded the project and left the community (evaluation).

Suggestions for Promoting Higher-Level Thinking and Problem-Solving

In this lesson, students engage in self-evaluation so they can view situations from the community's perspective. Just as important, for varying lengths of time, they immerse themselves in the community.

Pre-lesson activities should introduce students to anthropology (e.g., definitions, educational preparation). For example, students can read the work of cultural anthropologists like Margaret Mead or interview an anthropologist at the closest university to gain a better understanding of immersing oneself into another culture, building relationships, and building trust (knowledge-transformation). Students also need instruction in research skills (such as information-gathering and building relationships and trust) (comprehension and knowledge).

In addition to keeping a journal and learning about anthropology, students might create a documentary based on their experiences (synthesis-additive); or students can create a documentary based on key issues identified by community members (synthesis-social action). If students are assigned to read works by anthropologists, they can write a paper comparing and contrasting their experiences with those of the anthropologists (analysis-transformation). Students might also write a biography of a community elder or leader to share with classmates (application-additive).

Below, we present three additional lessons, each with two parts—part a and part b. According to Grant and Sleeter (1989, 1998), lessons 9a, 10a, and 11a represent traditional lessons, while lessons 9b, 10b, and 11b are at higher levels of multiculturalism. After presenting the lessons as they appear by Grant and Sleeter, we suggest ways to raise the thinking levels according to Bloom's Taxonomy. That is, where necessary, we add questions and activities at the analysis, synthesis, and evaluation levels. We also explain the strengths and shortcomings of each lesson. Lessons 9a and 9b focus on global cooperation, lessons 10a and 10b focus on slavery and resistance, and lessons 11a and 11b focus on music, specifically, the national anthem. For each lesson, we provide a brief critique and suggest ways to promote higher levels of thinking.

LESSON 9a *(Adapted from Grant and Sleeter, 1989, 1998)*

Topic: Global Cooperation
Subject area: Social studies
Grade levels: 3–4
Time: Two days
Objectives: Students will learn that different countries specialize in products for world trade. Students will value cooperation and interdependence.
Suggested procedures:

1. On a table, display items that come from different parts of the world, such as a banana, a rubber ball, a radio, and a wool sweater. Ask students if they know where the items are made (knowledge-contributions).

2. Explain that different countries produce different products, and that countries trade products so that people can enjoy more than just what is produced in their own country. To illustrate this, select about six different countries located in different parts of the world that produce different products. Point them out on a map and show pictures of their main trade products (knowledge-contributions).

3. Distribute blank world maps. Have students locate each of the six countries and post their own pictures or magazine cutouts of the countries' main products on the maps (knowledge-contributions).

4. Instruct students to locate items at home that come from different cultures (knowledge-contributions). Ask students to consider the following questions:

> What would happen if we stopped trading with a certain country? (analysis-additive)
>
> Why is it important for countries to cooperate? (comprehension-additive)
>
> Do individuals in the family or local community need to cooperate and trade for similar reasons? Can you give examples? (evaluation-additive)

Evaluation: Assess students' understanding of specialization, cooperation, and independence through class discussions.

LESSON 9b *(Adapted from Grant & Sleeter, 1989, 1998)*

Topic: Global Cooperation
Subject area: Social studies
Grade level: 3–4
Time: 2 days
Objectives: Students will appreciate the difficulties caused by maldistribution of products. Students will learn that they must give up something to gain something else. Students will value human life despite social and cultural differences. Students will develop cooperation skills.
Suggested procedures:

1. Divide the class into four groups. Have each group pick a country's name, draw a flag for their country, and draw or write a paragraph about its climate, land, and lifestyle (knowledge-contributions, knowledge-additive).

Table 5.4 Distribution of Four Products to Four Groups

	Group 1	Group 2	Group 3	Group 4	Total
Blankets	6	0	2	2	10
Bread	1	1	1	7	10
Fruit	2	7	0	1	10
Medicine	1	2	7	0	10

2. Distribute trade cards for four products — blankets, bread, fruit, and medicine — as shown in Table 5.4.

3. The groups now must decide which products are important to them and then trade in the trade center in the middle of the classroom. Only one person from each group can be in the trade center, but all trades must be approved by the entire country (analysis-contributions).

4. Take away one country's bread, due to bad weather, thereby creating a famine in that country. The other countries must decide whether to help the starving country. If they refuse, a flood will come to all except the starved country, which has the land with the highest elevation. The groups either cooperate or suffer from the floods.

5. Discuss the following questions with the class:

> How did you feel inside your group?
> How did you feel toward the other groups?
> What were the differences and similarities between the groups?
> What did the groups want from one another?
> What were the differences between products?
> How did you feel when the teacher took the bread?
> How did the rest of you feel toward this group?
> How did you solve the problem?
> Have you ever wanted something you did not get? What?
> How does that differ from wanting food or needing clothes?
> Have you had to sacrifice or trade to get what you want?
> Do your parents/guardians ever tell you to finish your food because there are starving children in their countries? Why do they say that?
> How could we help people who do not have enough?

6. Have children sit in a circle. Put some candy in a bowl and pass it

around the circle. No one can eat the candy until the bowl has made it all the way around the circle, but give this lenient rule: "You can take as many as you want." The bowl will probably not make it very far before it runs empty. At this point, give the problem to the students: "What are you going to do? Is it fair that a few have all the treats, while others go away without any? Does cooperating mean you do not always get your way?" This should reinforce the idea of thinking of others.

Evaluation: Assess students' willingness to cooperate and share through discussion and through their behavior when the candy is passed around.

Critiques of Lessons 9a and 9b

According to Grant and Sleeter (1989), lesson 9a teaches *about* cooperation, but it does not teach students to cooperate themselves (e.g., students work individually rather than with each other). In lesson 9b, students work together (e.g., the students constitute a country). Lesson 9a reinforces the idea that global specialization is beneficial to all, even though the economies of Third World countries are often devastated by shifting production from diversified products for local consumption to specialized products for trade. Often, wealthy countries are the main beneficiaries of global specialization. Lesson 9b does not criticize global specialization directly; neither does it reinforce it. This lesson directs students' attention to the distribution of goods and asks them to consider how people can work together to distribute goods more fairly.

Suggestions for Promoting Higher-Level Thinking and Problem-Solving

To tap social action, teachers might have students develop an activity that targets social improvement (e.g., raise money for poor or homeless families, volunteer for Habitat for Humanity, the Salvation Army, or similar organizations) (application-social action). Students can interview employees in international business or human service organizations to better understand the concept of global cooperation (application-additive; knowledge-additive). Going a step further, students can ask the individuals to share their perspectives on the rationale for global cooperation for a particular country (application-transformation). Students might make a list of objects in their homes to see which were made in another country (application-contributions) and discuss their feelings about this (analysis-transformation) (e.g., Does global cooperation take away jobs from U.S. citizens? If so, what can students do about the situation?) (application-social action). If most of the items in their homes come from another country, students can explore how this will affect their purchase decisions in the future (analysis-transformation). Students might also categorize the items and make a collage to share with classmates (application-contributions).

Students can also read articles on and write a report about global cooperation for a specific country (knowledge-additive; application-additive). More specifically, the report should include a discussion of the benefits and shortcomings of global cooperation for that country, along with benefits and shortcomings for the U.S. (analysis-transformation). Students can summarize and analyze trade agreements with such countries as Japan and Mexico (e.g., cars, toys, clothes, and food) (comprehension-contributions; analysis-contributions). Finally, students might analyze and evaluate the benefits of global cooperation from the perspective of wealthy countries versus impoverished countries (analysis-transformation; evaluation-transformation). Ideally, students would share this report/critique with political leaders or decision-makers (evaluation-social action) and/or create their own agreement to share with political leaders or appropriate professionals (synthesis-social action).

LESSON 10a *(Adapted from Grant & Sleeter, 1989)*

Topic: Resisting and Surviving Slavery
Subject areas: language arts; social studies
Grade level: 5–8
Time: Three class periods (spread out)
Objectives: Students will view slavery as an inhuman experience and an ugly part of our past. Students will describe the role that slavery played in moving the North and South toward the Civil War. Students will describe the Emancipation Proclamation as the formal end to slavery.
Suggested procedures:

1. In the context of studying life in the U.S. during the 1800s, have students read pages in the textbook on slavery. Discuss the extent to which Whites controlled the lives and destinies of slaves. Point out that there were a few slave rebellions, but that these did not weaken the institution of slavery. Also point out how the Underground Railroad helped many slaves to escape (knowledge-additive).
2. Later on, in the context of studying causes of the Civil War, have students read pages in the textbook on slavery as a cause. Review with students the Compromises of 1820 and 1850 and the Kansas-Nebraska Act, which tried to balance the number of slave states and

free states. Help students to see that there was tension between the North and South over slavery, but that compromises were often worked out in an effort to balance that tension (comprehension-additive).

3. Later on, in the context of studying the outcome of the Civil War, discuss the Emancipation Proclamation. Have students write an essay describing how they would feel, if they were slaves, when first hearing about it. Ask students to share their essays (application-transformation).

Evaluation: Assess students' understanding of the inhumanity of slavery and their appreciation of the Emancipation Proclamation through essays and discussions.

LESSON 10b *(Adapted from Grant & Sleeter, 1989)*

Topic: Resisting and Surviving Slavery
Subject areas: Language arts; social studies
Grade level: 5–8
Time: Five class periods
Objectives: Students will recognize that textbook accounts of slavery usually give little information about what slaves did to resist slavery. Students will describe several strategies that male and female slaves used to resist and survive slavery. Students will appreciate the active and creative roles that Black people played, and continue to play, to fight against oppression. Students will appreciate the literature about Blacks' resistance to slavery.
Suggested procedures:

1. Ask students to decide what they know about the experiences of slaves during slavery (knowledge-additive).

2. Have students read the social studies textbook account of Black slaves during slavery. Help them to realize that most accounts portray Blacks as helpless victims (knowledge-transformation).

3. Ask students what difference it might make to know what slaves actually did besides obey and suffer passively; that is, how might this knowledge affect their perceptions of Black people, and their understanding of history? Their understanding of oppressed people (knowledge-transformation)?

4. Divide the class into three groups. Explain that everyone will be given the same literature selections but that each group is to analyze them for a different purpose. Group 1 is to discover and list the strategies

that men used to survive and resist slavery; group 2 is to discover and list the strategies that women used to survive and resist slavery; and group 3 is to discover and list the strategies that slave owners used to overcome the slaves' resistance to slavery (comprehension-transformation). Some suggested literature selections include the following:

> Julius Jester (1968). *To be a slave.* New York: Dial.
> Dorothy Sterling (Ed.) (1984). *We are your sisters.* New York: W.W. Norton.
> Virginia Hamilton (1985). *The people could fly: American Black folktales.* New York: Alfred Knopf.

5. When students have finished the readings, ask each group to present and discuss their findings (application-additive). Groups 1 and 2 should have several resistance and survival strategies to share, and group 3 should have strategies that slave owners used to overcome the slaves' resistance.

6. Use this information to discuss the following:
   a. Many stereotypes of Blacks are based on Black resistance strategies; disassociating such strategies from their origin has been a White strategy for attempting to maintain White superiority (knowledge-transformation).
   b. Black people developed considerable strength and creative cultural adaptations in resisting and surviving slavery (knowledge-transformation).
   c. Blacks played a role in the destruction of slavery, contrary to what was taught in the past and sometimes even now (knowledge-transformation).
   d. Blacks continually had to resist the many efforts slave owners used to keep them in bondage (knowledge-transformation).
   e. Slave owners often used cruel and inhumane methods to force Blacks not to resist slavery (knowledge-transformation).

Evaluation: Assess students' understanding of the concepts of resistance and survival through initial discussion, textbook analysis, and analysis of literature selections. Assess students' appreciation of literature through small- and large-group discussions. Assess students' appreciation of the strength, determination, and creativity that Blacks have displayed historically and today in resisting oppression.

Critiques of Lessons 10a and 10b

Lesson 10a teaches about slavery in traditional ways, maintaining that slavery is part of the Civil War and American cultures of the past. Slavery is presented as an inhuman part of the past, and slaves are presented as victims who could do little to change their circumstances. That is, this lesson teaches children that Whites held all of the power, and slavery did not end until Whites decided that it should end. Equally problematic, lesson 10a suggests (incorrectly) that slavery ended with the Emancipation Proclamation, with little attention to continued injustices during Reconstruction (Grant & Sleeter, 1989).

Lesson 10b takes a different perspective; it views Blacks as strong and creative people who both sabotaged slavery and developed strategies for surviving slavery and oppressive conditions. It also recognizes that slavery was experienced in different ways by men and women (Grant & Sleeter, 1989). Similarly, lesson 10b connects the past and present actions of Blacks to resist, cope with, and overcome social injustices. Thus, Blacks are empowered in this lesson. Finally, the lesson uses multicultural literature as a major source of information, thereby authenticating the voices and experiences of Blacks.

Suggestions for Promoting Higher-Level Thinking and Problem-Solving

Any discussion of slavery can be awkward, for few Americans are proud of this part of our history. However, superficial discussions and exercises cannot do justice to this topic. The past must be examined honestly and thoroughly. Fostering higher-level thinking, creative thinking, and problem-solving in these lessons is possible. For example, students can examine the rationale for slavery and critique the decision to choose Africans for slave labor (analysis-additive; evaluation-additive). They might respond to the question, On what grounds was slavery justified (knowledge-transformation, comprehension-transformation)? Were these rationales justifiable at that time, and would they be justifiable now (evaluation-transformation)? What other means of labor could have been used (analysis-additive)? Using historical and/or legal documents, students can research Lincoln's position on slavery as well as that of Jefferson and other leaders (analysis-additive). How did other minority groups feel about slavery (analysis-transformation)? This analysis helps students to understand slavery from the point of view of other minority groups, thereby further increasing empathy.

Students can analyze slave revolts and discuss their significance in helping to end slavery (analysis-transformation). What tools and strategies did slaves use in the revolts, and to resist oppressive conditions (knowledge-contributions)? Do students think the revolts were justified (evaluation-transformation)? What other means of ending slavery did the slaves use (knowledge-contributions)? In what ways were slaves resilient? That is, how do the efforts and coping skills of slaves illustrate the human spirit for survival (analysis-transformation)?

Is it possible that slavery could happen again? Why or why not (analysis-transformation; evaluation-transformation)? What can be done to prevent the reoccurrence of slavery or slave labor (analysis-social action)? Students might also read the current events sections of newspapers and magazines to search for continued examples of enslavement of people of color (application-transformation), and develop plans to address these problems (application-social action).

Students can also read the biographies of abolitionists, looking in particular for their views on slavery and their efforts to end slavery (analysis-transformation). For increased understanding of slavery through the eyes of children (knowledge-transformation; comprehension-transformation), students can also read *Working Cotton* (Williams, 1992), *Follow the Drinking Gourd* (Winter, 1988), *Dear Benjamin Banneker* (Pinkney, 1994), *Narrative of the Life of Frederick Douglass, an American Slave* (Douglass, 1845/1997), *If You Traveled on the Underground Railroad* (Levine, 1988), and *If You Lived at the Time of the Civil War* (Moore, 1994).

Have students keep reflection journals of their readings (application-transformation). Suggested topics to reflect upon might include: How did slaves use songs to cope with the harshness of slavery (analysis-transformation)? How would students have coped with being a slave (analysis-transformation)? They can take on the role of Harriet Tubman—what were her coping skills and strategies (analysis-transformation) and how effective were these skills for someone who lacked resources and money (evaluation-transformation)? What do students think were the characteristics of abolitionists (analysis-transformation)? Ask students to create a poem or story depicting their perception of an abolitionist (synthesis-transformation). Generate a list of characteristics of qualities of people like Harriet Tubman, Frederick Douglass, or Benjamin Banneker (comprehension-transformation) and compare these qualities to their heroes (analysis-transformation). Should the President apologize to former slaves and their relatives? Why or why not (analysis-transformation; evaluation-transformation)? Is an official apology enough or sufficient to make amends (evaluation-transformation)? Have students to respond to this question: If you were the President of the U.S., what, if anything, would you do to help make amends for past social injustices like slavery (analysis-social action)?

LESSON 11a *(Adapted from Grant & Sleeter, 1998)*

Topic: Our National Anthem
Subject area: Music
Grade level: 6–10
Time: One class period
Objectives: Students will sing the national anthem. Students will explain why the national anthem was written.
Suggested procedures:

1. Pass out the lyrics to "The Star-Spangled Banner" and ask students to read them. Review the song's history and discuss the types of events at which the anthem is commonly sung (knowledge-contributions).
2. Play a recording of "The Star-Spangled Banner" and have students sing along. Then ask them to sing it without the aid of the recording (application-contributions).

Evaluation: Assess how well the class learns and sings the national anthem.

LESSON 11b *(Adapted from Grant & Sleeter, 1998)*

Topic: Our National Anthem
Subject area: Music
Grade level: 5–10
Time: Two class periods
Objectives:

1. Students will recognize the national anthems written by several American groups.
2. Students will describe the purpose of a national anthem.
3. Students will sing "The Star-Spangled Banner."

Suggested procedures:

1. Ask students to sing their school song. Have them discuss why they sing it and what their school song tells about the school (comprehension-contributions). Use this discussion as a basis for examining anthems.
2. Pass out the lyrics to anthems such as: (a) "The Star-Spangled Banner"; (b) "*Himno Nacional* (Mexican national anthem); (c) "Lift Ev-

ery Voice and Sing" (black national anthem); and (d) "Bread and Roses" (women's anthem). Arrange students into small groups and assign an anthem to each group. Have students write down what they think each anthem says about the group that wrote it and why they think the group wrote the anthem (analysis-transformation and evaluation-transformation).

3. Have each group report to the class, writing down key points on the board (knowledge-contributions). After they report on each anthem, tell the history of the anthem.

4. Discuss the following questions: If "The Star-Spangled Banner" is the anthem of all Americans, why have some groups written their own anthems (analysis-transformation)?

5. Play recordings of the anthem, asking students to sing along. Choose some favorites to learn as a class (knowledge-contributions).

Evaluation: Assess students' understanding of the purpose of a national anthem through class discussion. Assess students' ability to sing the anthems.

Critiques of Lessons 11a and 11b

Lesson 11a assumes that there is only one national anthem sung by Americans and uses it as the sole example of an anthem. Lesson 11b adds an analogue to an anthem from students' experience—the school song (Grant & Sleeter, 1998). It also draws on anthems from several different American groups to teach that there is more than one anthem. Lesson 11b also teaches what an anthem is by offering several examples and asking students to identify what they have in common. Further, this lesson includes multiple perspectives and asks students to work collaboratively to gain additional perspectives on the purpose of an anthem. While several of the questions and activities reach the transformation level, none reach the social action level.

Suggestions for Promoting Higher-Level Thinking and Problem-Solving

Students can compare and contrast the important ideas and concepts in each anthem (analysis-additive). That is, what is the main idea of each anthem? How do the themes differ for the various groups? Do students think it is "right" for different groups to have their own national anthem—is this "anti-American" (evaluation-transformation)?

Students can also conduct research to find out whether other groups in America have their own national anthem, and present their findings to classmates (application-additive). What factors have influenced minority groups to create their own anthem (analysis-transformation)? How are anthems signs of pride, identity, empowerment, allegiance, etc., for people (analysis-transformation)? What can students infer about each group based on their particular anthem (analysis-transformation)? What issue seems to be important to each group and why (analysis-transformation)?

Students can analyze the style of music for each anthem — In what ways do the melodies or rhythm differ for the various anthems (analysis-contributions)? What are some of the key features of Black songs, Hispanic songs, etc., and are they apparent in the anthems (comprehension-contributions)? What instruments are used in each of the anthems and how do they vary among the different anthems (knowledge-contributions)? Have students analyze the tone of the different anthems — do they hear hope, faith, or optimism? Do they hear despair or pessimism (analysis-transformation)? Why might this be the case (evaluation-transformation)? What can we learn about other cultures by listening to their music (analysis-contributions; analysis-transformation)?

In what ways, if any, can the National Anthem be changed so that it reflects the beliefs and themes of anthems from other cultures (analysis-transformation; synthesis-transformation)? Have students evaluate their school song to see if it is consistent with the U.S. national anthem and/or with anthems from other cultures (analysis-additive). What might students change, if anything, about their school song to make sure that it is culturally inclusive (analysis-social action; synthesis-social action)? Have students create a new school song that reflects their new insight and present it to the administration (synthesis-social action), along with a rationale for the new song (evaluation-social action).

Multicultural education is inadequate if students are not given opportunities to critically analyze and evaluate, and apply and synthesize what they have learned. It is primarily in this way that students reach higher levels of understanding and are able to transfer this understanding to the real world and complex issues, concepts, and topics.

LESSON 12: Multicultural Literature Unit

Topics: Discrimination, segregation, social action

Main goals: To increase students' understanding of racism and discrimination prior to desegregation, and to relate this understanding to current conditions. They will come to appreciate that children can make a difference in the world.

Specific goals: To use literature as a means of introducing students to and increasing their understanding of racial discrimination; to help students understand segregation and desegregation; to increase students' sense of empowerment and social action with literature that uses diverse children as a role model.

Grade levels: 3–6

Rationale for the unit: As the nation becomes increasingly diverse, students (all people) are being challenged and encouraged to live in a diverse world, a world that looks different from the time when our parents and grandparents were children.

This lesson encourages children to think about the past, our nation's history, so that the negative events are never repeated. Likewise, students have an opportunity to think about the future, about making the world a better place for us all. Burying or ignoring the past will not make it go away. The past is part of who we are and why we are. Remembering the past can make us stronger. *White Socks Only* (Coleman, 1996) tells the story of a child, now a grandmother, as she relives an event in her past prior to desegregation. This is an event that must not be repeated; it is an event from which we all can learn.

Book summary: A grandmother shares a true and significant event in her childhood with her granddaughter. The grandmother recalls facing discrimination in the South when she was not allowed to drink from a water fountain with a sign that read: "WHITES ONLY." Misunderstanding the sign, the girl thinks it is referring, literally, to white socks only, so she drinks from the fountain. The event ultimately results in the sign being removed, and changes the life of the town.

Pre-reading activities: Discuss important terms and concepts with students.

- What is segregation? Desegregation? Give examples of each.
- What was life like for Blacks during segregation? What about for Whites? What were Blacks not allowed to do before desegregation?
- When did segregation become unconstitutional, illegal?
- Talk to students about famous Blacks of this era — Rosa Parks, Ruby Bridges, Dr. Martin Luther King Jr., and others involved in the Civil Rights Movement. Many of these names will be familiar to students. Ask students to think about how the persons were similar — what were all of these persons seeking?
- Remind students that Ruby Bridges is one of a few children who helped to end segregation. Inform students that they are going to read about another child who influenced desegregation.
- Let children know that the book is written in Southern dialect. Share some of the words and phrases with students. Let students know that people speak differently in different parts of the country.

Vocabulary

Segregation	Porch
Plopped	Slinking down
Chime	Bandana
Plaits	Hobbled
Strutting	Desegregation

1. Place the words into categories based on parts of speech.
2. Use different tenses of the verbs in sentences.
3. Give the antonym and synonym for the words.

Social Studies (pre-reading)

1. Hold a discussion about the major events leading up to desegregation in 1954 (*Brown vs. Board of Education*). Place these events on a time-line. Let students look at the cover of the book and estimate when this story might have taken place. Plot this on the timeline. (Putting the events in a time frame will help students to understand the attitudes and beliefs of that time/era.)
2. As children read, ask them to think about time — how long ago did this incident take place? How about many years/decades ago?
3. The event/incident takes place in Mississippi. Where is Mississippi? Is this a Northern or Southern state? What is the state flower, bird, etc.? Who is the governor of Mississippi?
4. Inform students of different beliefs of the North and the South prior to desegregation. How did most southerners feel about Blacks prior to desegregation? How did many northerners feel about desegregation?
5. Talk to children about making generalizations. What is a generalization? Share an example of a syllogism with students so they can consider the consequences of "if then" thinking. For example:

   All dogs bark.
   Milo is a dog.
   Therefore, Milo barks.

   Hold discussions about the accuracy of this syllogism. Is the first premise true? Is the second premise true? Is the conclusion true? Let students create their own syllogisms or give them a list to evaluate.
6. Extend the concept of generalizations to slavery and the North and South. Did "all" people in the South want to keep slaves? Did "all" people in the North want to end slavery?

7. Ask students, "Do you think that children today can make a difference in improving society? How?"
8. What have you done that is courageous and made a difference in someone's life?
9. Research a young person in your town who has done a great and courageous deed. Send him/her a letter commending his/her efforts.

Lesson:

1. Who is the main character? What was she going to do with the eggs?
2. What is the story about? Retell the events.
3. What did she think the sign "WHITES ONLY" meant? What did it really mean? Do these signs still exist today? Why not?
4. Who was the Chicken Man? Why was he important in the story? When you first read about him, what did you think? Now that you've read the book, how has your perception/opinion of him changed?
5. What is the main idea or the moral of the story?
6. Capture the essence of the story by writing a newspaper headline.
7. Create a newspaper or TV interview about the incident. In small groups, have students develop interview questions for the little girl, her mother, Chicken Man, or another character.
8. What did Mama mean when she said: "Well, I guess you can go to town by yourself now 'cause you're old enough to do some good"?
9. Do you think the girl did "some good"? How did the girl's mistake/misunderstanding change the lives of people in her town?
10. The incident with the water fountain happened many years ago. How did the little girl's effort help *you* or affect *your* life today? Write a letter to the little girl. In the letter, express your appreciation.
11. What have you learned about segregation? Why is desegregation important in schools?
12. How can you/we "do some good" in our classroom? In our school? In our neighborhood?
13. Create a magic potion or solution that will cure the ills of prejudice and send it to the governor and President to help with their race relations programs.
14. What have you learned about yourself? Using a Venn diagram, compare yourself to the young girl—how are you similar and how are you different?
15. What did you like about the book? What did you dislike? What would you change about the book? (e.g., would you change the ending?)

Science:

1. Can you really fry an egg on the sidewalk? How can we find out?
2. Create a magic potion to cure prejudice. What would be the ingredients?

Visual and performing arts:

1. Have students reenact the incident. Let students role-play the characters and/or use tableau techniques.
2. Have students analyze and discuss the pictures. How has the author captured the emotions of the event?
3. Which picture did students like the most and the least? Why?
4. Examine the monuments shown in the book. Do a study of these monuments. Why do we create monuments? What other monuments have you seen?
5. Using clay or paints, make a monument of the little girl (and/or Chicken Man). What will you call the monument? Why might the little girl deserve to have a monument in her honor?

Interliterary link: Read *The Story of Ruby Bridges* (Coles, 1995).

1. How is the life of the child in *White Socks Only* similar to the life of Ruby Bridges? (Likewise, how is she similar to Rosa Parks?) Create a Venn diagram to show the similarities and differences. What characteristics and supports did each child have that enabled her to persevere? Do we still have those characteristics and abilities? How can we show this?
2. Have Ruby Bridges and the little girl meet on a TV show. What would they have to say to each other? Create interview questions for them. Who would be the interviewer (e.g., a student, Martin Luther King, etc.)?

Home connection:

• Have students to ask parents about their lives as children before 1954. What has changed since the parents were children?
• Have children interview grandparents. Did they ever see signs that read "WHITES ONLY"? When? Where?
• Ask parents to share memorabilia of that era.

SUMMARY AND CONCLUSIONS

Too often, low-level skills are relegated to students considered at risk for school failure, namely, minority and low SES students. Minority students are seldom exposed to the richness of academically rigorous curricula and instruction. In this chapter, we have provided recommendations, strategies, and lessons for improving the quality of instruction for gifted and minority students. Gifted students (indeed all students), we have argued, must be exposed to multicultural curricula and instruction in substantive and meaningful ways. The contributions and additive approaches (Banks, 1993, 1997) have never been and will never be sufficient for meeting the goals of a democracy. All students must be exposed to curricula and instruction at the upper end of Banks's model. Likewise, proponents of multicultural education must ensure that curriculum promotes higher-order thinking skills and problem-solving. An educated citizenry is able to apply, analyze, synthesize, and evaluate. They are able to recognize problems and to solve them. These skills are essential for school success; more importantly, they are essential for success in life.

By combining the work of Bloom and Banks, we have provided educators with the philosophy, strategies, and materials necessary to enhance their teaching and thus to improve students' learning. Unfortunately, gifted students may not be exposed to multicultural education; minority students may not be challenged cognitively. The synthesis of these two fields — multicultural gifted education — offers the greatest promise for providing students with the best that education has to offer. The lessons and units demonstrate that the curricular goals of gifted education and multicultural education can be combined to provide students with an education that is diverse, challenging, and empowering.

CHAPTER 6

Counseling Students from a Multicultural Perspective

We must feel good about who we are before we can feel good about others.

—Ponterotto & Pedersen (1993, p. 39)

INTRODUCTION AND OVERVIEW

Just as gifted education and multicultural education have proceeded along parallel paths, so too has the counseling of gifted students and minority students. This chapter focuses on counseling aimed at meeting the affective, social-emotional, and psychological needs of students who are gifted *and* culturally diverse. We present an overview of both counseling fields and offer recommendations for synthesizing them. We also summarize the Affective Taxonomy (Krathwohl, Bloom, & Masia, 1964) and draw implications for counseling students based on this model. We then provide recommendations for integrating multiculturalism into counseling using multicultural literature. Thus, the primary intervention in this chapter is bibliotherapy. Finally, the chapter contains a case study to help apply concepts and strategies. The case involves a middle-class Hispanic American male, Ramirez, who faces barriers to racial identity.

COUNSELING GIFTED STUDENTS

Efforts designed to address the affective, psychological, and social-emotional needs of gifted students span several decades, but are comparatively new. Terman (1925) and Hollingworth (1926) were among the first writers to recognize the special needs of gifted students. Terman's longitudinal study of middle-class White children helped to dispel the myth that gifted children were inherently well adjusted. Likewise, one of Hollingworth's greatest contributions is calling attention to the potential gap between a gifted child's intellectual and emotional development.

According to Colangelo (1991), it was not until the 1950s that concerted counseling efforts and initiatives were targeted at gifted students. Scholars highlighted the ignored issues related to suicide, depression, perfectionism, self-concept, self-esteem, anxiety, and poor peer relations among gifted students. Nonetheless, some four decades later, the field of counseling gifted students remains in its infancy. In particular, few counselors have addressed the social and emotional needs of gifted students, and the issue of affective development is conspicuously absent in most books on gifted education.

Just as troubling, less than a handful of articles focus exclusively or specifically on counseling gifted diverse students from a social-emotional perspective (see Ford, 1995b; Ford, Harris, & Schuerger, 1993). Books that focus on counseling gifted students often contain a perfunctory chapter on "special populations," a term that has become synonymous with "minority" (most often Black) children.

A few studies have explored school counselors' awareness of issues confronting gifted students, as well as their preparation to work with this student population. Findings indicate that school counselors (and psychologists) lack formal preparation to work with gifted learners. For example, Klausmeier, Mishra, and Maker (1987) found that most school counselors considered their preparation in recognizing gifted students to be less than average, and their training with minorities and low social-economic groups to be below average or completely lacking. In a study of university counselors, only 10% reported training in working with gifted learners (Ford & Harris, 1995). Further, the majority of the counselors in this study were unaware of (or indecisive about) the differential issues hindering the achievement of gifted Black and White students. Progress has been made. Recently, the National Association of Gifted Children (NAGC) published a position paper on the affective needs of gifted children. This document, presented in Figure 6.1, provides guidance and direction to school personnel on meeting the affective needs of gifted students. NAGC asserts, "It is imperative that those who provide services have experience in understanding the impact of giftedness on a child's development . . . These services include counseling that addresses the increased incidence of perfectionism, unrealistic goals, emotional intensity, moral concerns, and the resultant stress and lower achievement in the gifted population" (NAGC Position Paper, 1995a). Albeit less specific, the position paper also acknowledges that gifted minority children have additional affective needs that require consideration.

**Figure 6.1 NAGC Position Paper: Addressing the Affective Needs of Gifted
   Children**

Educational and counseling programs must provide all children with opportunities to
develop understanding of themselves and their role in society. Because, by definition,
gifted children differ significantly from others, these programs should be responding to
the social-emotional or affective characteristics that distinguish gifted students from
others. Furthermore, since significant differences also exist within the gifted population,
appropriate services need to be designed and implemented to respond to individual
differences.

Characteristics such as emotional and moral intensity, sensitivity to expectations and
feelings, perfectionism, lofty goals and standards for themselves and others, and deep
concerns about societal problems at an early age are found in a proportionally higher
incidence among gifted and talented children. Those who have disabilities or differ in
other ways, including culturally, linguistically, or socio-economically, may have
additional affective needs.

NAGC believes that gifted children also require appropriate affective services, including
gifted-focused counseling interventions and career-development guidance programs, if
they are to develop to their potential. NAGC recommends that these services be designed
to:

- Provide orientation to gifted programming, including information about the selection
  process and social, emotional, and academic implications of giftedness.

- Enhance relationships with others, including both those who are gifted and those who
  are not.

- Assist with long-term planning, including opportunities to deal with issues related to
  multipotentiality.

- Provide counseling that addresses the increased incidence of perfectionism, unrealistic
  goals, emotional intensity, moral concerns, and the resultant stress and lower
  achievement in the gifted populations.

Some gifted and talented children, because of heightened intellectual and social-
emotional needs, may experience difficulties that require professional intervention.
NAGC believes that it is imperative that those who provide services at such times have
expertise in understanding the impact of giftedness on a child's development.

MULTICULTURAL COUNSELING

Like counseling in gifted education, multicultural counseling spans only
a few decades. Not long ago, the counseling profession came to recognize
that the theories, techniques, strategies, and interventions taught and used by
counselors were inadequate for working with minority groups (Ponterotto,
Casas, Suzuki, & Alexander, 1995).

The importance of considering socio-cultural characteristics in counseling was first addressed by Wrenn (1962), who warned of the dangers of be-

coming "enculturally encapsulated," that is, viewing and interpreting the experiences of culturally diverse clients from one's own ethnocentric and monocultural viewpoint. More specifically, Wrenn cautioned against counselors imposing their culturally laden goals, values, and practices upon clients from diverse backgrounds. Seven years later, the Commission on Accelerating Black Participation in Psychology was established to direct its efforts to deal with barriers that Blacks encountered in the profession. In 1970, APA established the Office of Black Students' Psychological Association to address the needs of Black students (Ponterotto & Casas, 1991). Many other efforts ensued, including attention to other minority groups and females (see Ponterotto & Casas for details). Ultimately, the Association for Multicultural Counseling and Development approved a document outlining the need and rationale for a multicultural perspective in counseling. These standards appear in Sue, Arrendondo, and McDavis (1992).

A major thrust of multicultural counseling is its focus on one's perception of self as a racial being, yet other issues, namely racial identity, are central to multicultural counseling. Hence, numerous theories of racial identity have emerged, and are discussed below.

CENTRAL ISSUES TO ADDRESS IN COUNSELING MINORITY STUDENTS

Students of color have unique or special issues that must be addressed early and consistently in counseling. Central among these issues are underachievement, racial identity, and discrimination. Relative to social-emotional and affective needs, counselors may represent the only or primary source of professional support for students who underachieve, have poor self-perceptions, and face social barriers (e.g., racial injustices, low expectations).

Underachievement

It is an unfortunate reality that too many minority students have dismal educational outcomes—poor test scores, high dropout rates, high truancy rates, and high suspension rates. Underachievement is a complex phenomenon, a process that develops over time and is difficult (but not impossible) to reverse, especially if left unattended for some time (Diaz, 1998). Negative school outcomes can be attributed to poor academic self-concepts, numerous social-emotional needs, and socio-demographic risk factors.

Academic Self-concept. Although often considered a single global appraisal of one's overall worth, self-concept is recognized currently by many researchers (e.g., Cross, 1995; Harter, 1982) as consisting of several separate domains, including general/global, academic/intellectual, athletic, physical appearance, and social. Self-concept, or the cognitive assessment of one's abilities in comparison to others, is a widely studied variable assumed to have direct bearing on students' academic achievement. A person's self-concept is one of the single most important variables in an individual's life.

Whitmore (1980, 1986) found that one cause of underachievement in gifted children is not a lack of cognitive skills, but rather the perceptions students have about their ability: (a) to fit in socially; (b) to satisfy the expectations of parents and teachers; and (c) to perform basic academic tasks in the usually prescribed manner. These concerns hinder students' academic self-concept, making success in school even more unlikely. For instance, Ford (1992, 1993, 1995a) noted that many underachieving Black students hold paradoxical or inconsistent attitudes and behaviors about achievement. On the one hand, they hold positive beliefs about achievement; on the other hand, their behaviors do not support or match their beliefs. Fordham's (1988) research sheds additional light on this dilemma for Black adolescents. Similarly, Ogbu (1994) and Diaz (1998) explain in detail the achievement dilemmas for other students of color.

Social Self-concept. Children's social-emotional and educational problems often relate to an inability to fulfill their basic needs (Maslow, 1968). One of our basic needs is the desire to belong and to feel loved (Glasser, 1986). As described in chapter 1, minority students are socially oriented, as reflected by strong fictive kinship networks and large extended families. There is a strong need to belong and for affiliation, and also a need to bond with others who share similar concerns and interests. This need for group affiliation, however, can have unfortunate ramifications when an anti-achievement ethic is espoused by the peer group.

Our schools seldom address the social-emotional needs — self-esteem and belonging — of students. Although counselors recognize the interrelation of the social-emotional and cognitive domains of development, programs for gifted students appear to have largely neglected this area of development (Barnette, 1989, p. 525). Li (1988) demonstrated that many studies purporting gifted students to have higher self-concepts investigated only the general domain, rather than such specific domains as social self-concept in which gifted students frequently score poorly. Whitmore (1980, 1986) noted the feelings of alienation and isolation gifted children experience due to their unique abilities. Ford (1989), for example, reported that gifted elementary students expressed embarrassment, guilt, and even confusion about their academic success, which had negative effects on their peer relationships.

Diaz (1998) also found that social factors significantly and negatively impact achievement among talented Puerto Rican students.

Being placed in situations with students (and teachers) who look, speak, and behave differently can negatively influence one's social self-concept, as explained by the social comparison theory:

> . . . in the absence of objective standards of comparison, people will employ significant others in their environments as bases for forming estimates of self-worth and, given the choice of relatively similar or dissimilar others, they are more likely to select similar others as the bases for social comparison. (Coleman & Fults, 1985, p. 8)

Social Injustices and Discrimination

It is futile to deny that prejudice is a prevalent and persistent problem in schools and society. Minority students may experience racism on a daily basis, a problem students bring into the classroom. Students who are unable to cope effectively with injustices or prejudice (of any kind) are unable to work effectively in school. Learning is seriously hindered. Persistent racism conquers the spirit of students of color. Too many minority students receive negative input about their ability to achieve academically. Such low expectations may come directly from teachers, parents, or peers. The source of the messages aside, such injustices weaken an important facet of self-concept in minority students.

Psychological Issues

Self-perception plays a major role in school achievement and behaviors. However, traditional theories of self-concept have yet to include racial self-concept as a component, despite the reality that race is central to the self-concept of many people of color (Cross, 1995). People of color confront issues of race on a daily basis and thus struggle with this aspect of self. For instance, Lee's (1996) qualitative research highlighted the racial dilemmas facing some Asian Americans (Koreans), Diaz (1998) studied Puerto Rican students and such dilemmas, and Ford, Harris, and Schuerger (1993) discussed the racial confusion faced by some Black students. More than 400 studies have addressed racial identity among Black students, calling attention to its critical role in the psychological well-being of Blacks. As previously noted, Ponterotto and Pedersen (1993) devoted an entire book to the topic of racial identity and its implications for White students and students of color. Their underlying premise is that racial understanding and appreciation are lifelong developmental processes that begin with a healthy sense of one's own racial identity.

Racial Identity. Racial identity concerns one's self-concept as a racial being, as well as one's beliefs, attitudes, and values relative to other racial groups (Cross, 1995). By age three or four, children know their race, and by the time they enter school, the implications of racial group membership and status become even more salient (Helms, 1994). Few empirical studies on self-concept have been conducted using gifted minority students as the primary subject group, and school counseling approaches rarely operate from a multicultural orientation; thus, counselors may find it difficult to promote positive racial identities among minority children.

Racial identity theories exist for each major minority group. However, space limitations prohibit a detailed discussion of each theory. We focus on Black, Asian American, and Hispanic American students. Readers are encouraged to examine racial identity theories for White and other minority students in Ponterotto and Pedersen (1993).

Black Racial Identity. In his revised model of racial identity, or the psychology of Nigrescence, Cross (1995) described more completely how African Americans progress and regress in the process of becoming Afrocentric. According to the model, Blacks in stage I (Pre-encounter) hold one of at least three attitudes toward race: (a) low-salience attitudes; (b) social stigma attitudes; and (c) anti-Black attitudes. Those holding a low-salience attitude do not deny being physically Black, but they consider their blackness as having an insignificant role in their daily lives, their well-being, or how they define themselves. Cross contends that these individuals are unlikely to give much thought to race issues, and appear unaware of such problems. Overall, they view themselves as "human beings who just happen to be Black" (p. 98). African Americans who hold social stigma attitudes not only have low-salience attitudes, they also see their racial orientation as something to be ashamed of and negotiated. By default, race is attributed some significance, but not in the positive sense. Anti-Black attitudes constitute the third and most extreme type of Pre-encounter individual. Such persons see their racial status as negative, loathe other Blacks, feel alienated from other Blacks, and do not perceive the Black community as a potential resource or support base.

All three Pre-encounter types favor European cultural perspectives, such as beauty, art, communication modes, and academic preferences. In essence, many have been socialized to be bicultural, but they do not necessarily hold pluralistic and multicultural notions. Some, for instance, may consider multicultural education to be unnecessary, wasteful, or inferior (Cross, 1995, p. 103). Cross contends that Pre-encounter attitudes transcend social class boundaries, with low-salience, social stigma, and anti-Black attitudes being expressed at all socio-economic (SES) levels.

In stage 2 (Encounter), the individual experiences an "identity metamorphosis" (p. 104) in which a major event or series of events induces cognitive dissonance. These events, either positive or negative, tear away at Pre-encounter attitudes and push them toward increased awareness of their status as a racial being. The encounter, therefore, results in great emotionality, guilt, anger, and anxiety for having minimized or denied the significance of race. Similarly, they feel anxious upon realizing that there is another level of blackness to which they should aspire.

Stage 3 (Immersion-Emersion) represents what Cross (1995) refers to as the "vortex of psychological Nigrescence" (p. 106). African Americans in this stage begin to rid themselves of their raceless identities and begin constructing their new frame of reference. Yet this stage is also characterized by anxiety, primarily about becoming the "right kind of Black person" (p. 106). Equally problematic, all that is White is perceived as evil, oppressive, and inhuman, while all that is Black is proclaimed superior.

In the immersion phase, African Americans immerse themselves in the world of blackness. For example, they attend political or cultural meetings that focus on Black issues, along with issues of justice and equity. This stage is energized by rage, guilt, and a developing sense of pride. The individual accepts his or her self as a racial being. Common themes are selflessness, dedication, and commitment to Blacks. They may experience creative, inspirational bursts of energy that communicate the richness of their racial heritage. Taken to the extreme, African Americans in the immersion stage have difficulty controlling the impulse to confront White authority figures, even on a life-or-death basis. That is, the threat of death is not feared.

In the emersion phase, there is a marked decline in the racist and emotional attitudes. This leveling-off occurs when African Americans encounter a role model, for instance, who displays a more sophisticated and calmer persona. Through role models, Blacks learn to abandon romantic and romanticized notions of blackness toward a deeper and more serious understanding of Black issues.

The fourth stage (Internalization) is marked by the integration of a new identity, an identity that is more authentic and naturalistic. This identity includes high salience to blackness, which can take on several manifestations, including biculturalism. An internalized identity serves several functions: (a) to defend and protect the person from psychological problems associated with living in a society where race matters; (b) to provide a sense of belonging and social affiliation; and (c) to provide a basis for interacting and communicating with people, cultures, and situations beyond the world of blackness (Cross, 1995).

The fifth and final stage (Internalization-Commitment) is characterized as action-oriented. Here, African Americans devote much time and energy, perhaps a lifetime, to finding ways to translate their personal sense of blackness into a plan of action, a commitment to Black affairs and improving the circumstances of African Americans.

Although a stage model, Cross (1995) acknowledges that individuals can regress or get stuck at one stage. Whether they regress, become stuck, or progress through the stages of racial identity depends, in large part, on the individual's personality, support base, resources, and his or her experiences.

Hispanic American Racial Identity. Arce's (1981) research focused on Chicano racial identity and describes the processes whereby Chicanos stop thinking of themselves as Chicanos. Reaching this stage of identity involves two types of self-awareness: (1) cultural awareness and (2) political awareness. Cultural awareness represents increased pride in one's language, heritage, and cultural values. Political awareness represents the knowledge of Mexican people's history in the U.S., along with an awareness of the impact of discrimination or prejudice on one's group.

Unlike Cross (1995), Arce does not name stages in the racial identity of Chicanos. However, his transitional descriptions are consistent with other theories of racial identity. Ponterotto and Pedersen (1993) noted that the stages could be classified as: (1) forced identification; (2) internal quest; (3) acceptance; and (4) internalized ethnic identity.

During the first stage, forced identification, students are identified by the general terms "Hispanic" or "Mexican American" by others. Those who adopt this imposed identity find at some point that it stimulates a search for one's cultural roots — a quest for self-understanding relative to race (stage 2). This search leads to an acceptance of one's group, and contributes to increased pride and commitment (stage 3). In the final stage, Chicanos develop a deeper, more substantive sense of affiliation and belonging to one's group, and a desire to contribute to its overall well-being.

Asian American Racial Identity. In 1981, Kim examined the process by which Asian Americans resolve their identity conflict relative to their dual identities as Asians and Americans. The sample included third-generation Japanese American women. Unlike Cross (1995), Kim's model is developmental. "Ethnic awareness," the first stage of racial identity for Asian Americans, occurs during elementary school as students interact with family and community members. Kim found that initially, greater family support and exposure to Japanese culture contributed to positive racial identities and self-perceptions. However, as Japanese persons interact more with other racial groups, they progress toward the next stage of racial identity. For most of the women sampled, this interaction and progression were likely to be negative.

"White identification" represents the second stage. Japanese students begin to develop a heightened awareness that they are "different" from their White classmates. Racial prejudice contributes to these negative feelings. Feelings of inferiority, according to Kim's model, are internalized; thus, students at this stage attempt to adopt or internalize White values. Further, they begin to alienate themselves from other Asian Americans. Adopting this White frame of reference often results in decreased interactions with other Asian Americans, increased efforts in academic pursuits, and increased efforts to gain approval from White students. Lee (1996) discussed similar identity issues among Korean American high school students.

In the third stage, called "awakening to social political consciousness," students develop a new perspective of themselves, namely seeing themselves as a minority in society. Like Cross (1995), Kim notes that a significant event can push students into this stage of awakening political awareness. For Kim's subjects, a major event included the Civil Rights Movement. In this stage, Japanese Americans rid themselves of their White identity and reassess White standards (e.g., of beauty, success, etc.). They move toward a positive self-concept in which feelings of inferiority and oppression decrease.

The next stage, "redirection to Asian American consciousness," is characterized by a stronger and more positive minority orientation. Students embrace their racial identity more fully and immerse themselves in their cultural and racial heritage. However, as in Cross's immersion-emersion stage, Asian Americans feel angry, resentful, and outraged. They may view White racism as playing a major role in their identity difficulties, particularly during earlier stages.

The final stage of the model is called "incorporation." Students' identity is strong, balanced, and secure. Along with stronger and more positive racial identity, individuals now recognize and appreciate their other identities (e.g., gender).

Similarities Among Racial Identity Models

Ponterotto and Pedersen (1993) identified the following similarities among the various racial identity models:

1. *Pre-exposure/pre-contact* — lack of self-awareness of self as being a racial being; unaware of social expectations and roles relative to race; oblivious to racial issues; has not yet begun to explore racial identity; unconscious identification with whiteness; and unquestioned acceptance of stereotypes about minority groups

2. *Conflict* — Increased knowledge about race-relations that is facilitated by contact with minority groups. A central conflict is conformity to majority norms and humanistic, as well as humanistic or non-racist values

3. *Pro-minority/anti-racism* — Increased compassion for minorities, and strong feelings of guilt for previous low salience attitudes attached to race. This stage may include overidentification with and paternalistic attitudes toward other minority groups

4. *Retreat into White culture* — Retreat from situations that stimulate conflict; re-retreat into same-race contact for comfort, security, and familiarity

5. *Redefinition and integration* — Acknowledge more responsibility for maintaining racism while having an identity that is nonracist and healthy, as well as flexible and open.

Recommendations

An important responsibility of counselors is to help students to develop effective racial identities. The philosophy of existentialism is helpful when working with gifted minority students. That is, given the many issues facing these students, they may experience an existential crisis — Who am I? How do I feel about my race and heritage? What does it mean to be gifted? Most adults know what it is like to lack meaning or a sense of purpose.

Reality therapy is also valuable for addressing issues surrounding self-direction and independence, and can teach gifted minority students to take increased responsibility for their behaviors. Reality therapy asserts that all behavior is internally motivated, and that individuals must learn to take responsibility for their choices and behaviors. Reality therapy, therefore, reeducates and empowers students to identify their needs, wants, and goals; to establish realistic behaviors necessary to attain these goals; and to explore negative school experiences. Reality therapy can help gifted minority students to explore the need to belong and to be loved, the need for power and control, and the need for freedom. Counselors can help gifted minority students to establish and evaluate their present behaviors, to develop a plan of action to cope effectively with specific situations and immediate concerns, and to make a commitment to take action.

The final approach that we will discuss is Krathwohl, Bloom, and Masia's (1964) Taxonomy of Educational Objectives — the affective domain. Our observations of classrooms and discussions with educators reveal that this Taxonomy is often ignored in schools; if not ignored, it is given less attention than Bloom's Cognitive Taxonomy (Bloom, 1956). Yet giftedness is both an affective and cognitive entity, so many of the goals, objectives, and theories in gifted education and multicultural education must address the affective needs of students. This Taxonomy has five levels: (1) *receiving/attending;* (2) *responding;* (3) *valuing;* (4) *organization;* and (5) *characterization of a value* (Table 6.1).

The lowest level of the Affective Taxonomy is receiving/attending, which is divided into three subcategories. Awareness is the lowest subcategory. It includes being conscious of what is being taught and taking it into account. However, it does not imply that the student can verbalize what contributed to the awareness. The next subcategory is willingness to receive, which involves a neutral or suspended judgement toward what is being taught. The highest subcategory is controlled and selected attention. Here, the student attends to the information and is not distracted by other stimuli.

At the next level, responding, students voluntarily seek information about what is being taught, and they find pleasure in learning. Responding includes the subcategories of acquiescence in responding, willingness to respond, and satisfaction in response. Acquiescence in responding implies obedience or compliance and passivity. Students do not initiate behaviors, nor do they avoid them. Willingness to respond implies that students are more voluntary and active. They are beginning to make choices to respond. With satisfaction in response, enjoyment takes place; students derive some type of pleasure and a feeling of satisfaction with learning.

In valuing, the third level, students demonstrate a sense of responsibility for learning; they are invested in learning and value what is being taught. Again, there are three subcategories — acceptance of value, preference for a value, and commitment. Acceptance of a value indicates that what is being taught has worth or significance to the students. However, it is the lowest level of valuing, where commitment is not definite. Increased commitment and valuing come at the next subcategory, preference for a value. The student both indicates a value for what is learned and shows commitment. Finally, commitment, the third subcategory, implies an even stronger consistency between values and behaviors.

The next level, organization, occurs when students are able to examine basic assumptions, form judgments, and develop personal goals. This, unlike the previous levels, is more of a conscious effort to make decisions. It is the level at which students are organizing a value system. The first subcategory of a value, conceptualization of a value, indicates that the student is able to see how one value relates to another. In organization of a value system, he/she coordinates different values to patterns and relationships. They try to balance different and opposing values into a less complex and more consistent schema.

The final level, characterization of a value, represents the point at which students have a personal philosophy of life that is demonstrated in their be-

Table 6.1 Taxonomy of Affective Educational Objectives

Category	Subdivisions	Affective Objectives
Receiving/ Attending	Awareness Willingness Controlled and selected attention	Observes; recognizes; is aware of; develops sensitivity to. Accepts others; develops tolerance; listens carefully; recognizes persons as individuals. Ability to use discrimination skills; shows appreciation; alert to values.
Responding	Acquiescence in responding Willingness to respond Satisfaction in response	Shows a willingness to comply, to observe rules and regulations. Voluntarily seeks information. Finds pleasure in learning (e.g., listens, reads).
Valuing	Acceptance of a value Preference for a value Commitment	Develops a sense of responsibility. Values what is being taught; values learning. Committed to learning; is invested in learning (e.g., listens, reads).
Organization	Conceptualization of a value Organization of a value system	Analyzes basic assumptions; forms judgments; develops personal goals; establishes a conscious base for making decisions. Examines role of democracy in conserving natural resources; accepts own potentialities and limitations; is without prejudices; develops techniques for conflict management; accepts responsibility for future.
Characterization of a value	Generalized set—the basic orientation that allows individual to act consistently and effectively in a complex world Characterization—one's personal philosophy of life demonstrated in behavior	Reverses judgments or changes behavior in light of evidence or facts; confidence in ability to succeed. Develops a code of behavior based on ethical principles consistent with democratic ideals; behaviors and beliefs are consistent.

Adapted from Krathwohl, Bloom, & Masia (1964)

haviors. They have a code of ethics that guides their behaviors, and their beliefs and behaviors are congruent. There are two subcategories — generalized set of values and characterization. The first, generalized set of values, represents a consistent reaction to situations and contexts. These values help to guide students' actions and decisions. In the last subcategory, characterization, students have a philosophy of life, a worldview that impacts their behavior and choices.

The Affective Taxonomy reinforces the central role of these affective needs and development on student outcomes; thus, it must be incorporated into models and theories of counseling (and education, as discussed in chapter 5). For instance, considerable research indicates that school success depends heavily on students' interests, sense of responsibility, sense of self-efficacy, ability to make effective choices, ability to manage conflicts, and ability (or willingness) to follow school rules. School success also depends on students' coping skills, listening skills, and value or belief systems. Counselors (and teachers) can use the Affective Taxonomy to understand students' achievement motivation and interests, and to develop interventions based on the affective variables.

Essentially, we support an eclectic and developmental approach to counseling whereby counselors consider the individuality of students relative to their needs and concerns. Counselors must be willing to redefine the counseling situation so that communication, change, and growth are possible.

PREVENTION AND INTERVENTION STRATEGIES

The types of approaches to counseling students are limitless. We focus primarily on bibliotherapy, the use of literature to promote self-understanding and awareness (racial pride), persistence and resilience, and social relations. Below, we present more than a dozen annotations of books categorized by grade level and major concepts.

Literature/Bibliotherapy

Bibliotherapy for gifted students has been recommended in several publications (e.g, Hebert, 1991; Kyung-Wong, 1992; Reis & Dobyns, 1991). Halsted (1994), for instance, reviewed approximately 300 books with gifted characters or with issues common to students identified as gifted. Like Halsted and others, we think bibliotherapy represents a potentially powerful tool for counseling students. Unfortunately, few efforts have used bibliotherapy as an intervention with gifted minority students.

Kyung-Wong (1992) noted that bibliotherapy has four stages: (1) Identification—the reader sees similarities between him/herself and the character in the literature; (2) Catharsis—the reader allows emotions and internal conflicts to surface; (3) Insight—the reader makes connections with the characters and issues; and (4) Universalization—the reader understands that he/she is not alone, that his/her problems are not unique. We add a fifth stage, Action, which represents the essence of bibliotherapy—behavioral and cognitive change. In this final stage, readers are able to act upon this new information and understanding. If students are unable to act upon this newfound insight, the effectiveness of the intervention is questionable. Action will not necessarily be immediate; for some students, time will be needed for the information to set in. We have read books whose impact was immediate or more distant, more out of touch with students' reality.

In terms of racial identity issues, students should be exposed to such books as *Maizon at Blue Hill, Eggbert: A Slightly Cracked Egg, I Wish I Were a Butterfly, The Missing Piece, I Hate English,* and *The Ebony Duckling.* These books focus on identity concerns and help students to resolve and cope with such problems.

Below, we describe these books using an annotated approach. Table 6.2 summarizes the books by topics and concepts, and recommended grade levels. All of the literature is multicultural or has concrete application to multicultural themes, concepts, and issues. Where appropriate, we have selected books with gifted minority characters. This was a challenge in that few books have gifted or achieving minority students as their central character. Other appropriate books appear in Chapter 5.

LITERATURE FOR GRADES P–3

Ross, T., & Barton, R. (1994). *Eggbert: The Slightly Cracked Egg.* New York: The Putnam & Grosset Group.

Eggbert is rejected by other foods in the refrigerator because he has a slight crack. He leaves the refrigerator in search of a place where he can be accepted. Eggbert eventually learns that many things with cracks can be beautiful. The central theme is self-acceptance by appreciating one's differences. Also important is the concept of peer relations and social pressures. We have designed the following activity to facilitate students' discussion and critical thinking relative to differences and diversity.

Self-concept/self-pride: How did Eggbert feel when others did not accept his slightly cracked shell? How do you feel about this? Why did Eggbert leave? What did Eggbert see as he traveled? What did he learn? What did you learn about yourself? What have you learned about friendships?

Table 6.2 Bibliotherapy: Sample of Multicultural Literature for Gifted Students

Literature	Grade Level	Demographics of main character	Central themes or concepts
The Ugly Duckling	P–3	Black duck who is rejected by family and other ducks	Self-concept, peer pressure, family support
The Mixed-Up Chameleon	P–3	Chameleon who changes to many things that it sees	Self-concept
Corduroy	P–3	Bear who is missing a button	Self-concept, friendship
Do You Want to Be My Friend?	P–3	Mouse who can't find a friend	Friendship, persistence
I Wish I Were a Butterfly	P–3	Cricket who does not like itself	Self-concept, peer pressures, friendship
A Color of His Own	P–3	Chameleon who does not like being different	Self-concept
Maizon at Blue Hill	4–6	Gifted, Black, low SES, female	Racial pride, achievement, persistence, friendship
Yang the Youngest and His Terrible Ear	4–6	Chinese male who does not like playing music; SES seems to be middle-class	Expectations, friendship, stereotypes
The Gift-Giver	4–6	Gifted Black male, low SES	Self-confidence, independence, friendship, achievement
Gifted Hands	9–12	Gifted Black male, low SES	Achievement, effort, persistence, self-concept, family support
Malcolm X	9–12	Black males, low SES	Racial identity, persistence, social action
Blue Tights	9–12	Gifted Black female, low SES	Achievement, self-concept, self-pride

Note: A few of the books for P–3 students focus on important multicultural themes and concepts; they are not necessarily multicultural. Several of these books are also discussed in Chapter 8 and are recommended for use by families.

Activity: The most important message that should be conveyed in this activity is that "the outside may be different, but the inside is often the same."

- Boil two eggs.
- Paint one of the eggs and cover it with glitter.
- Leave the other egg unpainted.

1. Ask students: "Which egg is pretty"? (Or "Which is prettier?")
2. Most likely (but not guaranteed), students will choose the painted/colorful egg. Whichever egg is chosen, ask students to explain their choice ("Why do you think it is prettier?").
3. Ask students: "Which egg tastes better? Why?"
4. "What does the outside of the egg have to do with the inside?" "Just because it is pretty outside, does that mean it is pretty inside?"
5. Crack the eggs. Ask students to look for differences on the inside.
6. What do students see? What does this mean?
7. Ask students: "What have you learned about yourself from this activity and book?"

Howe, J. (1987). *I Wish I Were a Butterfly.* New York: Harcourt Brace Jovanovich.

A cricket is convinced that he is ugly because a frog told him so. A spider (The Wise One) tries to convince the cricket that he is not ugly; however, it is a difficult task. Eventually, the spider gets the cricket to play music. A butterfly hears the music and wishes it were a cricket. A number of topics can be discussed with students, particularly self-concept/self-pride, peer pressures, and friendships.

Self-concept/self-pride: Ask students to think about why the cricket thought he was ugly. Why did he believe what the frog said? What makes a person or thing ugly? Ask students to consider how the book focuses on the concept "Don't judge a book by its cover." How can we make sure that we have high self-concepts?

Peer pressure: Why do people tease others? How is teasing others like trying to hide one's own faults? What can we do in our classroom and school to increase respect?

Friendships: What are the qualities of a good or real friend? How was the spider a friend to the cricket? How can you be a friend to someone else?

Hoffman, M. (1991). *Amazing Grace.* New York: Dial.

Grace is a creative and confident young Black girl. She loves to act and perform in plays. When performing, Grace dreams of having the most exciting role. When Grace's teacher requests volunteers for the play *Peter Pan*, everyone wants the title role. One classmate tells Grace that she cannot play Peter because she is a girl. Another student says Grace cannot play Peter because she is Black. Grace decides to audition, despite their comments. Grace's mother and grandmother encourage Grace to audition, reminding her that she can do anything. Grace's grandmother takes her to see a production of *Romeo and Juliet* in which Juliet is played by a Black woman. This inspires Grace even more. Grace auditions and receives the role of Peter. The book is a reminder to young children that they should have dreams and goals, and they should pursue them despite barriers and challenges. The story also stresses the role of family support in students' success and motivation.

Giftedness: How is Grace gifted? How does she show this? Is Grace proud of her abilities?

Persistence and motivation: Grace is discouraged by other students in the book. How does she handle this peer pressure? How does Grace's family help her to be persistent? Do Grace's motivation and persistence pay off? What advice can you give other students about dreaming and working to achieve those dreams?

Discrimination: What types of discrimination does Grace face? How does she handle it? Do you think the students were right or wrong in their comments to Grace? What have you learned about stereotypes? What can you do to avoid stereotypes and to avoid discriminating against others?

LITERATURE FOR GRADES 4–6

Woodson, J. (1994). *Maizon at Blue Hill.* New York: Delacorte.

Maizon is a gifted Black pre-adolescent who is raised by her grandmother in a working-class neighborhood in Brooklyn, NY. Although Maizon's best friend is also gifted, Maizon is the only student to receive a scholarship for admission into the private school in Connecticut. When Maizon sees the school's brochures and arrives there, she questions the lack of diversity. Where are the Black girls? Eventually, Maizon meets five other Black students. However, she is still filled with fear—fear about leaving her grandmother, losing her best friend, and losing her identity. She second-guesses herself—is she smart? Is she cool? Is she a traitor? Readers will identify strongly with Maizon, for the story seems so real, so authentic. They will empathize with Maizon as she confronts her feats and searches for self-determination. Key topics for discussion might focus on achievement, peer relationships, racial discrimination, and racial identity.

Achievement and persistence: How is Maizon an achiever? How is she an underachiever? When did Maizon begin to question her abilities? Do you think Maizon took advantage of the opportunity to get a better education? Would you have accepted the scholarship? Would you have left the school? Why did Maizon decide to leave? Do you support her decision?

Racial identity: What is racial pride so important to Maizon? What does she do to try to maintain her identity as a Black person? How does Maizon's racial pride affect her friendships with students at the private school?

Peer relationships: Do you think the White students were sincere in trying to make friends with Maizon? Were the Black students sincere? In what ways might Maizon have overreacted to both groups of students? How would you have handled making friends? Can people who are culturally different be friends? What are some of the strengths of cross-cultural friendships?

Discrimination: Give one or two examples of discrimination faced by Maizon. How did she handle this? How would you have dealt with the situation? What factors contribute to discrimination? How can we overcome stereotypes and discrimination?

Hansen, J. (1989). *The Gift-Giver.* New York: Houghton Mifflin.

This novel describes the friendship that develops between several Black fifth-graders, particularly Amir and Doris. Amir is new to the school and somewhat different from the other students. He is serious, thoughtful, studious, and quiet. Just as interesting, Amir is a nonconformist. He does not worry about or succumb to peer pressures.

Because he has been shuffled from foster home to foster home, Amir has a keen sense of insight into human behavior. The concept of "wise" comes to mind when reading the book. This ability to understand others, to look into the soul of others, is what quickly attracts Doris to Amir. Eventually, other students are taken with Amir's interpersonal and intrapersonal intelligences, his independence, and his academic achievements. When Amir is sent to another foster home at the end of the book, he is sincerely missed. They ask, "How could somebody who only smiled and looked like he was always seeing inside of things, make a bunch of us feel so strange when he isn't there?" This is a warm story about friendships and achievement that addresses urban realities and gives readers a sense of hope. Several topics can be highlighted: giftedness, achievement, and independence.

Giftedness: What does "gifted" mean? What types of giftedness were discussed in the novel? How is Amir a "gift-giver"? What did he give his classmates—how did he use his gift(s) to help his classmates grow? What types of gifts do you have? How can you use your abilities in productive ways?

Achievement: What is achievement? What do we mean when we say that a person has "achieved"? How have the main characters learned to achieve? How are they different from their experiences with Amir? Among your peers, in what ways do you encourage achievement? How is academic success accepted in your classroom and school? In your home? What can you do to make sure that you are an achiever?

Independence: How did Amir show his self-confidence and independence? How do you feel about his ability to avoid peer pressure? How do you avoid peer pressure? In what ways did Amir's independence help him to be successful?

Namioka, L. (1992). *Yang the Youngest and His Terrible Ear.* New York: Brown.

This is an amusing yet serious novel of a tone-deaf Chinese American male in a musical family. Since Yang cannot play music and does not want to, he (along with a newfound friend) plots ways to inform Yang's family that he does not want to play music. Instead, Yang prefers baseball, which his family does not value. Instances of stereotyping appear in the book, but they are subtle. The book's strength rests in helping students to follow their dreams, to be honest, and to develop rather than avoid cross-cultural friendships.

Expectations: Were Yang's parents expectations realistic? How do you feel about their emphasis on music? What pressures did their expectations place on Yang? Although much of the mood is written with a sense of humor, how can family expectations be negative?

Cross-cultural friendships: Is it difficult to make friends with someone who is different from you? Can a person be a best friend with someone from another culture? How did the two boys show that they were true friends? 'What have you learned about cross-cultural friendships?'

LITERATURE FOR GRADES 7–8

Sebestyen, O. (1968). *Words by Heart.* Boston: Little, Brown.

The main character is Lena. Lena's Papa has high hopes for his daughter, so he moves his family from the post-Reconstruction South to the West, where it is believed that a Black family may have greater opportunities to succeed. However, Papa's willingness to work brings resentment from Mr. Haney, who loses his job to Papa. Further, Lena learns that not everyone rejoices with her when she wins the scripture-reciting contest. The family is learning that prejudice exists in the West, it is just more subtle than in the

South. This new understanding means that the family will still need extraordi-
nary fortitude to survive.

While racial prejudice is the theme of this book, Lena's giftedness adds
another dimension. The combined themes emphasize factors influencing the
ability of Blacks to grow and develop to their potential. Gifted Black students
may see a version of their own struggle in Lena's story, and all gifted students
can recognize Lena's and her father's acceptance of the responsibility to appreciate and use one's gifts, despite barriers and setbacks. At least two concepts can be used for bibliotherapy—identity, and perseverance or resilience.

Identity: If you were in Lena's position, do you think you could make it?
What would be your greatest asset? What would be your greatest liability?

Perseverance/resilience: What barriers did Lena face? How does Lena cope
with barriers? What does Papa teach Lena that will help her to survive? What
else do you think she will need to get through the next few years? What strategies do you use to cope with difficulties? What important message did Papa
teach Lena, in terms of what he said and how he lived? How was he a role
model for his daughter? What have you learned from the book that could be
useful to you in reaching your goals? What challenges might you face as you
grow up to be a productive person, making full use of the abilities you have?
How are you doing so far?

Williams-Garcia, R. (1991). *Fast Talk on a Slow Track*. New York: Dutton.

The is a realistic story of a Black high school male coming of age during the
1980s. Denzel lives in a middle-class neighborhood in New York. Although
he is the high school valedictorian, Denzel resents being placed in a special
preparatory program for minority students admitted to Princeton. He deliberately does poorly in school so that he won't have to return. However, after
one month of selling items from door to door and getting beat up after trying
to swindle a customer, Denzel rethinks his decision about Princeton. He begins to study and gets involved in an African American student group. Eventually, Denzel realizes that wit is not enough to excel and achieve academically.
He puts his mind to studying, and resists drugs, girls, and other distractions.
The book is one of few in print that focuses on a gifted Black male, which
makes it essential reading. Major topics for discussion can focus on achievement and effort.

Achievement and effort: Why does Denzel resent the special program at
Princeton? Do you think his criticisms are justified? How would you define
the term "effortless success"? How does this term describe Denzel? Is success
without effort admirable, in your opinion? How much time and effort do you
devote to studying? What events lead Denzel to conclude that wit is not

enough to reach one's potential? What do you think are the most important "ingredients" for success?

Betancourt, C. Y. (1991). *More than Meets the Eye*. New York: Bantam.

This is another contemporary, realistic novel of school and community life. The main characters are Liz, a gifted student, and Ben, her Chinese American classmate, who is also gifted. Liz's parents are afraid that Ben, the school's top student, will get special treatment from teachers because of stereotypes about Asian Americans. Negative peer pressures confront Ben, who is called such names as "Slanteyes" and "Chinaman" by one student. Issues of parental pressures, stereotypes, and discrimination appear in the book. For instance, one teacher thinks Ben can communicate with a Cambodian student because they are both Asian. Students will also be exposed to cross-cultural relationships as Liz and Ben become close friends. Potentially important topics include coping with discrimination (perseverance/resilience), identity, and peer relationships.

Peer relationships: What barriers did Liz and Ben face as they sought to establish friendships? How can negative peer pressures hinder cross-cultural friendships? In what ways did the two characters cope with these pressures? Do you think their strategies were effective? What would you have done differently?

Identity: What do you know about Chinese Americans and their culture? What identity issues did Liz confront? What about Ben? How did they come to have stong(er) identities?

Perseverance/resilience: What events posed barriers to Ben in school? Do you think he handled them well? What factors eventually led to Ben's success?

LITERATURE FOR GRADES 9–12

Williams-Garcia, R. (1988). *Blue Tights*. New York: Dutton.

This book is a contemporary and realistic portrayal of a Black adolescent coming of age in an economically diverse neighborhood in New York City. Colleen, 15, is gifted in visual and performing arts. She is at odds with her mother, who was never married. Colleen is often the recipient of jeers from slimmer and higher-income classmates. She also feels put down by her dance teacher, who frequently comments on Colleen's physique (large behind and thighs). At the end of the book, readers learn that this teacher had high expectations for Colleen, but did not communicate them effectively.

A chance encounter introduces Colleen to an African dance ensemble and the lead role in one of their plays. An understanding but demanding teacher encourages Colleen with high expectations and constructive feedback. The experience with the African dance ensemble ultimately helps Colleen to overcome her insecurities and increase her commitment to dance (e.g., practice, discipline, etc.).

In several instances, events are bleak but hopeful. For example, Colleen overcomes negative peer pressures and poor relations with her mother. The book addresses contemporary issues — sex, teen pregnancy, gossip, and teen jargon. Students will identify with these issues. Important topics for counseling are identity, peer relations, and perseverance/resilience.

Identity: In what ways is Colleen gifted? Does she value this ability? Do others value her ability? What concerns does Colleen have about herself? Can you relate to these issues? How does Colleen handle these concerns in (a) constructive ways and (b) destructive ways? How does self-perception relate to aspirations?

Peer relations: How do peers have a positive influence on Colleen? How do they have a negative influence on Colleen? Identify a negative example of peer pressure in the book and evaluate how Colleen handled the situation. What would you have done in that situation. What can students do to decrease negative peer pressure in their schools?

Perseverance/resilience: Do you think Colleen was persistent in her efforts to dance? What factors eventually influenced her successful outcomes? What have you learned about persevering?

Carson, B. S. (1992). *Gifted Hands: The Ben Carson Story.* New York: Harper.

Ben Carson, the renowned Black neurosurgeon, presents his biography in this moving novel of resilience and faith. Carson shares his childhood — growing up in poverty in Boston, living in a single-parent home with his brother and mother (who has a 3rd-grade education), being angry and violent as a child, and succeeding despite all of these factors. He shares the low expectations of some teachers and the high expectations of others. In particular, he attributes his success to his mother because she set high expectations and standards. Central topics for discussion include resilience and family support.

Resilience: Ben faced many barriers to achievement throughout his life. What were these barriers? Identify barriers in his home and his school. How were Ben's relationships with peers? How did Ben overcome the different barriers? What is the most important message of the book?

Family support: Despite his mother having a 3rd-grade education, she instilled certain values in her children. What were these values? How did she help Ben to turn his life around?

ADDITIONAL STRATEGIES

Many of the lesson plans using the books above relied heavily on questioning strategies. Of course, students must be given other opportunities to demonstrate their understanding of the literature and concepts. For instance, drama, music, and art are effective strategies for engaging gifted minority students. These creative outlets address minority students' learning styles and aesthetic appreciation (see Ford, 1995b, for details). Likewise, poetry can be used to promote identity. In particular, works by Langston Hughes, Rita Dove, Zora Neale Hurston, Maya Angelo, Nikki Giovanni, and Pleasant De-Spain often focus on themes of achievement, self-determination, hope, identity, achievement, and family, which serve to empower gifted minority students.

Biographies can also enhance students' racial identity, motivation, and achievement. For example, most books on Malcolm X depict his life in various stages of racial identity (e.g., Myers, 1993). These stages are consistent with Cross's model. Students witness Malcolm's transformation from self-hatred to self-love, from a socially imposed identity to a self-imposed identity, from an other-identity to self-identity. Students also learn about Malcolm X's strategies for coping with trials and tribulations, his high achievement orientation, and his sense of self-determination.

The human dimension of counseling (and teaching) cannot be underestimated, as is discussed throughout this chapter. Mentors and role models can promote hope, faith, and optimism. These individuals can be community members, school personnel, or students. Torrance's (1998) most recent publication reinforces the central role that mentors play in the lives of gifted minority students, as does Ladson-Billings's (1994) book on the key role that Black teachers play in the academic and affective life of students.

Given the values that many minority cultures place on families and social relations, family and group counseling may be more appropriate and effective than individual counseling. Thus, counselors should work with all family members to address students' concerns. Similarly, support groups should be developed so that minority students feel more at ease and less alone in the counseling situation. These groups may have to be gender- and race- or culture-specific. For those minority students contending with racial identity issues, it might be difficult to share concerns with White students, and males may feel more open with other males. As the case study below illustrates, counseling must be diagnostic and prescriptive.

THE CASE OF RAMIREZ

Ramirez, a 13-year-old Latino male, currently attends high school in a middle-class community. Ramirez's parents (a dentist and a homemaker) brought him to counseling because of anger and fighting. During counseling, Ramirez often reflects upon his school experiences. Ramirez attended a predominantly minority public elementary school in grades K–3. He has happy, positive memories about these school years, and often boasts about his school achievement. His mother indicated that Ramirez was placed in the district's gifted education program in the second grade. At one point, he participated in the school's academic challenge program, earning most of the points for his winning team.

The family moved to a predominantly White suburb when Ramirez was in the 4th grade. Shortly thereafter, his parents began to notice a significant decline in Ramirez's interest in school and academic performance. Ramirez, for example, no longer made the honor roll, nor was he interested in doing so. His teachers, all of whom were White females, expressed concern that Ramirez was a behavioral problem—he often disrupted class, failed to follow directions, seldom completed assignments, talked out of turn, and thrived on his status as the "class clown." Ramirez had a different point of view. He described his teachers as mean, unfair, and boring. He reported that many of the teachers ridiculed and embarrassed him. He complained that the teachers were insensitive and seemed to enjoy demeaning Hispanics. Ramirez also recalled being teased by both Latino and White students, many of whom could not understand why Ramirez spoke "proper English." Ramirez was teased most often when he visited friends in his former neighborhood.

By the end of the first grading period, one teacher requested that Ramirez be referred for special education evaluation. Ramirez's parents were shocked—how could their son be identified as gifted in one school and referred to special education in another? They refused to have Ramirez evaluated. They held numerous meetings with administrators and teachers regarding why Ramirez was not placed in the gifted program, as he had been identified earlier. Unable to resolve this issue and their differences with several teachers, Ramirez's parents transferred him to another school in Grade 5. The school was also predominantly White and middle-class, and the problems were similar. Teachers complained that Ramirez talked too much and asked too many questions, particularly about minority groups and issues of justice. For example, Ramirez questioned teachers when they stated that Christopher

Columbus discovered America; he questioned their constant focus on slavery, and their inattention to the contribution of Hispanics to American history. Ramirez also expressed frustration and anger at being what he called a "token" at certain times during the school year. For instance, he recalled having to be the "expert" on all issues related to Hispanic Americans. One student asked Ramirez to explain "Why do so many Hispanics commit crimes?" Another student wanted to know why "Hispanics have so many kids?" Others asked how his parents could "afford a nice house and to live in their neighborhood?"

Much of what Ramirez discussed in counseling had not been shared with his parents. Thus, they thought that Ramirez was adjusting well to the new school, although his grades were lower than they expected. They did not know that Ramirez had attempted to buy friendships and peer acceptance. During one counseling session, Ramirez described how he stole money from his parents so that he would "always have it to show the White students." He stated, "I did not want them to think that I was just another poor Latino kid." When this did not work, that is, the teasing, isolation, and rejection continued, Ramirez became more frustrated and angry. When his parents brought Ramirez to counseling, he had been suspended for fighting.

Questions to Consider

1. What are Ramirez's major concerns?
2. What needs are Ramirez trying to fulfill?
3. What factors have contributed to these difficulties?
4. How could these difficulties have been prevented?
5. How can you, as a counselor or teacher, help Ramirez to deal effectively with his concerns?
6. To what extent will you, as a school counselor, involve peers, teachers, and family members in the counseling process?

Suggested Interventions

To the extent possible, intervention strategies must be tailored to students' individual needs. Figure 6.2 presents general guidelines for working with students experiencing difficulties similar to Ramirez. Intervention strategies for Ramirez are categorized into four areas: (a) individual needs; (b) family factors; (c) peer factors; and (d) school factors.

Individual Needs. Recommended strategies at the individual level should focus on improving Ramirez's self-understanding, particularly his racial identity. Ramirez appears to have a need for greater understanding of

Figure 6.2 Suggested Intervention Strategies for Ramirez

Problems/Issues	Suggested Strategies
Negative or poor racial identity	Multicultural curriculum and instruction; bibliotherapy and/or cinematherapy; role models and mentors; provide opportunities for students to discuss concerns related to perceived injustices related to race; counseling for self-esteem and self-affirmation
Low teacher expectations	Teachers (and other school personnel) seek substantive training in multicultural education
Poor relations with teachers	Teacher self-examination of beliefs and attitudes held about racially and culturally diverse students

Affective classroom environments; student-centered classrooms (e.g., positive regard) |
Poor peer relations; feelings of isolation and not belonging	Decreased competition; group and cooperative learning activities and strategies; increased social interaction (e.g., extracurricular activities); class discussions about students' concerns
Learning styles conflict with teaching styles	Teachers are willing to adapt their teaching styles to students' learning styles; students are taught to be bicognitive
Poor motivation; intrinsic motivation greater than extrinsic motivation	Teachers seek to increase student interest and engagement; culturally responsive teaching is espoused; social-emotional factors explored; cultural factors examined; increased use of intrinsic rather than extrinsic rewards; provide constructive feedback on performance and behavior
Underachievement	Examine factors contributing to poor achievement or the discrepancy between potential and performance, between ability and effort
Family achievement orientation and involvement	Schools encourage and actively seek family involvement; family members considered partners in their children's education; parent education programs available in the school

himself as a person of color, as well as a need for others to see Latinos in a positive manner. Thus, as the figure indicates, intervention for Ramirez should be based primarily on multicultural education and counseling, with the goal of increasing and nurturing his identity as a racial being. Bibliotherapy is a powerful tool for personal growth. Ramirez might first be introduced to theories of self-esteem, self-concept, and racial identity. This "introduction to psychology" can be followed by bibliotherapy or cinematherapy, which uses literature and movies to increase self-awareness. Many books discussed in chapters 5 and 8 can help Ramirez: (a) to better understand the relationship between self-esteem, self-concept, and racial identity; (b) to examine feelings, thoughts, and behaviors at the various stages of racial identity; (c) to compare and contrast his experiences with others; (d) to explore how the issues faced by Malcolm X (and others) contributed the leader's growth and sense of social responsibility; (e) to see that growth is possible with the support of significant others; and (f) to examine how one can learn to become stronger or resilient in the face of negative events and failures. Finally, Ramirez can write his own biography, a strategy that may prove cathartic.

Social or Peer Relations. Negative peer relations can occur in different ways — conflict between minority and White students; conflict within a minority group (e.g., among Latino or Mexican American students); and conflict between minority groups (e.g., between Black and Hispanic American students). Ramirez's concerns relate to the first two types of peer conflicts — he feels isolated from White students and rejected by Hispanic American students.

Teachers can improve peer relations between minority and White students using numerous strategies, for example, by encouraging Ramirez to participate in extracurricular and social activities. Other strategies may consist of creating buddy systems and using cooperative learning. The use of social and cooperative learning to improve the educational achievement of these students was recommended by Diaz (1998). Counselors and teachers can also build a sense of community using such books as *Seven Blind Mice, Swimmy,* and *Imani in the Belly*. These books all focus on the role of social relationships and teamwork in achieving goals and objectives. For example, in *Swimmy*, a school of fish join forces to keep from being consumed by larger fish. The collective efforts of the mice in the *Seven Blind Mice* help them to discover that the creature they once feared is an elephant.

Essentially, school personnel must act upon rather than ignore, deny, or minimize racial injustices in their classrooms. If negative, stereotypical statements are not addressed, White students may perceive that their statements are valid or justified. Ponterotto and Pedersen (1993) provide numerous exercises to help students understand and cope with social injustices in their school or classroom. Counselors must work with teachers to increase students' understanding of and appreciation for differences and similarities. Several books listed in the resource section of this book can also be used by students to achieve mutual understanding and respect. For instance, with K–3 students, teachers might use *The Crayon Box That Talked* to introduce, reinforce, and extend topics of diversity, cooperation, and interdependence. In the book, crayons are initially unappreciative of other colors. The crayon box helps them to see their individual and collective value. Students in grades 4–6 can read *The Great Blueness,* in which a wizard makes everything in the town blue. When the town gets tired of this color, he makes everything yellow, and so forth. Eventually, he makes the world full of different colors, which the people appreciate.

To deal with conflicts between students, particularly conflicts regarding an anti-achievement ethic (e.g., doing well means "acting White"), Ramirez will need the assistance of mentors and role models. He needs to see, hear, and learn from successful Hispanic students and professionals who have confronted and overcome similar difficulties. Finally, counselors may wish to begin a student support group specifically regarding social issues and relationships. These meetings can be held during lunch hours or after school.

Family Factors. Family involvement does not seem to be a major problem in Ramirez's case. His parents appear to be very interested in his educational well-being. However, teachers can encourage them to participate in the school's parent–teacher association, and develop other appropriate home–school partnerships. Counselors, within the limits of confidentiality, can share Ramirez's concerns with his parents. They can help their son to find additional mentors and role models in the community; further, they can read selected books with Ramirez. Chapter 8 presents a more detailed discussion of family involvement and student achievement.

School Factors. A student-centered, culturally responsive classroom provides a safe, nurturing place in which to learn. Such an environment is particularly important for minority students, who are often racially and culturally different from their teachers. Teachers and counselors must work together to address Ramirez's academic *and* affective needs. To better understand how it feels for Ramirez and other minority students in the gifted program, school personnel should interview former and current minority students about their experiences. What are/were their school-related concerns? How could these problems have been either avoided or resolved?

Classroom rules often help students to establish acceptable social norms. Included in the list of classroom rules must be respect for peers, and there must be policies regarding discrimination, harassment, or other injustices.

Students must understand that the school does not tolerate such inequities. Teachers must also model the attitudes and behaviors they wish students to emulate. For example, students who see others treated unfairly are likely to treat peers in this way. Finally, as stated throughout this book, the school must provide an education that is multicultural—from curriculum and instruction to staff diversity to staff development in multicultural counseling.

Prevention

Much of our effort in education seems to focus on intervention. Intuitively and logically, however, prevention seems to be the optimal solution to many of the issues confronting minority students. How could some of the issues facing Ramirez have been avoided or *prevented*? Early family involvement in the recruitment and retention of minority students in the gifted programs is essential for ensuring a better goodness-of-fit between students and services. For example, family members should be involved throughout the identification process, not only in completing forms, but also in learning about gifted education services. How often are parents encouraged or required to visit the gifted program prior to and during student placement? An orientation to the gifted program allows parents and students to observe demographics. For instance, do parents know that their child will be the only (or one of a few) student of color in the program? Is this a concern for parents or the student? Is lack of teacher diversity in the gifted program a concern for caregivers or students? These questions focus on race, but parents and students can observe the gifted program for other relevant concerns, if any[16].

SUMMARY AND CONCLUSIONS

This chapter focused on some of the primary issues facing gifted minority students, specifically, underachievement, racial identity, and social-emotional issues. Poor peer relations, low self-concepts, poor racial identities, and environmental risk factors can work to the detriment of gifted minority students. Counselors have many roles and responsibilities that call for increased attention to barriers to gifted minority students' achievement and psychological health. Along with teachers, counselors can have a significant impact on gifted minority students. Finally, it was emphasized that counselors should recognize both individual and group differences among *all* students.

Like all human beings, students of color need understanding, caring, respect, and empathy. With this basic awareness as well as appreciation, counselors can begin the process of effective counseling and guidance, which requires multicultural counseling approaches and strategies. It is incumbent upon school counselors to help gifted minority students to manage and appreciate their gifts, to manage negative peer pressures, to make appropriate educational choices, to learn effective coping strategies, to accept failure, and to set realistic goals and expectations.

With an understanding of racial and cultural diversity, counselors can better serve this student population by celebrating diversity and advocating for the human rights of all students. The strategies and interventions presented in this chapter emphasize the importance of developing the whole child. This includes focusing on the needs and concerns of gifted students in general and on minority students. The problems facing children of color are complex, as are the solutions. With counselors joining teachers as advocates, mentors, and role models, minority students will be better prepared to achieve in school and life.

The aforementioned recommendations only touched upon some suggested strategies for intervention and prevention. Teachers, with the assistance of counselors, must tailor strategies to those factors affecting the individual student. For some minority students, racial identity is not a major concern. Some students are not pressured by peers, nor are they concerned about social relations. However, for those students who do experience these difficulties, counselors and teachers play an important role. As Ladson-Billings (1994) noted, teachers are often required to be more than a "teacher" for minority students; they must be an advocate, mentor, role model and, sometimes, surrogate parent. Many children of color, children like Ramirez, need the guidance and support that teachers can and must provide as they endeavor to help children, *all* children, reach their potential in school and in life. Teachers must focus their efforts on both the recruitment *and* retention of minority students in our gifted programs.

CHAPTER 7

School Personnel Preparation in Gifted Education and Multicultural Education

It is easy to be a bad teacher.
It is hard to be a good teacher.
It takes time to be a great teacher.

INTRODUCTION AND OVERVIEW

This chapter addresses two important components of multicultural gifted education — teacher diversity and school personnel preparation. Our rationale is simple: The best camera in the world will not produce the best pictures if the photographer lacks formal training in photography. Likewise, the best education cannot be provided if school personnel lack formal preparation. As President Clinton noted in his 1997 State of the Union address, "to have the best schools, we must have the best teachers . . . and we should challenge more of our finest young people to consider teaching as a career."

The goals of this chapter are twofold. First and foremost, the goal is to inspire educators of gifted students to adopt multicultural education as an integral component of the school, from assessment to curriculum and instruction to hiring practices. Throughout this book, rationales for this goal have been provided. A second goal is to encourage all school personnel to seek substantive and continuous preparation in multicultural education. Realistically and unfortunately, the first goal cannot be achieved without the second goal. We need educators who are prepared in multicultural education so that multicultural education can become fully integrated into the educational process.

Having laid the foundation for multicultural gifted education in the previous chapters, we hope that educators can answer the following questions: *Why* do we need multicultural education? *Who* needs an education that is multicultural? *What* is an education that is multicultural? *Which* kinds of multicultural education are most important for students? *When* is multicultural education needed? *Where* is multicultural education needed? *How* can we effectively implement multicultural education in gifted education?

Any discussion of school personnel preparation is incomplete without a discussion of minority teachers. The scarcity of racially and culturally diverse teachers is a major and persistent issue in education nationally, particularly given projections that the representation of minority teachers is declining while the number of minority students is increasing. The representation of minority teachers in gifted programs, however, has received little attention in the literature. Accordingly, this chapter provides data on the under-representation of minority teachers in both general education and gifted education.

Owing to the limited information available on minority teachers in gifted education, we reason by analogy, drawing implications from the general education literature to gifted education. Similarly, since the majority of research and writing have focused on Black teachers, we use Black teachers more often as a case in point, and draw implications for other teachers of color.

In essence, while we need more teachers of color in classrooms, students also need educators who are culturally competent. We ask the question, How can multicultural education be implemented effectively without the support and experience of teachers? The answer is simple — without the support and skills of school personnel, multicultural education cannot become a reality. Multicultural education can be implemented more effectively when school personnel are trained to be more culturally aware and competent. Thus, we recommend specific goals, objectives, and strategies for teacher education preparation and staff development.

AN OVERVIEW OF THE MINORITY TEACHER SHORTAGE

The recruitment and retention of minority teachers in education has already received extensive attention in mainstream and special education. Specifically, between 1983 and 1990, hundreds of reform reports discussed the shortcomings of education in the U.S. (e.g., National Commission on Excellence in Education, 1983). One major item was the recruitment of a teaching force that reflects the nation's racial and cultural diversity, and the preparation of teachers to be both culturally aware and instructively effective. This national decline has important implications for the fields of gifted and multicultural education.

The education profession has a severe shortage of minority teachers, and their numbers are steadily decreasing. Paradoxically, there is an inverse relationship between the percentage of minority students and minority teachers

Table 7.1 Trends in the Representation of African American Teachers, 1970–1994

Year	Percentage
1970	12.0
1971	8.1
1976	8.0
1981	7.7
1986	6.9
1991	8.0
1994	9.2

Source: American Association of Colleges for Teacher Education (1994); Gay (1993); National Educational Association (1991).

Table 7.2 Percentage of Teachers and Students by Race/Ethnicity

Race/Ethnicity	Teachers	Students
White	86.0%	68.0%
Black	9.2%	16.0%
Hispanic/Latino	3.1%	12.0%
Asian/Pacific Islander	1.0%	3.0%
Native American/ Alaskan Native	.7%	1.0%

Source: American Association of Colleges for Teacher Education (1994).

(Table 7.1). Although minority students represent a large percentage of the school population (about 32%), less than 15% of the teaching profession is African American, Hispanic American, Asian American, and American Indian combined. More specifically, the Hispanic/Latino teacher representation is 3.1%, the Asian-Pacific Islander representation is 1%, the Black teacher representation is 9.2%, and the Native American and Native Alaskan teacher representation is .7% (American Association of Colleges for Teacher Education, 1994) (see Table 7.2).

Minority teachers fulfill many needs of students and schools. They are more than teachers in the traditional sense. Directly or indirectly, minority teachers serve as mentors, role models, disciplinarians, advocates, cultural translators, and surrogate parents for minority students (Ladson-Billings, 1994). Teachers of color are also positive role models for White students. Given the promises minority teachers hold for all students, the need to diversify the education profession is obvious. According to Kennedy (1991),

Minority teachers do much more than literally teach content. They also personify content. They stand as models for what it is like to be an educated person. . . . If we want students to believe that they themselves might one day become scientists, writers, or mathematicians or that they might be mentors, guides, and educated people, then they need to see diverse examples of such people, including at least one who looks like they look. (p. 660)

Administrators and policymakers must make a commitment to recruit and retain minority teachers; they must develop strategies and efforts that target teacher diversity (see Ford, Grantham, & Harris, 1996, 1997). A major step toward attracting minority teachers to gifted education is to create an atmosphere that values diversity, respects diverse students, and promotes pluralism, as described in earlier chapters.

Many efforts exist to entice minorities into teaching, including forgiveness loans, mentoring programs, training in test-taking skills, and increased peer and professional contact with minority students; however, these efforts alone have little positive residuals for improving the representation of minority educators. Further, minority students need academic and vocational support that includes counseling, mentoring, and tutoring. Minority students must be carefully monitored for academic progress, academic skills, and test-taking skills to ensure their successful completion of certification requirements, including standardized tests. Early interventions must be in place for those at risk for poor educational outcomes.

Data indicate that few Black students, including those identified as gifted, aspire to teach (e.g., Ford, 1993, 1996; Ford, Grantham, & Harris, 1996). Equally alarming, teachers are not encouraging gifted students to enter teaching. In a recent survey, Langdon (1996) found that 8% of the teachers reported that they would discourage their brightest students from teaching; another 42% of the teachers reported that they would encourage gifted students to consider other fields before deciding on teaching. If these widespread sentiments persist, gifted and minority students may need vocational guidance that exposes them to teaching as a viable career or option. School counselors, gifted program personnel, and university personnel in gifted education can form partnerships to address this recommendation. For instance, minority students at all levels can be paired with college students, teachers, or university faculty members who serve as their mentors. As mentors, college students and educators can provide vocational guidance and advice on an early, continuous, and long-term basis. Mentors can help minority students deal effectively with bureaucratic policies and procedures, with academic advisement (for example, taking required courses and taking courses in the correct sequence), submitting paperwork on time, gaining increased information about scholarships and internships, identifying and resolving problems, and networking. Similarly, exposing gifted minority students to minority educators through internships, practica, and mentorships in gifted education can help can increase their interest in and knowledge about teaching.

The problem of recruiting and retaining a diverse teaching force is complex and resistant to simple or single-approach solutions. Ultimately, much of the encouragement and incentive to recruit and retain minority teachers must come from school boards, administrators, and educators in public schools with gifted programs, as well as the faculties and deans at teacher education institutions. The educational pipeline needs to be repaired at all levels.

COMPETENCIES NEEDED BY EDUCATORS OF GIFTED STUDENTS

Concerns regarding teacher competencies in gifted education abound. Almost every introductory book in gifted education devotes attention to characteristics of gifted education teachers. Nonetheless, many gifted students are being taught by teachers who have little to no formal preparation in gifted education. In many states, validation, certification, and degrees in gifted education are not required. Accordingly, the National Association for Gifted Children (NAGC, 1994a) issued a position paper on competencies needed by teachers who work with gifted students. Teachers need to possess:

1. a knowledge and valuing of the origins and nature of high levels of intelligence, including creative expressions of intelligence;
2. a knowledge and understanding of the cognitive, social, and emotional characteristics, needs, and potential problems experienced by gifted and talented students from diverse backgrounds;
3. a knowledge of and access to advanced content and ideas;
4. an ability to develop a differentiated curriculum appropriate to meeting the unique intellectual and emotional needs and interests of gifted and talented students; and
5. an ability to create an environment in which gifted and talented students can feel challenged and safe to explore and express their uniqueness

In addition to these competencies, gifted education teachers must possess competencies associated with good teaching and learning in general (e.g., modeling, openness, curiosity, and enthusiasm). While the position paper does not specifically address the different intelligences, teachers of gifted students must also be able to meet the needs of students gifted in leadership and visual and performing arts.

MULTICULTURAL COMPETENCIES NEEDED
BY SCHOOL PERSONNEL

The desire to integrate multicultural education in one's school represents a personal and professional commitment. This commitment requires time, effort, and persistence. A lack of preservice and/or inservice preparation to work with diverse students must not be used as a rationale for not integrating multicultural education into classrooms and schools. Without the support and skills of all school personnel, multicultural education cannot become a reality. Indeed, increased diversity among school personnel, modifications in curriculum and instruction, and philosophical changes can be implemented more effectively when school personnel are trained to be more culturally aware and competent.

Clark (1997) noted that educators prepared from a multicultural perspective are better able to identify strengths rather than weaknesses in minority students. They understand that behaviors unique or special to a cultural group can serve as indicators of high-level abilities to conceptualize and organize phenomena. Similarly, these educators seek alternative, more equitable tests and instruments to identify gifted minority students. Further, they understand that giftedness exists in all human groups, regardless of racial background and other socio-demographic variables. This latter statement supports the notion that manifestations of giftedness are contextually dependent — what is gifted in one culture is not necessarily gifted in another. Finally, preparation in multicultural education increases the ability of teachers and counselors to understand the social-emotional needs of gifted minority students (Ford & Harris, 1995).

Sue, Arrendondo, and McDavis (1992) hold that culturally competent professionals have the following core characteristics: self-awareness and understanding; cultural awareness and understanding; social responsiveness and responsibility; and culturally sensitive techniques and strategies.

Self-Awareness and Self-Understanding

Culturally competent educators seek greater self-awareness and understanding regarding their biases, assumptions, and stereotypes. This self-awareness comes from understanding one's own cultural values and norms, and in an understanding of how individuals are a product of their culture (as described in chapter 1). Self-awareness helps educators to recognize how their assumptions and biases influence their teaching and relationships with minority groups.

Cultural Awareness and Understanding

Culturally competent educators seek to understand the worldviews (i.e., values and norms) of minority students without negative judgments. Educators do not have to adopt these views, but they respect them as different and legitimate rather than as inferior or otherwise substandard. Thus, a philosophy of pluralism prevails among culturally aware educators. At its best, multicultural education must move from the stage of tolerance for cultural differences to a point where educators truly embrace what Greene (1993) describes as "the passions of pluralism" (p. 13).

To state the obvious, we are teaching in a nation of unparalleled diversity. Through self-understanding, educators become more informed of how attitudes and prejudices affect teaching and learning. Just as with children, our sense of self-worth influences our work. Our self-awareness influences the way we relate to children. Our personal histories reflect biases about how "other" people live, work, and play. Our own family culture helps to shape the way we feel about children who live differently, behave differently, and learn differently than we do. Without firsthand knowledge or experience, we have probably developed strong feelings about children from backgrounds that are different from our own and otherwise unfamiliar. In many subtle ways, we communicate this to the children in our schools.

Socially Responsive and Responsible

Culturally competent educators attempt to increase multicultural awareness and understanding among *all* students. These educators practice multicultural education, even in racially homogenous settings (e.g., predominantly or all-White classrooms, schools, and communities). The shortage or absence of minority students in the gifted program, school, community, or state is not used as an excuse for inattention to multicultural education. Socially responsive educators are also activists who seek positive changes on behalf of minority students. As advocates, such teachers seek equity in all areas of the educational process; they address inequities in materials, instruments, policy, and so forth.

Culturally Sensitive Techniques and Strategies

Culturally competent educators attempt to deliver more effective education to minority students. Thus, education is relevant, appropriate, and sensitive to students' diverse needs. In general, such educators adopt principles of learning that meet the academic, social-emotional, and psychological needs of minority students. Much of their efforts are directed at achieving the highest levels of multicultural education — transformation and social action (Banks, 1993, 1995, 1997).

Essentially, educators who espouse multiculturalism create an education aimed at achieving pride, equity, power, wealth, and cultural continuity (Lomotey, 1990). Culturally competent teachers, therefore, go beyond the subject matter — they encourage minority students to value achievement, as well as to understand the personal value, the collective power, and the political consequences of academic achievement rather than failure (Foster, 1992). Teachers engage *all* students in reflections about life's realities. In particular, they help minority students to make the connections between what they know and live in a structured yet eclectic, supportive, nurturing, family-like classroom. Culturally competent teachers integrate the realities of students' lives, experiences, and cultures into the classroom, while validating and affirming students' identities (Ladson-Billings, 1994).

TEACHER EDUCATION IMPERATIVES

Teacher education institutions hold the primary responsibility of preparing future teachers for school life. The National Association for Gifted Children (1995b) has developed an extensive list of standards to guide graduate programs in gifted education. In terms of knowledge and understanding, teacher preparation programs must develop future teachers who have the following competencies and skills (see NAGC, 1995a, for the complete list of standards and competencies):

1. *Knowledge and understanding of:* (a) principles of human development and the nature of individual differences; (b) the social, cognitive, emotional, and environmental factors that affect the development of giftedness; (c) a variety of methods for identifying and assessing students; (d) current and seminal research related to learning theory, giftedness, and creativity; (e) theoretical models, program prototypes, and educational principles that offer appropriate foundations for developing differentiated curricula for gifted students; and (f) the unique potentials of gifted students from underserved populations, including but not limited to gifted females and those who are disabled, racially or ethnically diverse, economically disadvantaged, and/or underachieving; and
2. *Educators must have the ability to:* (a) interpret and apply knowledge related to the needs of gifted students; (b) identify and assess the unique needs of gifted students; (c) act as a change agent in social, cultural, political, and economic environments inhibiting services to gifted students;

(d) vary teaching styles and instructional strategies to help gifted students meet their individual needs; (e) develop in gifted students the attitudes and skills needed to become independent, lifelong learners, to self-evaluate, and to set and pursue appropriate personal and academic goals for future success; and (f) create an environment in which giftedness can emerge and gifted students can feel challenged and safe to explore their uniqueness.

Just as important, schools must provide future educators with field experiences in a variety of settings; these settings must expose future educators to the diversity that exists within the gifted population. This exposure increases the probability that educators will effectively plan instruction for and provide direct services to gifted students from different cultural backgrounds. Finally, for purposes of this chapter, NAGC called for greater efforts by teacher preparation programs to recruit and retain minority students.

We believe the following recommendations are essential for enhancing educators' competence in working with gifted minority students.

1. *Personal Exposure and Experience:* (a) Educators must increase their self-understanding, which requires involvement in experiences that allow them to examine their own cultures, and to better understand the concept and significance of culture; and (b) educators must examine their beliefs and assumptions regarding gifted and minority students.
2. *Cultural Exposure and Experience:* (a) Educators must have opportunities and experiences that expose them to cultural and racial diversity in the U.S. and its schools. In many cases, these experiences cannot take place by reading books and articles. This exposure and experience in diverse school settings must be early and ongoing; and (b) educators must have early and ongoing experiences that expose them to gifted and minority students.
3. *Linguistic Exposure and Experience:* Educators must have early and ongoing experiences with linguistically diverse gifted students; educators must understand the importance of language and the implications of bilingualism and limited English proficiency in student learning.
4. *Social Exposure and Experience:* Educators require substantive preparation and direct instruction in dealing effectively with prejudices in school settings, particularly reducing racism, sexism, and classism in attitudes, assessment, and curriculum.
5. *Multicultural Curriculum and Instruction:* Educators must learn how to design, implement, and evaluate multicultural curricula and instruction for all students, regardless of ability. (Similarly, counselors and researchers, as

discussed in other chapters, must foster multicultural counseling and research).

6. *Learning Environment:* Educators must know how to develop supportive,
   affirming, and nurturing environments for diverse students of all ability
   levels.

In terms of self-awareness, educators might discuss how they see themselves in terms of socio-demographic variables — ethnicity, gender, language,
culture, and socio-economic status. They might be asked to participate in
community and cultural events, such as those described in chapter 5, and then
to reflect on these experiences. A central question to increase insight is: "How
does it feel to be a 'minority'?" Educators can also keep reflective journals and
write essays regarding their educational and social experiences with minority
groups (including the media). Likewise, future educators can write a critical
review or critique of an article, book, or film on minority issues (e.g., tracking,
ability grouping, poverty, and underachievement). The critique should include changes in attitudes and beliefs toward diverse groups. In terms of goals
and objectives, educators must:

1. Acquire a basic understanding of the literature and research in gifted education and multicultural education. Topics will focus on definitions and
   theories of giftedness, identification and assessment, programming, curriculum and instruction, and social and emotional needs.
2. Understand the various needs (e.g., academic, social, psychological, cultural) of gifted minority learners.
3. Understand the influence of the family, school, and peers on gifted minority students relative to achievement.
4. Understand the differential needs of gifted males and females, as well as
   the needs of culturally and ethnically diverse gifted students. Options for
   course projects or papers might include:
   • Prepare a critique/evaluation of your district's gifted education pro-
     gram, with an emphasis on gifted minority students.
   • Design a model for identifying gifted minority students in your partic-
     ular school or school system. Include rationales for the procedures and
     the instruments selected.
   • Prepare an in-depth case study of a gifted minority student, including
     assessment, diagnosis, and program planning.
   • Develop an inservice program for teachers on identifying and assessing
     gifted minority students.
   • Develop a set of mini-courses for meeting the academic and social-
     emotional needs of gifted minority students.
   • Develop a catalogue or list of resources (people, places, events) that

can be used to meet the educational and/or social-emotional needs of gifted minority students.

- Develop a presentation or workshop for administrators on the need for programs for gifted minority students.

Options for course projects or papers in courses on the " Social and Emotional Needs of Gifted Students" might include:

- Shadow a school counselor who is working with a gifted minority student.
- Design a strategy/model for helping a particular group of gifted minority students cope with psychological or socio-emotional concerns.
- Prepare an in-depth case study of a gifted minority child (or adult), including counseling and program planning for that individual.
- Develop an inservice program for the teachers regarding the socio-emotional needs of gifted learners.
- Develop a packet of activities designed to meet the affective needs of gifted students in general or a specific group of gifted students.
- Develop a program to inform parents and family members about the socio-emotional needs and development of their gifted children.
- Develop a catalogue or list of community resources (people, places, events) that can be used to meet the socio-emotional needs of gifted minority students.
- Prepare a brochure for counselors, encouraging them to seek special/ additional preparation in working with gifted students.
- Conduct a mini-survey with a minimum of 10 participants that explores their perceptions and beliefs about the socio-emotional concerns of gifted minority students (participants must come from one of the following groups: counselors, teachers, families, or gifted students).

PROFESSIONAL DEVELOPMENT IMPERATIVES

Becoming a competent educator is a lifelong process. It is a continuous search for self-improvement and professional improvement that does not end with formal education. Educators must, therefore, continue to seek experiences that help to refine their skills and abilities to work with gifted and minority students. For example, while school personnel in gifted education often join such organizations as NAGC and Council for Exceptional Children (CEC) (and their subdivisions), they can also join such organizations as the National Association for Multicultural Education, Black Child Development

Organization, Association for Multicultural Counseling and Development, Association of Black Psychologists, and so forth. These organizations are devoted to ensuring the highest standards of education for all students, particularly students of color.

Paley's (1989) *White Teacher,* Peters's (1987) *A Class Divided Then and Now,* Ladson-Billings's (1994) *Dreamkeepers: Successful Teachers for African-American Children,* MacLeod's (1995) *Ain't No Makin' It,* and Kozol's (1991) *Savage Inequalities* are highly recommended for educators who seek insight and self-understanding as they work with minority students. Gould's (1981) *The Mismeasure of Man* should also be read for its candid, historical, and research-based discussion of theories of intelligence and the testing of minority groups. Similarly, such films as *Eye of the Storm* and *Children in America's Schools* provide a thorough discussion of school life for minority students and low-SES students. In terms of self-awareness, educators should also discuss the concept of White privilege, perhaps using the work of McIntosh (1988, 1990). McIntosh focuses on White privilege and male privilege, a discussion that can raise students' levels of consciousness about the relationship between racial status and power.

Important topics in pre-service education must focus on cultural diversity relative to values, norms, and traditions, as well as minority students' learning and identity. Cultural values, norms, and traditions were discussed in chapters 1 and 5, as were learning styles and preferences. Likewise, social-emotional and psychological issues (e.g., racial identity) were discussed in chapter 6. Staff development can focus on many of the topics listed above. A few of these topics are addressed in Figure 7.1, entitled "Intelligence Myth Quotient." This information can be used to help determine the direction for staff development.

SUMMARY

At least two issues must be addressed in terms of professionals working in school settings — educational preparation and teacher diversity. Teacher preparation programs and professional development must prepare future and current educators for working in schools that are more diverse than ever before.

Nationally, minority teachers are underrepresented in education, and their numbers are declining steadily. Conversely, minority students are increasing rapidly. Minority teachers hold much promise for improving the academic and affective well-being of minority students. Specifically, the recruitment and retention of minority teachers into gifted education represents one promising way to address school failure and alienation among minority stu-

Figure 7.1 Intelligence Myth Quotient

True	False	Statement/Belief
		A child's IQ score is a strong indicator of adult success.
		IQ scores are the most frequently used tool in identifying gifted students.
		IQ scores are the most accurate identifier of gifted students.
		Cultural bias is a major weakness in intelligence tests.
		Genetics provide the primary contribution to superior intelligence.
		Higher IQ scores guarantee a person's ability to perform higher-status jobs (e.g., doctor, lawyer, engineer).
		Black students have lower IQ scores than White students.
		Most mental retardation is the result of heredity.
		Memory is the best index of human intelligence.
		College graduates are more intelligent than non-college graduates.
		There are multiple kinds of intelligence.
		IQ scores between identical twins tend to be the same.
		Verbal ability is the best single predictor of IQ.
		IQ remains constant from birth to death.
		Males have higher IQ scores than females.
		Poverty has no impact on intelligence or IQ scores.

Note: This figure focuses on intellectual giftedness, but can be modified to address other types of giftedness.

dents. This effort could also increase the representation of minority students in gifted education (Ford, Grantham, & Harris, 1997).

Effective teaching requires knowledge of both the subject matter and students, including their cultural backgrounds. Cultural knowledge includes knowledge of the nature, functions, and processes of culture and knowledge related to particular cultural groups. As has been acknowledged for some time, there is no "one best educational system," as some have proposed. Liberating the dominant culture from its ethnocentrism is the first step toward providing real opportunities to those who are culturally diverse.

CHAPTER 8

Minority Families and Gifted Education

The ruin of a nation begins in the homes of its people.
—Ghanaian proverb

Thousands of articles and hundreds of books, reports, and programs have focused on families and education. A significant percentage of these publications and initiatives focus on family involvement and its impact on student achievement. One theme threads through these works—families play a central and critical role in their child's education. Our reading of the literature suggests that: (a) most efforts address the role of schools and organizations in increasing family involvement; (b) most efforts target family involvement in the early years—preschool to upper elementary; (c) few publications target family empowerment—giving families the tools and strategies to promote and sustain their children's achievement; (d) few efforts target families of gifted students; and (e) few works and initiatives target minority families and concerns that may be unique to their context (e.g., racial identity). While certainly essential, these efforts are insufficient and inadequate. That is, efforts must provide families with the knowledge and skills to promote student achievement, and efforts must address issues specific to minority families.

This chapter addresses the needs of minority families with gifted children and provides suggestions for helping to increase or refine their involvement. We answer the following questions: What is family involvement? How can families be involved meaningfully in their children's education? What strategies promote student achievement and healthy self-perceptions? How can literature be used as a means of promoting student achievement and self-perceptions? Undergirding each of these questions is attention to achievement, self-worth and self-perception, and persistence and resilience.

THE CONTEXT: MINORITY FAMILIES

The Children's Defense Fund (CDF) (1998) identified significant and troubling issues facing families of color. Minority families are more likely to

170

live in poverty, to be headed by single-parent mothers, and to have mothers with lower educational levels than White students. On this last point, the CDF (1998) reported that *every* school day, more than 2,000 babies are born to mothers who are not high school graduates—1,810 are White, 465 are Black, 970 are Hispanic American, 71 are Asian American, and 34 are American Indian (CDF, 1998).

While these issues are not unique to minority families, they call attention to the importance of contextualizing strategies—tailoring strategies and initiatives—to meet the individual needs of minority families. In essence, there is a critical need to promote literacy among people of color, so many of whom have the highest illiteracy rates in the nation. There is also a need to promote racial pride among minority groups, for far too many wrestle with poor racial identities (e.g., Cross, 1995).

Likewise, schools must understand that risk factors such as those described by the CDF play a major role in decreasing family involvement in schools. As Maslow (1954) noted, meeting basic needs (food, shelter, safety) takes precedence over higher-level needs (e.g., need for achievement). While poverty must not be used as an excuse to limit family involvement (or to accept low family involvement), poverty must be understood as a powerful barrier to family involvement and student achievement. And lack of family involvement should not be equated with lack of concern on the part of families. Many minority families do not have the luxuries that come with middle-class status. For instance, their jobs are less secure and their pay is lower. Additional money for tutors is not an option for those in poverty. Schools must, therefore, be responsive, creative, and persistent in their efforts to involve and support minority families. Whatever efforts are adopted to increase and sustain minority family involvement in school settings, three things are clear—we must find ways to involve families at home, families must understand that they *can* make a difference in their children's academic life, and families must believe that schools care about their children.

A CRITICAL NEED: MINORITY STUDENT ACHIEVEMENT AND LITERACY

On a daily basis, the Children's Defense Fund raises the conscience of U.S. citizens with its reports on "Key Facts About American Children." In its most recent report (February 11, 1998), CDF presented the following statistics on poverty:

- 11.1% of White children are poor.
- 39.9% of Black children are poor.

- 40.3% of Hispanic children are poor.
- 19.5% of Asian/Pacific Islander children are poor.

Just as disturbing, of all poor children, 31.5% are Black. Other social issues take their toll on the quality of student life and achievement. Not only is the U.S. changing demographically relative to race and culture, it is changing in family structure. The CDF (1998) reports that 27% of all children live in single-parent families, and a larger portion of them are minority groups. With single-parent status comes poverty, role strain, and the need to meet survival or subsistence needs.

To state the obvious, the effects of these conditions show up in students' lack of school completion. The CDF (1998) reports that *every* school day, 2,489 White students drop out of school, as do 606 Black students and 967 Hispanic American students. Data were not presented for Asian American and American Indian students.

Virtually all of the data presented above focus primarily on low-SES minority students. An important question is, "How does SES impact intelligence test scores?" That is, do higher-SES minorities fair better than their lower SES counterparts in IQ and/or achievement tests? According to experts in the field of intelligence (see *The Wall Street Journal*, 1994), Black students from prosperous families tend to score higher on IQ tests than Blacks from poor families. However, the irony is that Blacks from higher SES families score, on the average, no better than Whites from poor families! Thus, we cannot assume that higher SES Blacks do not share the dilemmas facing lower SES Blacks. Higher income does not guarantee higher educational and social outcomes for Black students.

Because less information is available on higher SES minority students, educators, decisionmakers and policymakers may make erroneous generalizations — generalizations that lead to lowered expectations. According to Rodriguez and Bellanca (1996), Shade, Kelly and Oberg (1997), and many others, these social factors are used as *excuses and justification* for low teacher expectations for poor and minority students.

WHAT IS FAMILY INVOLVEMENT AND WHY IS IT IMPORTANT?

Family involvement has been defined and described in many ways. For example, family involvement that impacts achievement can be minimal (such as fundraising or field trips) or substantive (such volunteering in classrooms and participating on decisionmaking committees). Further, family involvement can take place in school settings or at home (e.g., monitoring homework, setting times for study). More specifically, family involvement ranges

Figure 8.1 Typology of Family Involvement

Type 1 Basic obligations of families	These obligations relate to the child-rearing practices of the family and the positive home conditions that relate to school success.
Type 2 Basic obligations of schools	Schools encourage communication with families.
Type 3 Involvement in school	Parents serve as volunteers in the school and classroom.
Type 4 Involvement in learning activities at home	Parents monitor and assist their own children at home.
Type 5 Involvement in decisionmaking, governance, and advocacy	Parents have participatory roles on boards, committees, site management teams, etc.
Type 6 Collaboration and exchange with community organizations	There is a sharing of responsibility for children and families across agencies and institutions.

Source: Adapted from Epstein (1997)

from superficial to substantive, from temporary to permanent. Epstein (1997) summarized the several levels of family involvement (see Figure 8.1), which range from families fulfilling their basic obligations to families working with community agencies.

Schools often encourage families to become involved in parent–teacher organizations, to help with fundraisers, and to help with newsletters and other communications. Seldom do families serve in an advisory or decision-making capacity. However, when Comer (1988) transformed family involvement in several school programs so that family members held key decision-making roles, students had higher academic outcomes.

Table 8.1 summarizes a seminal study on low-SES Black families and student achievement. In 1983, Clark found approximately a dozen factors that distinguished high-achieving from low-achieving Black students—amount of school contact, distinct role boundaries, parents' role in schooling, child's role in school, consistency of rule enforcement, family contact with school, and family's achievement-orientation values and behaviors. Essentially, parents of high achievement were more involved in their children's education, both quantitatively and qualitatively.

As Clark (1983) noted, family involvement (partnerships between homes and schools) helps to improve student outcomes, including grades,

Table 8.1 Quality of Success-Producing Patterns in Homes of Black High Achievers and Low Achievers

Key Factors	High Achievers	Low Achievers
School contact	School contact initiated frequently by parents	School contact initiated infrequently by parents
Parents' psychological and emotional status	Parents are psychologically and emotionally calm with child	Parents in psychological and emotional upheaval with child
Child's psychological and emotional status	Child is psychologically and emotionally calm with parents	Child is less psychologically and emotionally calm with parents
Parents' role in schooling	Parents expect to play a major role in child's schooling	Parents have lower expectations regarding their role in child's schooling
Child's role in schooling	Parents expect child to play a major role in his/her own schooling	Parents have lower expectations regarding child's role in his/her schooling
Role boundaries	Parents establish clear, specific role boundaries and status structure with parents as the dominant authority	Parents establish blurred role boundaries and structures
Post-secondary expectations	Parents expect child to get post-secondary education	Parents have less expectations for child to get post-secondary education
Family achievement-oriented rules	Parents have explicit achievement-centered rules and norms	Parents have less explicit achievement-centered rules and norms
Family achievement-oriented behaviors	Parents engage in deliberate achievement-oriented training	Parents seldom engage in achievement-oriented training
Students' acceptance of norms	Students show long-term acceptance of norms as legitimate	Students have less long-term acceptance of norms
Family contact	Infrequent conflict between family members	Frequent conflict between family members
Parent consistency	Parents consistently enforce and monitor rules	Parents have inconsistent standards and exercise less monitoring of child's time
Nurturance and support	Parents provide liberal nurturance and support	Parents are less liberal with nurturance and support
Child's knowledge	Parents defer to child's knowledge in intellectual matters	Parents do not defer to child in intellectual matters

Source: Adapted from Clark (1983)

test scores, attendance, and classroom behavior. However, many schools rightfully lament that students who need the most family involvement have the least. Certainly, role strain and economic problems serve as barriers to minority family involvement. Just as important, but seldom addressed, is the reality that many (perhaps most) families *do not know how to be involved*. They may lack the cultural capital, the educational experiences, and the sense of empowerment so important to creating family–school partnerships. Thus, as discussed below, family education programs are essential if family involvement is to increase and if families are to truly impact their children's academic achievement.

INVOLVING FAMILIES IN LITERACY: SUGGESTIONS FOR SCHOOLS

As the previous section noted, family involvement comes in many forms and can take place within and outside school walls. Strategies for involving minority families in their children's education were provided in Ford (1996). Rather than repeat this information, we will focus on strategies for promoting minority family involvement in literacy. The suggestions also focus on components of family education programs.

Family Education Literacy Initiatives

Schools wishing to promote family education programs targeting literacy can adopt numerous strategies. In particular, they can:

- Create literature and literacy workshops for families. Presenters should help families to understand different genres of literature (e.g., poetry, folk tales, fables, etc.). The workshop should also help families: (a) to choose interesting and high-quality multicultural books; (b) to create projects/activities related to the literature; (c) to ask higher-level thinking questions; and (d) to promote problem-solving skills.
- Assign a staff member (or family member) to coordinate local family literacy initiatives, such as working with libraries and bookstores to create programs for families, finding authors to speak to families, creating themes of the month, and so forth.
- Always include a literature and literacy section in the school newspaper that targets families. An annotated bibliography that includes activities and questions for discussion would be ideal.
- Create a literature club that meets monthly so that families can share

new books with other parents and discuss how they use those books with children.

- Take a survey of students to identify their favorite books; distribute the information to families and encourage them to introduce students to the books.
- Take a survey of families regarding their favorite books; share this information with other families.
- Invite parents (and grandparents) into the classroom to share their favorite books with students.
- Invite families to visit the classroom to watch teachers modeling effective teaching with literature.
- Send a brief list of suggested books home with grade reports.
- Talk about books and literacy during conferences with families.
- Always have books displayed in a showcase near the office and/or classrooms.
- Encourage families to volunteer at the school's library.
- To make books accessible to families, run a small bookstore (or loan library) that contains copies of all books recommended to families.
- Make a video about family literacy using students in the school.

Why the focus on families and literacy in this chapter? Perhaps Keeshan (1996) said it best:

As parents, one of our principal functions is the giving of values. Just as we place healthy food on the table to foster strong bodies, so we must foster strong minds and characters by the menu of values we place before our children. The values we choose to teach our children are lived out in the wider experiences that can be found in the stories we tell and the books we read with our children. (p. 10)

MINORITY FAMILY INVOLVEMENT: STRATEGIES AND RECOMMENDATIONS

If families are to be truly involved in their children's education, they (like educators) must have knowledge, strategies, and skills for helping their children. Teachers acquire knowledge, strategies, and skills in formal educational settings (e.g., colleges and universities). Conversely, families seldom receive formal training in rearing and educating their children. In this section, we offer a few strategies and recommendations for filling in this gap.

Choosing High-Quality Multicultural Literature

Choosing books that will interest and engage children is not an easy task. Choosing high-quality books is even more challenging. Families must know how to choose high-quality literature and literature containing important multicultural themes and concepts.

- The information is accurate and does not have distortions, such as stereotypes and exaggerations
- Images of people of color are positive, realistic, and authentic
- Minority groups play a central role in the book (e.g., are the main characters)
- The literature is likely to increase the child's self-awareness and self-understanding
- The literature is likely to increase the child's understanding of others
- The literature provides opportunities to dialogue and interact with others
- The literature provides opportunities for solving problems
- The literature provides opportunities for critical thinking

Relevant Multicultural Literature, Concepts, and Topics

Dozens of topics can be addressed when families read with their children (e.g., divorce, family structure, sibling rivalry, self-esteem, etc.). Even more topics are possible when discussing minority families. Our work with minority children, primarily those who are underachieving, suggests that four topics are essential: (a) families and student achievement; (b) perceptions of giftedness and ability; (c) racial pride; and (d) social relations. After reading each book, children should always be asked, "What have you learned from reading this book?" and "What have you learned about yourself?" With these two basic questions, children can increase their insight and self-awareness. Further, where appropriate, ask the children to think about how they might solve the problem(s), which facilitates problem-solving skills. Finally, talk with children about acting upon this newfound knowledge and insight. That is, how will they try to handle peer pressures, how will they treat others, and so forth? Many of the books in this chapter appear in chapters 5 and 6 (see Table 6.2.)

1. *Fostering Self-Understanding Through Self-Pride* (Grades P–4). Self-understanding and self-pride are important factors that affect student achievement. There are hundreds (perhaps thousands) of books that families can use to increase their children's understanding of and appreciation for self.

Some books have subtle messages regarding racial pride; others have overt messages. In both instances, discussions should lead children to make connections between self-pride and racial pride. For instance, in *The Ugly Duckling*, students may not initially notice that the duckling is dark and that this is the reason for others' rejection. Nonetheless, this is one of the most overt examples of racism in books for very young children. On the other hand, the bear *Corduroy* is rejected because of a missing button. How is the button analogous to race? How is this like rejecting someone based on skin color differences (or some other difference)?

Anderson, H. C. (1979). *The Ugly Duckling*. New York: Harcourt Brace Jovanovich.

In this classic, a duckling is rejected by his family and taunted and teased by other ducks because he is different. Specifically, he is dark (black) and the others are light. The duckling, feeling rejected and unaccepted, leaves the pond. Eventually, the duckling finds a swan family who accepts him; the duckling grows up to be the most beautiful swan of all.

Topics for discussion: peer pressures, family support, fairness, and equality.

Peer pressures: Why did the ducklings tease and taunt the duckling? How do you feel about this? Would you have teased the duckling? How would you handle being teased because you were different?

Family support: How do you feel about the duckling's family? Do you think parents would really treat their children differently? Why or why not? What advice would you give the parents about how they treated the duckling? What do you think of the swan family? What does adoption mean?

Fairness: Was the duckling treated fairly? Did he deserve to be treated unfairly? How can we treat others better? What rules can we make at home about treating others fairly?

Equality: What does "ugly" mean? Why was the duckling considered "ugly"? Do you think he was ugly? What makes someone "ugly"? Were the lighter ducklings better than the dark duckling?

Mendez, P. (1989). *The Black Snowman*. New York: Scholastic.

Two Black brothers, Peewee and Jacob, find a kente cloth, which they use to help dress their black snowman. They question whether a snowman can be black. With the magic of the kente cloth, the snowman comes to life and teaches the boys many important lessons about their history and life. Of the many concepts, the most central is racial pride.

Racial pride: Why do the boys have a difficult time accepting the reality that a snowman can be black? Is snow always white? What things come to mind when you hear the words "black" or "dark"? Why do you think negative events or phenomena are often associated with darkness? What things or concepts come to mind that are dark *and* positive? What does the kente cloth symbolize to Africans and African Americans? How does knowing your history help to improve your self-image?

2. *Fostering Social Skills and Relationships* (Grades P–3). Much data indicate that peers have a forceful and significant impact on minority students' achievement (e.g., Diaz, 1998; Fordham, 1988; Fordham & Ogbu, 1986; Lee, 1984). High-achieving minority students are often burdened with negative peer pressure in at least two forms: (a) they may be rejected by minority students who accuse them of "acting white" and (b) they may be isolated from White students.

The ability to build social relations and to avoid succumbing to peer pressure is one of the most important challenges that children face. It is also an important lifelong skill. While schools often focus on building students' social skills, they cannot do this alone. They need the support and assistance of families. The following books can be used in homes (and schools) to promote strong social skills among minority students.

Freeman, D. (1968). *Corduroy.* New York: Viking.

A teddy bear, Corduroy, is missing one button on his corduroy overalls. Other children won't buy him. One day, a little girl notices him in the store window and wants to buy him. When she takes him home, he finally feels loved. Discuss such topics as making friends and feeling special.

Making friends: Why do you think the other children would not buy Corduroy? Why didn't the storeowner give Corduroy a button? Is a missing button a good reason not to buy the bear? Why do you think the little girl liked Corduroy? Would you have bought the bear with the missing button?

Feeling special: Why was Corduroy special? How are you special or unique? Is being different okay in some cases? What would happen if everyone were the same, exactly the same? How would you feel if I looked like all the other mothers in the world? How would you know me? How would I know you? What lessons have you learned about differences?

Carle, E. (1971). *Do You Want to Be My Friend?* New York: Harper.

A little mouse is looking for a friend. He is very persistent and goes from animal to animal. After asking all the animals, he finally finds a friend in another mouse. The very simple story has several important concepts that can be discussed, including friendships and persistence.

Friendships: Why did the mouse want a friend? How do you think the mouse felt when he could not find a friend? Why do people need or want friends? How do you choose your friends? How do you approach other children you don't know? Is it okay to be friends with someone who is different from you in some way? What advice can you give the animals about being friends with the mouse?

Persistence: Do you think the mouse was persistent? How did he show this? Do you admire the mouse's persistence? Would you have been as persistent? Did the persistence pay off? How was the mouse like the engine in *The Little Engine That Could?*

3. Promoting Family Literacy (Grades 1–3).

Rahaman, V. (1997). *Read for Me, Mama.* Honesdale, PA: Boyd Mills Press.

A young Black child, Joseph, loves to read. He really likes reading with his mother. When he is young, his mother is able to hide the fact that she cannot read. She uses excuses about being busy, tired, and so forth. As he gets older, the boy realizes this. He finds a way to help his mother learn to read and to love it. Finally, when he asks his mother to read to him, she can. The compassionate story helps families to discuss literacy and family support.

Literacy: Why might Joseph's mother be unable to read? Why don't some elderly Black persons know how to read? How does Joseph's mother seem to feel about her inability to read? Why is the ability to read so important?

Family support: How does Joseph support his mother when he learns that she cannot read? Why does he want her to learn to read? How would you help a family member (or other person) who could not read?

4. Increasing Family Support (Grades 1–3).

Williams, V. B. (1986). *A Chair for My Mother.* New York: Greenwillow.

A young Hispanic American girl works with her mother at a diner a few days a week. She is saving her money for a special gift for her mother. Unfortunately, they lose all their possessions in a fire. Nonetheless, the girl is optimistic. The family rebuilds their life and eventually buys the special gift—a chair for her mother; a chair large enough for the family to fit in. Key themes include family support and perseverance.

Family support: How would you describe the family's relationship? What makes them a close family? What are the characteristics of a close or supportive family? How can we make our family more supportive of each other?

Perseverance: What does the book tell us about dreams and hope? How did the family finally buy the chair? What does the chair symbolize to the girl? What does it symbolize to you?

5. *Setting Realistic Family Expectations* (Grades 1–6). Just as teacher expectations have a significant impact on students' self-perception and achievement, so do family expectations. During the formative years and throughout their childhood, children are learning about the expectations that others have of them. Verbally and non-verbally, these messages are communicated. Two books have been selected to illustrate the role of unrealistic and excessive expectations on students. As stated earlier, a balance is needed — too many expectations can be as damaging as low expectations.

DeCesare, A. (1996). *Anthony the Perfect Monster.* New York: Random House.

Everybody thinks that Anthony is perfect, especially his mother. Anthony spends so much time trying to be perfect that he does things he really doesn't like (such as eating spinach). His classmates don't appreciate Anthony's perfect behavior, clothes, answers, etc. After watching a TV show about a monster, Anthony decides that he does not want to be perfect. He causes lots of trouble in the school, which no one likes. Eventually, the students like him, and his mother accepts that he is not perfect. His teacher says, "Nobody can be perfect, no matter how hard he tries. It's a lot easier to be yourself . . . and a lot more fun." Parents can discuss expectations with children, as well as the need for self-acceptance.

Expectations of self and others: Why did Anthony try to be perfect? Who was he trying to please? How might attempting to be perfect be a sign of low self-concept? How realistic is it to try to be perfect? What problems can perfectionism cause? What is the difference between trying your best and trying to be perfect? Which is achievable? What advice can you give Anthony's mother about expecting him to be perfect?

Namioka, L. (1992). *Yang the Youngest and His Terrible Ear.* New York: Brown.

As described in chapter 5, this is an amusing yet serious novel of a tone-deaf Chinese American boy in a musical family. Since Yang cannot play music and does not want to, he and his new friend (a White boy) devise ways to inform Yang's family that he does not want to play music. Yang prefers baseball, which his family does not value. Instances of stereotyping appear in the book, but they are subtle. Topics for family discussion include aspirations and expectations, cross-cultural friendships, honesty, and stereotypes.

Aspirations and expectations: What does Yang prefer to do in his spare time? How does this differ from his parents' expectations? Why do his parents seem to value music so much? Who do you support—Yang or his parents? Why?

Honesty: What do you think of Yang's plan to inform his parents of his desire to play baseball? Is it easier to be honest or dishonest with parents? Why? Was there an easier way to inform Yang's parents of his wishes? What advice can you give Yang and his parents about listening to each other and making compromises?

Stereotypes: What stereotypes appear in the book about Chinese students? How does Yang feel about this? How would you feel if someone held stereotypes about you? What can be done to decrease or eliminate stereotypes?

Cross-cultural friendships: What is a friend? How do you feel about people from different cultural groups being friends?

SUMMARY

Few educators would disagree that families play a central role in the education of their children. However, few families, especially minority families, are as involved as schools wish. One barrier to family involvement may be that schools (rather than minority families) tend to define the type and level of involvement that families can have, specifically in school settings. For instance, families are often asked to participate in fundraising initiatives and on field trips, some are asked to participate in the classrooms as tutors and aides, but few are asked to play a major role in decisionmaking. A second barrier may relate to concerns that minority families have about participating in schools (see Ford, 1996). For example, minority families who have had negative school experiences may be very hesitant to participate in school settings. Further, some families may hold the misperception that it is the school's sole responsibility to educate children.

A third barrier rests in families, especially those in poverty, using their limited time and resources to fulfill basic needs. Thus, families in poverty, so many of whom are people of color, do not participate in schools at the same rate as upper-SES families. How the schools respond to these differential needs and priorities is telling. How flexible are schools in accommodating families torn by the ravages of poverty and unsure of their role in school settings? What perceptions (or misperceptions) do schools hold about families who are not involved in school settings?

Another barrier to family involvement may rest in the lack of knowledge and skills that families need in order to be involved. It is one thing to say, "We want you to be involved in your child's education." It is another thing to help families to do this. Family education programs offer promise in this regard. As with teacher education programs, family education programs can give families the sense of empowerment to share in the ownership of their children's education, achievement, and school outcomes. All of this is to say that family involvement is a shared responsibility. Both partners require formal and ongoing preparation to promote, nurture, and sustain students' achievement.

CHAPTER 9

Research and Evaluation from a Multicultural Perspective

INTRODUCTION AND OVERVIEW

When all is said and done, schools must participate in evaluation and research to better understand the impact of their efforts and impact. Research and evaluation efforts help schools in at least two ways: (a) to improve accountability and (b) to take corrective actions. This chapter addresses evaluation and research with minority groups and minority issues in mind. We share concerns about research conducted with minority students and offer recommendations. Likewise, we offer suggestions for schools that wish to evaluate their efforts with gifted minority students.

The need for this chapter stems from the recognition that there is a long history of research conducted on racially and culturally diverse populations. Increasingly, racially and culturally diverse populations have come under the scrutiny of researchers, particularly White researchers. Yet research by African Americans and other minority groups has all but vanished from the pages of major journals (Graham, 1992). In fact, most of the research conducted on minority groups is conducted by White researchers. A lingering question among minority scholars has been, Can White researchers conduct bias-free or value-free research on participants who are racially and culturally different from themselves? This question stems from several concerns. Underlying the many concerns are issues of objectivity and cultural understanding. That is, minority groups may question the extent to which White researchers or others who do not share their cultural heritage can understand their culture and thus place results in context.

Ideally, research (and evaluation) is supposed to be objective rather than subjective, from the statement of the problem to the interpretation of the results. Can research be bias-free or value-free, especially when conducted by researchers who are racially and culturally different from their sample or subjects? Is such research a reality or an ideal? The notion of research being free of values and biases has been seriously challenged; important questions have been raised about the appropriate relationship between scientific research, ob-

184

jectivity, and the role of researchers' values and beliefs (Kimmel, 1988). We examine these issues in this chapter, urging researchers to recognize that bias-free research is an ideal, not yet a reality. We also suggest recommendations for more research and evaluation in gifted education programs.

SCHOOL SELF-EVALUATION AND MINORITY STUDENTS

As noted in chapter 4 and elsewhere (Ford, 1996), many articles point to the poor performance of minority students on standardized tests as the major barrier to their being underrepresented in gifted education. Few articles and studies have examined other factors in the underrepresentation of minority students in gifted education. Specifically, school policies, practices, and procedures play a part in minority student underrepresentation, and unless schools engage in self-evaluation, this situation is likely to persist.

As researchers and consultants to many school districts, we frequently hear a statement that echoes in the halls of many school buildings: "We have a hard time identifying gifted minority students because they don't test well." We see several problems with this statement.

First, it assumes cause–effect or causation; that is, the statement can be interpreted as "low test scores cause underrepresentation." A more accurate statement is that students with lower test scores tend not be identified as gifted, particularly when test scores are the sole or primary source of identification information. Another interpretation of the cause–effect statement, one that is quite troubling, is that "because minority students don't test well, they are not gifted." This statement and associated beliefs place a great deal of faith in the validity of tests. A third interpretation is also possible. With this interpretation comes the assumption that the responsibility for poor performance rests within the students rather than within the test itself. Essentially, the statement fails to reflect the reality that many environmental or situational factors influence test scores. According to Weschler (1991),

It cannot be presumed that the array of tasks, standardized and presented as the WISC-III can cover all of an individual's intelligence . . . other determiners of intelligence, nonintellective in nature, also help shape how a child's abilities are expressed. These nonintellective factors . . . include attributes such as planning and goal awareness, enthusiasm, attitudes, field dependence and independence, impulsiveness, anxiety, and persistence. . . . [We] must consider an individual's life history (e.g., social and medical history and linguistic and cultural background) as part of any good assessment . . . [It is] important to take into account factors other than intellectual or cognitive abilities. (pp. 2–3)

In sum, the statement or assumption that the poor test scores of minority students cause underrepresentation does not adequately explain the persistent and pervasive underrepresentation of minority students in gifted education. This conclusion led us to the purpose of this chapter — a call for school districts to evaluate how other factors (i.e., policies, practices, and procedures) impact minority student underrepresentation. Four scenarios are used to illustrate our concerns:

1. A school district's policy specifically states that the WISC-III or Binet 4 are the only two intelligence tests that can be used in the identification process. Yet the district is aware that African American and Hispanic American students in the district are not performing well on either test.
2. A school district takes gifted education referrals from teachers only. Yet the district is aware that teachers are not referring students of color for identification and screening.
3. Only students who have an achievement test score in the 95th percentile are screened for gifted education services. Yet the district is aware that no minority student has scored above the 85th percentile.
4. To receive gifted education services, students must maintain a B average. Yet the district is aware that minority student achievement averages less than a B.

These scenarios may seem too unrealistic or exaggerated to be taken seriously. However, we have witnessed each scenario on more than one occasion. In some instances, test performance has been a significant factor in minority student underrepresentation. However, other factors, such as those described in the scenarios, have also contributed to underrepresentation. Simply put, there is a need to evaluate the role of policies, practices, and procedures in minority student underrepresentation and underachievement.

Three of the most significant challenges for school districts are: (1) to determine what information is needed to conduct a *comprehensive* self-evaluation; (2) how to analyze the results; and (3) how to use the results. A critical review of a district's enrollment in gifted education, particularly relative to racial status, is the cornerstone of self-evaluation. This self-evaluation helps to determine whether policies, practices, and/or procedures are legally sound. For instance, the use of teachers as the sole source of referral or nomination may be legally sound, but is questionable if teachers underrefer certain groups or types of students (e.g., minority students, underachievers, males, etc.). Likewise, the use of test scores in the identification and placement process may be legally sound, but a particular test or instrument may be invalid and unreliable (and useless) for certain students. The continued use of this test, while legal, seems questionable.

Components of Self-Evaluation

Evaluation, as defined by Worthen, Borg, and White (1993), is the formal determination of a thing's worth, value, or quality. Evaluations in school settings often focus on the educational value, worth, or quality of programs, projects, and processes. Worthen and colleagues contend that "evaluation perhaps holds more promise than any other approach in providing schools with information they need to improve their practices" (p. 624). In particular, we focus on formative evaluations whose purpose is to improve programs and policies. We focus on the effectiveness of quality of policies, practices, and procedures relative to identifying and placing students in gifted education programs. Although we focus exclusively on issues associated with minority student underrepresentation, schools might wish to focus on this issue as one aspect of a larger self-evaluation. In essence, it is not enough to say that minority students are underrepresented in gifted education; we must find out why, and seek ways to correct the problem. Below, we present an overview of five issues that require examination relative to minority students; other topics for gifted education self-evaluation appear in Buchanan and Feldhusen (1991) and Callahan and Caldwell (1995).

1. *Extent of Minority Student Underrepresentation.* Debates abound regarding what constitutes "underrepresentation" and when underrepresentation is "severe." For example, if Hispanic Americans represent 25% of the school district but 10% of the gifted program, is this a significant discrepancy? If they represent 15% of the gifted program, is this a significant discrepancy? According to Chinn and Hughes (1987), underrepresentation is severe if the percentage of minority students in the school and gifted program is more than a 20% discrepancy. Nationally, Hispanic students represent 9.4% of the school population, but 4.7% of gifted education. This would, using Chinn and Hughes's criteria, represent a severe discrepancy.

2. *Gifted Education Classification.* To date, we have not been able to locate national data on how minority students are classified once identified as gifted. We often see an overrepresentation of minority students in the areas of creativity and visual and performing arts. In a recent study, Black students represented 23% of one school district and 8% of the gifted program; noteworthy is that most of those Black students who were identified as gifted were classified in visual and performing arts (Ford, 1995a).

An examination of both within- and between-group classification might also prove insightful. It is quite possible that a district is successful at identifying African American students, but less successful with Hispanic American students. We have also noticed classification issues relative to grade level, socio-economic status (SES), and gender. Specifically, relative to grade level, Ford (1995a) found that Black students in one school district were identified as gifted in elementary school, but no Black students in middle and high school were identified as gifted. We have not found national data on minority student classification by grade level, SES, or gender.

3. Referral Rates and Sources. An important question to include in a self-examination is the extent to which teachers refer or underrefer minority students for identification and placement. For instance, do White teachers underrefer minority students? Do minority teachers underrefer minority students? Again, grade level, SES, and gender trends must be explored. Similarly, what role do minority parents play in the referral process, as well as other aspects of identification and placement? Do minority parents underrefer their children? Are instruments completed by parents user-friendly (e.g., take into consideration literacy rates) or barrier producers (e.g., time-consuming, complex, abstract)?

4. Identification and Assessment Instruments. As stated in chapter 4, most of the work on underrepresentation centers on test performance. As part of the self-evaluation process, schools will need to examine whether all instruments (tests, checklists, referral forms, etc.) are:

1. valid and reliable;
2. used appropriately (e.g., examiner follows directions, examiner is qualified/trained to administer the tests, examiner is qualified to interpret results in a culturally sensitive manner); and
3. appropriate for use with minority students (e.g., norms include representative sample of minority students, the test is not considered discriminatory, etc.). For a more comprehensive list of issues related to minority student assessment, see Ford (1996), Frasier, Garcia, and Passow (1995), and Frasier et al. (1995)

5. Student Outcome Data. A considerable number of reports and studies have revealed the disproportionate failure rates of minority students; and many gifted students are underachieving at high rates. Little is known about the outcomes of gifted minority students. Do gifted minority students fare better than minority students not identified as gifted? Do they have higher graduation rates? Higher achievement rates (e.g., tests and grades)? Lower suspension and expulsion rates? Do they attend college at higher rates?

Is the rate of underachievement less? In addition to asking these questions in general, evaluation must be specific. For example, these questions must be asked by gender, SES, and age, as well as between minority groups. In essence, are the outcomes for gifted minority females more positive than those for gifted minority males? What role does SES play in these outcomes — are higher SES gifted minority students achieving better than other minority students? Do certain gifted minority groups fare better than others?

In Appendix C, we present a checklist for self-evaluation targeting multicultural variables. The checklist was developed by the National Council for the Social Studies Task Force on Ethnic Studies Curriculum (1992). When reading the guidelines and using them as a checklist, respondents answer in three ways. First, respond "yes" or "no" to the item. Second, indicate how important/necessary you believe this guideline to be. Finally, indicate whether the item is within your control as a teacher (counselor, administrator, etc.).

CONDUCTING RESEARCH WITH MINORITY GROUPS

In the previous section, we focused on gifted education evaluation. In this section, we focus on another important topic — research conducted on (or with) minority students.

Objectivity Issues

Historically, students in research courses have been taught that research is indeed objective, that science is and must be objective. One traditional view of research was that the only values to influence research were the scientific values placed on truth and objective methodology, a view that prescribed complete detachment of personal values from research. Researchers are perceived to be cool, detached, impassive, and dispassionate observers of phenomena that have no emotional meaning for them. More specifically, researchers have been expected to be paragons of objectivity and passionless purveyors of the truth (Kimmel, 1988, p. 126). Without such objectivity, the results are considered invalid and unreliable.

Achieving scientific objectivity is an onerous task, one that requires superhuman characteristics. One must not become personally or emotionally invested in the study, interpretations must not reach beyond the data, conclusions must not be value-laden, and so forth. Yet we all have some level of both professional and personal investment in our work, including research. We consciously or subconsciously hope that our hypotheses will be supported (e.g., parent involvement has a positive impact on student achievement), that one variable predicts another (e.g., SAT scores predict college achievement), that relationships are significant (e.g., GPA and achievement test scores are highly correlated), that one intervention is more effective than another, and that the experimental group will have different outcomes than the control group. Imagine a study whose results showed that urban Black students had significantly higher IQ scores than suburban White students. When the expected results are not found, there is some level of disappointment and concern—what went wrong? What could the researchers have done differently? Should another statistical analysis have been used? How will the results be explained to and received by the scientific community? As Cyril Burt demonstrated, a researcher may even resort to unethical practices when results conflict with preconceived notions (Gould, 1981). There are, of course, other alternatives. For instance, the researcher may choose not to publish the results, may seek a larger sample size, may modify the measures for another study, or may replicate the study.

Researchers must be aware that ethical conflicts and moral dilemmas are inevitable. As human beings, we are not free of biases; we bring our values, attitudes, and beliefs into our work, be it teaching or research. If such biases did not exist, there would be less need for Human Subjects Committees. For example, the influence of teacher expectations on student outcomes is well researched. Teacher expectation literature serves as a case in point. This literature provides educators with much data on the effect of low expectations on Black students' achievement. Conversely, less is known about the effects of researcher and interviewer expectations, probably because of our zeal for achieving the ideal—scientific objectivity. Nonetheless, biases, ethical decisions, and moral judgments are affected by our own cultural and personal characteristics, interests, and beliefs. Essentially, an objective methodology guided by a utilitarian set of ethical standards cannot always overcome the initial biases associated with individual decisionmaking (see Kimmel, 1988, p. 125). As Gould (1981) noted:

> Science, since people must do it, is a socially embedded activity. It progresses by hunch, vision, and intuition . . . Much of its change through time does not record a closer approach to absolute truth, but the alteration of cultural contexts that influence it so strongly. Facts are not pure and unsullied bits of information; culture also influences what we see and how we see it. (pp. 21–22)

We must work toward the realistic goal of reducing biases in ourselves and our work. Personally, we can seek greater awareness and understanding about biases, stereotypes, and misperceptions regarding minority groups. Ample opportunities for increased cultural competence and sensitivity are available via literature, conferences, and educational institutions that focus on multiculturalism. We can also become more involved in the lives of minority groups. Ideally, such involvement takes place with ethnographic research; alternatives include seeking the assistance of a minority person to serve as a mentor or cultural translator. For example, we often ask colleagues to critique our work, not only for editing, but also for inaccuracies in assumptions and conclusions, for polemic literature reviews, and other potential barriers to quality and equity.

Researcher Demographics

It is essential for the research team to be as racially and culturally diverse as early as possible at all stages of the study—from the literature review, statement of the problem, and research design (including sampling, methodology, instrument development, and data collection) to interpretation. A few years ago, the senior author reviewed a manuscript in which the author argued that the lower IQ scores of Blacks compared to Whites is largely due to Blacks being genetically inferior; conversely, the lower IQ scores of Whites compared to Asian Americans was due to environmental factors. What guides the different assumptions and interpretations? Would this conclusion have been reached had the research team been all Asian American and African American? Or had the team included these groups of color? Further, what factors—stereotypes, biases, etc.—might have led to this conclusion?

The following biases may be less blatant: (1) a few years ago, we attended a national conference presentation in which the speaker stated that most Black mothers do not value education and achievement for their children; (2) in a manuscript submitted for publication consideration, the author stated that most Black families are dysfunctional; (3) in a different manuscript under publication review, we found the instrument to be problematic—all items pertaining to Hispanic American fathers were worded negatively, while those for White fathers were worded positively; and (4) in several articles, we note that authors examine gender differences but ignore racial differences.

In the first example, two studies from the early 1970s were the sole source of the conclusion; in the second example, the author also stated that the results were generalizable to all people of African descent; in the third example, about 60% of the respondents were Black and 30% were female; in the last example, conclusions were based on a sample size of 26. These are contemporary examples from a long list of manuscripts, published articles, and conference presentations that inappropriately stereotype, generalize, and draw unfounded conclusions regarding persons of color.

The following biases are even less blatant. Several studies today, as in the past, refer to students of color as "disadvantaged." For example, gifted minority students are found in the ERIC database as "disadvantaged gifted." Many other students are automatically given the label "at risk" because they are persons of color, without attention to their socio-economic status, health, parental educational level, family structure, family achievement orientation, and other factors that place students at risk for poor educational and social outcomes. Such global and unqualified labels as "disadvantaged" and "at risk" are offensive and demeaning for those groups to whom the labels are applied; they send subtle and not-so-subtle messages that are humiliating and hurtful, and biased.

Are these insensitivities the result of malice? of oversight? of lack of cultural awareness? of lack of understanding? or of several of these factors? Are the insensitivities conscious or unconscious? Regardless of their sources, minority groups are negatively affected. Essentially, the field has little valid and reliable research on minority students, little research that is useful.

MULTICULTURAL COMPETENCE: RECOMMENDATIONS FOR RESEARCH

How can researchers become more culturally competent? Personal *and* professional growth are essential for working with minority students. We must acknowledge that as researchers, we are human and, therefore, infallible and subjective. Thus, we must begin the difficult process of looking inward for the sources of biases. What assumptions do you hold about African Americans? Hispanic Americans? American Indians? Asian Americans? males and females? In what ways might these preconceived notions affect your research? How willing are you to change negative perceptions? Will you look for biases in your own work and the work of others?

With increased insight and awareness, researchers are more likely to seek, receive, and provide constructive feedback regarding minority groups; they become more proactive in their willingness to ask for the assistance of diverse persons throughout the research process. In essence, culturally competent researchers seek equity through bias-reduced research.

There is little that researchers can do to foresee how their work will be used or interpreted, yet they must try to make the best possible prediction of how their work will be used and, to the greatest extent possible, try to protect those who are the focus (directly and indirectly) of the research. We must also take special care to note the limitations of our study and its results. Researchers should also inform readers of known consequences of the results that should be considered. Equally important is that we must avoid hasty conclusions and interpretations. Finally, researchers must be willing to assume some responsibility for the knowledge they generate, and seek the guidance or assistance of those who can point out sources of biases and other problems. Conducting bias-free research is certainly an ideal and worthy endeavor. However, bias-reduced research is a reality that is within our grasp and our control.

SUMMARY AND CONCLUSION

The overwhelming majority of research conducted on or with minority groups is conducted by White Americans. Research is not a neutral process, for it is conducted by human beings who, ideally, are bias-free, but realistically cannot be. It takes a great deal of effort to conduct research that is untainted by biases, yet this ideal must be our goal. One of the first and most effective steps to achieving this ideal is to confront biases. Then we can begin the process of improving research with minority groups.

The questions presented in this chapter do not represent an exhaustive list of items for research and self-evaluation. They serve as a basis for helping school districts to consider the many variables that contribute to minority student outcomes, particularly underachievement and underrepresentation. The findings can help increase and improve services to gifted minority students. Research and self-evaluation may reveal the need to adopt a broader, more inclusive definition of giftedness, and to create a broader range of services for gifted students. Schools may find that instruments deemed valid and statistically reliable nonetheless fail to identify the strengths and abilities of certain groups of students. Other schools may find that a sole reliance on teacher referrals may not be an effective procedure. A different school may find that parental checklists are too complex and time-consuming.

Without comprehensive, ongoing self-evaluations, we may examine problems in isolation and fail to gather a complete picture of important issues. We thus pick away at problems, place a Band-Aid on them, and never really get to the task of addressing minority student underrepresentation and underachievement in a systematic and systemic way. In short, school personnel must be proactive and willing to examine the issues discussed in this chapter and elsewhere, in order to increase the participation of minority students in gifted programs. Perhaps the most important question to consider in this type of self-evaluation is: "How might schools — via policies, practices, and procedures — contribute to the underrepresentation of minority students in gifted programs?" Just as important, we must seek valid and reliable research with groups of color.

CHAPTER 10

Case Studies and Scenarios for Reflection

INTRODUCTION AND OVERVIEW

This chapter presents three case studies and several scenarios for reflection and reinforcement. The cases and scenarios are based on actual children and events. Much support exists in higher education for using case studies to teach important concepts and skills, particularly reflection, problem-solving, application, and evaluation. Two of the three cases in this chapter include recommendations for intervention. We have intentionally left one case and the scenarios without interventions. It is our hope that sufficient information has been provided in the previous chapters to allow readers to identify major issues facing gifted children of color and to develop appropriate prevention and intervention strategies.

THE CASE OF ANDREA

Andrea is a 5-year-old Mexican American female who attended an inner-city elementary school for gifted children.[17] Her mother and father are professors at a private university. Andrea's performance in school was not progressing as expected by her parents. Teachers expressed concern over Andrea's lack of achievement and were considering additional evaluation to confirm Andrea's giftedness.

Andrea was the only Mexican American student in the entire school, and there were no teachers of color. Andrea's primary language was Spanish, although she was quickly learning English from her bilingual class. Spanish instruction was offered twice a week for 30 minutes. At the beginning of the school year, Andrea would converse in Spanish with the Spanish teacher, but after a few months, she began to participate less and less. In an effort to be more inclusive, teachers would often ask Andrea how to say various words in Spanish. Andrea would respond quietly with the correct Spanish words. Language arts, including reading and writing, were emphasized in Andrea's school. A variety of methods were employed to teach reading—phonics, whole language, and so forth. However, Andrea was not progressing as quickly as her classmates. To facilitate Andrea's English, teachers suggested that the family speak only English at home.

Andrea usually played by herself. However, the dramatic play center was the one place where Andrea's classmates would include her. Students would assign Andrea to the role of nanny or housekeeper.

A new girl, Jamie, joined the classroom. Jamie was very attractive and extremely bright, as demonstrated by her very advanced reading, linguistic, and math skills. Jamie, who was not accepted into the group initially, gravitated toward Andrea. Teachers could not understand their friendship. They did not consider Andrea to be Jamie's intellectual peer. However, Jamie and Andrea's friendship generated a confidence that resulted in both of them becoming more extroverted and risk-taking. They really enjoyed working together. Nonetheless, as Andrea's academic performance improved, teachers became suspicious. They expected high-quality work from Jamie, but attributed Andrea's improvement to cheating. Andrea was often asked if she actually did her own work or if someone helped her. After a couple of months, Andrea's work began to deteriorate. When Andrea's parents voiced concern over this, teachers suggested that perhaps Jamie had been helping Andrea. They pointed out that Andrea's performance was much lower before Jamie came along.

Over the next few weeks, Andrea completely withdrew from social relations with teachers and classmates, including Jamie. She completed her work, but seldom participated in class. Eventually Andrea's parents withdrew her from the program. Andrea's teachers were surprised, but supported the decision. They thought the program was too academically rigorous for Andrea.

Needs and Intervention

Social-Emotional Needs. Soon after entering school, Andrea learned that she was different from peers and teachers. There were no other Mexican American students or teachers. Her lack of proficiency in English exacerbated matters. There were two persons with whom Andrea could truly communicate—Jamie and the Spanish teacher (whom she saw for a very short time during the week).

With the absence of other Mexican American children and staff, it becomes even more important that cultural diversity is presented through the inclusion of multicultural education and counseling. Andrea needs to have an opportunity to learn how her people and culture contributed to the history of her state and to the world. Similarly, other students can gain increased cultural awareness and understanding.

As noted in chapters 5 and 6, bibliotherapy, or literature that uses culturally relevant literature, can prove invaluable to minority students. Johnson et al. (1995) provide a sound literature lesson addressing identity for 2nd- and 3rd-graders. The lesson begins with teachers providing mirrors for each student. Students are directed to look into the mirror and to think of two changes that they would like to make about themselves. A major goal of this component is to help students to understand that how one looks is not as important as what type of person one is. That is, the outside matters less than the inside.

Next, students read *The Ugly Duckling* and create a literature web for the book. (Students can also read *Cuckoo/Cuco, Eggbert: The Slightly Cracked Egg*, and other books mentioned in previous chapters.) The web is followed by class discussions. Students are asked: What is the "problem" with the duckling in the story? How was the duckling treated different from the other animals? What is the main idea of the story? Do you agree with the hen's description of how to recognize a true friend? And what does the following statement mean to you—"A good heart never becomes proud"? Students provide examples to explain their interpretation of the quote and readings. Students are also asked reasoning questions: What reasons are given by the other animals for rejecting the duckling? What evidence is there that the duckling's mother also rejected him? And how does the concept of "the pain of being different" relate to this story?

Students keep a response journal where they write about an experience in which they felt the "pain of being different." They complete a vocabulary web, and make a change matrix to serve as a basis for later discussions. As part of a homework assignment, students develop an argument for the acceptance of differences in our society; they cite three examples of present-day individuals or groups that are treated like the "ugly duckling"; and they give reasons for accepting individual differences. Finally, as an extension, students can explore the meaning of beauty, create a collage of the three most beautiful things in their lives, or share (in writing) why they are beautiful.

Counseling through student support groups can be very effective in helping culturally diverse students develop a sense of belonging and an opportunity to develop successful strategies for dealing with inadequate social relations (e.g., feelings of isolation, rejection, etc.). Unfortunately, the limited number of minority students prevents this particular school from providing a support group. Thus, an alternative is to provide students with role models and mentors with whom they can relate. This might be an older student in the school or a community member. Students get an opportunity to develop a relationship with someone who is contributing positively to the community. Mentors and role models provide an opportunity for children who are isolated to have some sense of belonging and shared understanding. Andrea's teachers might have this role model(s) and mentor(s) visit the classroom on a weekly or monthly basis (e.g., read to students, help with homework, etc.).

Finally, teaching strategies may need to be altered to meet Andrea's learning styles. As indicated in chapter 1, some minority groups thrive in less competitive learning situations. Specifically, Andrea and her classmates might benefit from social and cooperative learning groups. Cooperative learning serves both academic and affective goals — students learn from each other, and they learn to work together.

Language Needs. Andrea was bilingual, with Spanish as her primary language. The burden of communicating with peers and teachers who only spoke English was often placed on this young child. While an effort was made to include Spanish within the classroom, it was done in a "touristic manner," or superficial way. That is, Spanish was not incorporated into the curriculum. In several instances, teachers did not validate Spanish as a legitimate language. They treated it as a novelty, which sent a strong message to Andrea that Spanish, which was her primary language, was not very important. Essentially, this practice devalued Spanish in Andrea's eyes. It was also evident that Andrea did not want to bring attention to her linguistic differences by only using Spanish when requested. When Andrea's parents stopped speaking Spanish, as recommended by her teachers, it created confusion in terms of family expectations. Andrea lives in a bilingual home, but was forced to choose which language should be used.

The integration of languages into curriculum provides an opportunity for bilingual students to learn effectively. The validation of students' language and linguistic styles contributes to the development of positive self-esteem and identity in culturally diverse students. Thus, teachers might have spent more time and depth on each language. This approach serves two purposes: first, it exposes students to many languages; second, it does not place students like Andrea in the awkward situation of being the focus of additional and unwanted attention. Classrooms and schools should also have books in multiple languages. For example, *My Day/Mi Dia* (Emberley, 1993), *My House/ Mi Casa* (Emberley, 1990), *Cuckoo/Cucu* (Ehlert, 1997), *Moon Rope* (Ehlert, 1992), and many other books are in both Spanish and English. Likewise, Feelings (1971, 1974) has written two award-winning books on counting and the alphabet in Swahili (*Moja Means One* and *Jambo Means Hello*).

While the teachers were working in a gifted education program, they still seemed to have difficulty understanding that a lack of English proficiency does not necessarily mean a lack of intelligence. At one point, they contended that the gifted education program was too academic for Andrea. As noted in chapters 5 through 7, teachers, counselors, and administrators need training in diversity and multicultural education to become more culturally aware and sensitive to the needs of minority students and their families. In particular, as discussed throughout this book, Andrea's teachers need training in teacher expectations, varying instructional strategies, meeting affective needs, meeting cultural needs, and working with minority families. Teachers must have the opportunity to examine their own values. They must be able to identify how their own cultural belief system impacts their attitude and expectations of culturally diverse students. Andrea was very much aware of the disbelief of her teachers concerning her work and was confused about what they expected from her. The suggestion that someone else "helped" her was a direct insult to her ability and integrity. The result was social and academic disengagement by Andrea, an already lonely and confused child.

Like many school districts nationally, Andrea's school lacks teacher diversity. School administrators must work diligently to increase the number of minority staff in their schools. Strategies for increasing teacher diversity were discussed in chapter 7.

THE CASE OF MARCUS

Marcus is a 14-year-old African American male. His father works in construction and his mother works in a florist shop. He currently attends an inner-city gifted magnet program. He is one of four Black students in the program.

In elementary school, Marcus reported feeling isolated from other students, primarily because he was much larger than his classmates. Marcus's achievement in math was excellent. Language arts, especially reading, were difficult for Marcus. Due to his high performance in math, teachers felt that he was not really trying in language arts and that he was lazy. He eventually was placed in remedial reading in the fourth grade. The teacher's aide was able to work with Marcus and he was returned to his regular classroom at the end of fourth grade. Marcus's progress in language arts continued; by fifth grade, he had maintained a high B average.

Marcus was recommended for the gifted program by his parents. They felt very strongly that he learned quickly and needed to be challenged. With resistance from his 2nd grade teacher, who felt that Marcus was bright but not gifted, Marcus was given the Raven's *MAT* and the *Cognitive Abilities Test* (CogAT). Due to the discrepancy of results on the Raven's and the CogAT (Raven's at the 98th percentile and CogAT at the 75th percentile), further testing was given, eventually resulting in Marcus qualifying for the gifted program.

Marcus enjoyed the challenge of the gifted program in middle school. He was one of seven Black students, but was able to develop friendships with ease. The curriculum, although challenging, was not very inclusive of people of color. Marcus took it upon himself to infuse the curriculum with information from his own culture. Many of Marcus's friends began to distance themselves from Marcus and would ask him why he always had to talk about Blacks. Marcus felt very disappointed and hurt by his friends' comments, but decided not to back down.

When asked why he was so driven, Marcus shared how he was teased in elementary school for speaking "wrong" and not liking the "right music." He tried to change how he spoke and really tried to like the "right kind" of music, but he just couldn't do it. Marcus wanted to get people to see that there is no right or wrong in many things.

Most of his teachers enjoyed the information Marcus shared in class and even asked for resources and materials. Some did not appear to like the additional information and questioned the validity of his information and sources. This would motivate Marcus to bring in more information.

Marcus was performing very well in all of his classes. Marcus kept up his personal mission during the sixth and seventh grades, but by the eighth grade, his attitude appeared to have changed. Marcus shared that he was tired of trying to teach White people about himself and others. He said that he was tired of being the only African American in all of his classes and wanted to have more culturally diverse friends. Although he was eligible to attend an International Baccalaureate Program and had been aggressively sought after by recruiters, Marcus chose to attend a culturally diverse inner-city high school. He wanted to be with people more like himself and take classes where he would learn about other cultures. Marcus's family, although disappointed with his decision not to attend the International Baccalaureate Program, respected his wishes and decided to let him attend the school of his choice.

When Marcus's decision was discussed at a meeting concerning the recruitment of gifted students of color, it was used as an example of how Black parents are not really committed to their children's education.

Needs and Intervention

Identity Needs.   For the most part, Marcus has a strong, positive sense of self. One might place him in Cross's later stage of identity — internalization-commitment — for Marcus has been on a mission to make a positive contribution to society in the area of race relations. He is proud of being Black and wants others to understand and accept his pride and culture. Marcus has put out a blatant call for curricular modifications — he wants mirrors for himself and windows for other students.

Some of Marcus's energy and determination have been understood; some teachers have been willing to learn from Marcus; others have not. Marcus saw this lack of tolerance and interest as a challenge. To nurture this energy and strong racial identity, teachers can introduce Marcus (and other students) to Malcolm X, whose biography represents the epitome of Cross's model of racial identity. For example, in later life, Malcolm was committed to social action, to improving the lives of Blacks, and to improving race relations nationally and internationally. Students can also read about Benjamin Banneker, a self-taught scientist who was determined to achieve, and a host of other minority role models.

Social Needs. In this case, we recommend that school personnel target efforts at Marcus's classmates, providing them with the skills to be more culturally aware and competent. From the information presented in the case, Marcus's classmates feel uncomfortable with discussions that focus on diversity. Similarly, they do not see the need for such discussions. Directly and indirectly, these students have devalued Marcus's culture. For Marcus, this is a challenge and motivator; for other minority students, it may not be.

Activities that target students' perceptions and stereotypes are a good place to begin creating and maintaining a culturally responsive classroom. Initial activities might be general rather than race-specific. For example, gender and age stereotypes and discrimination can first be integrated into the curriculum. Students can view books, magazines, TV shows, newspaper articles, and other media for examples of such stereotypes and associated discrimination.

Schools with a service component to the curriculum can encourage students to work in minority communities or in social organizations that target students with backgrounds different from their own. For instance, students might volunteer as tutors in Chapter I and Head Start programs, as well as social work and community agencies (e.g., Salvation Army and Goodwill).

Class discussions on generalizations, stereotypes, and perceptions can increase students' insight, thus improving their understanding, receptiveness, and ability to deal with more complex issues associated with race and culture. Counselors, teachers, and administrators should also develop a support group for Marcus, as well as provide mentors and role models. Such organizations as the 100 Black Men (headquartered in Atlanta), National Association for the Advancement of Colored People (NAACP), and the National Urban League seek to improve the educational and social outcomes of minority groups. Similarly, many college and university programs target school-age populations (e.g., athletes serve as tutors, big buddies, etc.). Likewise, a network of other Black males can help students to cope effectively with their concerns. Students, with the support of a teacher, counselor, or administrator, can meet before, during, or after school on academic and nonacademic matters.[18] For example, students can tutor each other, and organize school events and fundraisers. It is essential that students have many opportunities to experience success in both academic and nonacademic ways. It is equally important that minority students have opportunities to make a positive, meaningful contribution to the school. Finally, it is important that other students see the positive efforts of students of color. Table 10.1 summarizes relevant prevention and intervention strategies in the areas of social-emotional and academic support.

THE CASE OF DEANNE

Deanne lived in an inner-city community that was 99% Black. Deanne was an honor student. As a 9th grader, she was president of the National Junior Honor Society and a straight A student. As a 10th grader, she received an academic scholarship (A Better Chance) to attend a private all-female high school about an hour from her home. This was the first year that the school had admitted students on academic scholarships.

Although Deanne was reluctant, her mother was eager for her to attend the school. When notice came home that Deanne had earned the scholarship, her mother was ecstatic. This was Deanne's "only chance to become somebody important, to win scholarships to college, and to move out of poverty." This was the key to upward mobility, a dream come true.

The first day of school was a challenge for Deanne in many ways. She was intimidated by the buildings—they were so old, so cold, and yet so beautiful. As Deanne got off the bus (public transportation), other students parked their expensive cars. Deanne's family did not own a car; few people in her neighborhood did. She was intimidated by the students—they were so rich and so snobbish. Deanne was the only Black student at the school on scholarship. The other two Black females were rich (or at least not on scholarship). She was uncomfortable and self-conscious around the other girls. They did not look at Deanne; they looked through her. She remembered one of her favorite cartoons as a child, Casper the friendly ghost. She remembered the duckling in *The Ugly Duckling* (Anderson, 1979). She felt like *The Invisible Man* (Ellison, 1952), which she had read over the summer. It was on the school's summer reading list and the title had intrigued Deanne. Before starting at the new school, Deanne could not completely relate to Ellison's character; how could a person be invisible, yet alive, breathing, thinking, and feeling? Surely, she thought, race could not render one invisible, meaningless, and insignificant? Now she knew that it could. A number of events answered these questions for Deanne. Students went out of their way to avoid Deanne. She ate lunch alone, she studied alone, and she completed class assignments alone, even when they were "group" assignments.

About two months after school began, the literature class was assigned *The Scarlet Letter* (Hawthorne, 1961) for reading. Just as Deanne now understood the insignificance felt by *The Invisible Man,* she understood what life could be like living with a scarlet letter. For Deanne, being Black had become her scarlet letter. She hated being poor, and being Black was even worse. The

Table 10.1 Prevention and Intervention Strategies for Gifted Minority Students

Strategy	Goal/Objective	Recommended Prevention/Intervention
Supportive strategies	To affirm the self-worth of students and convey the promise of greater potential and success; to provide social-emotional support	Provide opportunities for students to discuss concerns with teachers and counselors; Involve mentors and role models; Use mastery learning techniques; Decrease competitive, norm-referenced environments; use cooperative learning and group work; Use positive reinforcement and praise; Seek affective and student-centered classrooms; Set higher expectations for students; Use multicultural education and counseling techniques and strategies; Involve family members in substantive ways
Intrinsic strategies	To help students develop internal motivation; to increase academic engagement and self-efficacy	Provide constructive and consistent feedback; Give choices, focus on interests; Vary teaching styles to accommodate learning styles; increase student awareness of learning styles; Use concrete, active, and experiential learning strategies (e.g., role-plays, simulations, case studies, projects, internships); Use bibliotherapy and biographies; Use mentorships and role models; Use multicultural education and counseling
Remedial strategies	To improve students' academic performance in the specific area(s) of difficulty	Implement academic counseling (e.g., tutoring, study skills, test-taking skills); Teach time management and organizational skills; Use individual and small-group instruction; Use learning contracts, learning journals
Cognitive strategies	To improve students' thinking, metacognitive, and problem-solving skills	Raise level of instruction; Enhance metacognitive skills; Implement cognitive instruction (e.g., critical thinking, analytical thinking, creative thinking, and problem-solving skills)

Source: Adapted from Ford (1996)

teacher was so moved by Deanne's paper about the book that she asked Deanne to read it to the class. Deanne refused—how could she share her paper with students who were responsible for her misery and self-hatred? The teacher changed the grade from an A to an F.

For another assignment, students had to read Shakespeare's *Macbeth* and write a reaction paper. The teacher called a conference with Deanne. Her first question: "Who helped you?" she asked. "Did you use *Cliffs Notes?*" After denying that she had cheated, and offering to rewrite the paper in front of the teacher, Deanne was given an A. Deanne was also accused of cheating on a geometry test. She was the only student to receive a passing grade. At the end of the school year, Deanne was 75 pounds heavier and suicidal. Deanne transferred to her neighborhood school.

Questions for Discussion

Identify the major issues or problems in the case. What aspects of the learning environment seemed difficult for Deanne? What factors (e.g., social-emotional) may have influenced Deanne's decision to leave the school? What were teachers' academic expectations of Deanne? What role did race and/or economics appear to play in teachers' expectations? Is there any way that the school personnel might have anticipated students' reactions to Deanne? How might the school have prevented poor peer relationships between Deanne and her classmates? What is the school counselor's role in addressing issues faced by Deanne? How might school personnel (teachers, counselors, and administrators) have intervened to increase positive peer relationships? What is the role of school administrators in addressing the social climate of the school? What can they do to provide teachers with opportunities to work more effectively with gifted and minority students?

SCENARIOS FOR REFLECTION

Lee. During Black History month, a 2nd grade teacher was reading a book about Harriet Tubman to her students (10 Black, 13 White, and 3 Hispanic American students). Lee, one of the White students, made a derogatory remark about Blacks as the teacher read the book aloud. The teacher ignored him. He repeated the statement, in a rhyme this time. Not expecting this behavior from such a young child, the teacher ignored the statement again, and asked him to pay attention so that she could finish the book. Classmates seemed not to hear the statement or chose to ignore it.

How would you handle this situation? Would you ignore the incident? What is the teacher's role in addressing negative social behaviors like this?

What factors in this brief scenario will affect your decisions? React to the statement, "Inaction is action." In what ways can curriculum and instruction address the problem of student stereotypes and discrimination?

How might this incident influence other students now and in the future? How might school counselors become involved in this situation? Should parents/guardians of the students be informed of the situation at this point?

Renee. Renee, a 6th grader, attends a school that is predominantly Hispanic American. She has been a high-achieving student throughout elementary school. This grading period, Renee's grades have dropped from As and Bs to Cs and one D. Her parents have come to you, the teacher, because Renee is complaining about students teasing her for being a "brainiac." She is afraid of being ostracized for getting high grades, and has chosen to do just enough to get by.

Assume that you are Renee's teacher or counselor. How will you handle this situation? What other school personnel, if any, will you involve and why? How can families and school personnel work together to promote student achievement and to prevent and stop the anti-achievement ethic among many students?

Jarvis. Jarvis, an African American, is a new student in your 8th grade classroom. He comes to your class about 15 minutes late. The only seat available is next to Martin, a student known to bully others and to treat minority students with disdain. With hesitancy, you place Jarvis in the seat next to Martin. Martin moves his chair away from the empty seat with a great deal of noise. He states scornfully and loudly, "I don't want *him* sitting next to me!" Jarvis does not react. Several of the students chuckle.

What are your next steps? How will you handle this situation? Is there a reason to intervene? What message do we send students when we ignore social injustices? How can curriculum and instruction address this problem? Should this situation be handled at the classroom or school level?

Steve. Steve is one of five American Indian students in the school. This year, the school district is spending three days celebrating Columbus Day. Steve's mother opposes this, arguing that American Indians have little to "celebrate" regarding Christopher Columbus. She also states that Steve is upset about being taught that Columbus discovered America.

As a school administrator, what are your next steps? Should Columbus Day be celebrated? Are the concerns of Steve's mother legitimate? What compromises can you think of in this situation?

THEMES IN THE CASES AND SCENARIOS

Although students in the cases and scenarios attended different schools and were diverse in age and race, they share some experiences (see Table 10.2).

Table 10.2 Matrix of Themes in the Cases and Scenarios

	Language	Curriculum	Instruction	School or classroom demographics	Family	Teacher expectations and relations	Peer relations
Andrea	X	X	X	X	X	X	X
Marcus		X	X	X		X	X
Deanne		X		X		X	X
Lee		X			X		X
Steve		X		X			
Jarvis				X			X
Renee		X			X		X

Note: We recognize that the scenarios may be too brief to complete the matrix for Lee, Steve, Jarvis, and Renee. For example, Steve is American Indian, but no information is given regarding language background. Further, little information is provided on instruction in the scenarios.

Overall, the three most common issues relate to lack of school diversity, poor peer relationships, and inappropriate curricula. Specifically, students often experienced social-emotional difficulties, such as poor peer relationship (e.g., negative pressures, teasing, and rejection). In several instances, low teacher expectations were evident, contributing to poor student–teacher relationships and teacher–family relationships. This was most apparent in Andrea's situation.

Curriculum and instruction were also problematic for many students. For instance, Marcus wanted more multiculturalism integrated into the curriculum, and took on the task of doing this. Several students experienced lower achievement, decreased motivation and poor morale. A few of the students (and their families) responded to these events by withdrawing from the situation; however, they first tried to resolve their concerns with school personnel. The various cases highlight the reality that many variables influence students' cognitive and affective development. The cases reinforce the critical need for teachers to be both culturally aware of and culturally responsive to their students. Without this knowledge-base and accompanying skills, teachers are more likely to misunderstand and miseducate students of color. This notion is at least seven decades old, as discussed by Woodson (1933).

Afterword

Homogeneity is fine in a bottle of milk, but in the classroom, it di-
minishes the curiosity that ignites diversity.

—Paley (1989, p. 56)

It is an unfortunate reality that schools have not changed sufficiently to meet the dramatic changes that have occurred in the United States. Schools continue to operate as if conditions and demographics are the same as when the common school was first created. Yet it is within our reach and within our power to bring about change. Tinkering and Band-Aids are inadequate.

At its best, education accomplishes its mission of meeting the needs of its students. To date, this mission has not been met—too many students of color have been denied their right to an appropriate education, to an education that prepares them to succeed inside and outside of schools. Too often, these students have learned multiple curricula—the formal curriculum and the hidden curriculum (e.g., Apple, 1993; Giroux, 1983). Students have been taught an ethnocentric curriculum, one that presents mirrors for White children and windows for others. This curriculum sends devastating messages that wreak havoc on the self-perception, motivation, and achievement of minority students while affirming those of White students.

As noted in earlier chapters, multicultural education is more than a program—it is a process and a philosophy whose goals are consistent with democratic ideals. Multicultural education as a process, philosophy, and program must be systemic and comprehensive. That is, all facets of education must be multicultural—assessment, research, curriculum and instruction, teacher demographics, and family involvement. Likewise, all participants in the school community should be involved in the development of multicultural education—teachers, counselors, administrators, students, and families—and they require substantive and ongoing multicultural preparation.

Our goals and objectives in writing this book are simple. First, like other advocates of multicultural education, we wish to help students, teachers, and others in the school community to become more aware of themselves as individuals *and* cultural beings. Second, we wish to help the school community to become more culturally aware and competent. Third, we wish to integrate

207

multiculturalism throughout the educational process. Most important, we wish for every child to have the *opportunity* to reach his or her full potential. A mind is a terrible thing to erase.

For us, the debate about excellence *and* equity vs. excellence *or* equity is futile. Education can be *both* excellent and equitable. Equitable and excellent education exists when:

1. There are high expectations for all students, regardless of socio-demographic variables.
2. There is confidence that all children have the ability to learn.
3. There is respect for culturally diverse students and the culture they bring to school.
4. Schools are committed to preserving and enriching the culture children bring to school; they provide culturally responsive school settings.
5. Schools are committed to enhancing students' self-perception and dignity.
6. Educators are willing to learn more about diverse students.
7. Educators tailor education to meet the needs of their students.
8. Educators realize and accept that differences are not always deficits or disabilities.

For far too many educators, diversity represents both promise and dread; these seem to be the dichotomies that mark their work with children of color. All educators must examine their perceptions of students of color and how they feel about diverse cultures. It is essential that educators understand the reality that they, particularly teachers, are powerful and compelling figures in the lives of students — they are both role models and change agents. This understanding supports the philosophy that teaching is an act of faith in the promise of the future for *all* students. All students must have the opportunity to dream, as so many people of color tell us. Martin Luther King Jr. dreamed that one day the nation would rise up and live out the true meaning of its creed — that all men are created equal. He dreamed that the "sweltering heat of oppression" would be transformed into an "oasis of freedom and justice" (King, 1963/1997, p. 25). Our schools must share this dream and vision of what the United States and its schools *can* be for every child.

As discussed in chapter 6, the social, emotional, and psychological needs of students cannot be separated from the act of learning and the art of teaching. That is, teaching is a complicated profession because students bring many backgrounds, experiences, and personalities to the learning situation, and teachers are seldom prepared to work with (rather than against) these differences.

Schools have a crucial role to play in helping to create a society that is inclusive and pluralistic, one that goes beyond merely tolerating diversity and adopting color-blind philosophies. Education must celebrate and honor diversity. As with the rainbow, all the colors of the human race illuminate the magnificence of the human experience (Siccone, 1995, p. xiii). Multicultural education supports the long-term goal of transforming society and serves the more immediate objective of transforming schools. It provides the best opportunity to develop education that works for all students.

People of color must understand that it is a waste of time hating a mirror or its reflection, instead of stopping the hand that makes glass with distortions (Audre Lorde, as cited in Siccone, 1995, p. xvi). Multicultural education provides that support, that sense of empowerment and social action.

Several assumptions guide this work. First, the goals of multicultural education cannot be achieved unless teachers and educators assume responsibility for designing and carrying out a pluralistic curriculum. Teachers, as adults and classroom leaders, play the most significant and powerful role in shaping students' identities, and providing an environment where diversity thrives.

A second assumption is that all education is inherently multicultural, since it is experienced by and addressed to individuals who represent varied cultures. We must be responsive to and respective of these differences.

Third, a color-blind philosophy ignores not only color, but also culture. A color-blind goal to view all children in the same manner often has the reverse effect; when differences are ignored, problems associated with them may be exacerbated. This perspective is based on an erroneous assumption that to recognize race is to be racist. Thus, when a color-blind philosophy prevails, all groups are expected to conform, to assimilate into the mainstream. In essence, the richness of this nation's diversity is a treasure, a treasure that must not be buried.

A fourth assumption is that minority groups can retain much of their original culture and be multicultural at the same time. Thus, minority groups must learn to accommodate rather than to assimilate; they can walk that line between two cultures that may be very different in terms of norms, values, and beliefs. People often refer to this ability as "biculturality"; however, multicultural individuals are competent in more than two cultures.

A fifth assumption is that multicultural education contributes to or expedites excellence. The attainment of any degree of excellence is stunted by curriculum that is inaccurate and incomplete. Likewise, educational excellence cannot be achieved without educational equity. Equity entails equal opportunity for all students to develop to their fullest potential. Equity acknowledges that equal treatment cannot be given to students who have unequal needs; similarly, unequal treatment should not be given to students who have equal needs. There are many correctable inequalities of opportunity in our schools and gifted programs.

Sixth, in addition to excellence or high standards, multicultural education seeks high expectations for students. Students live up to our expectations, and they live down to our expectations. Teachers play a major role in removing the low ceiling of expectations often held for minority students. We must release minority students' opportunities and aspirations through high teacher expectations.

A seventh assumption is that school personnel can and must make education relevant to students. Teachers must understand the desires and values of their students; they must understand the inertia that afflicts minority students in school settings. How can we engage minority students? How can we increase the sense of community in schools, the feelings of belonging and engagement felt by minority students? Takaki's (1993) observation rings true here: We must ask ourselves, what happens to children when a teacher presents a portrait of America and certain children are not in it? Where are the mirrors?

Eighth, multicultural education is not only exciting, but also painful, for change is difficult. To truly implement an education that is multicultural, we must have an honest exchange of views on *real* issues. Multicultural education confronts the fact that we live in a society where race matters, a society with a history of White supremacy. Thus, multicultural education endeavors to "reduce the ignorance that breeds racism and to develop the understanding and actions people need to become antiracist" (Bennett, 1990, p. 17).

A final assumption is that our primary goal as educators is to foster the intellectual, social, and personal development of students to their fullest potential. This goal is to provide every student, not just some students, with an equal opportunity to learn and achieve. Thus, as an old saying goes, "We may not all hit home runs, but everyone should have a chance at the bat."

Throughout recent history, the United States has championed the cause of equity, hence our Constitution, Bill of Rights, and other documents that espouse principles of democracy, equity, and equality. Advocates of multicultural education have added their voices to the call for human rights to be met for all. In a democracy, as Clark (1997) noted, all citizens are promised that no barrier will be raised to their pursuit of health, happiness, liberty, and justice, for the fullest achievement of each of us must be encouraged. Kozol (1991) recognized that there is often a contest between liberty and equity: "There is a stunted image of our nation as a land that can afford only *one* of two dreams — liberty or equity, but not both. . . . Liberty and equity are seen as antibodies to each other" (p. 73).

Clark and Kozol remind us that gifted education must be multicultural. Likewise, in its most recent report on gifted education, the U.S. Department of Education (1993) offered several recommendations for action, many of which address the needs of minority students, including (1) increased access to preventive programs for minority students that address talent development and (2) expanded opportunities for minority students to participate in gifted education programs and advanced learning opportunities.

Schools must reaffirm the humanity, spirit, and dignity of all students. As Takaki (1993) noted, America's dilemma has been our resistance to ourselves — our denial of our immensely varied selves. But we have nothing to fear but our fear of our own diversity (p. 3).

In sum, multicultural gifted education moves beyond the rhetoric and recognizes that the potential for brilliance is sprinkled evenly across all ethnic groups. "When social conditions and school practices hinder the development of this brilliance among students outside the macroculture . . . the waste of human potential affects us all" (Bennett, 1990, p. 14). As Martin Luther King Jr. (1963/1997) stated so eloquently some three decades ago:

> When the architects of our republic wrote the magnificent words of the Constitution and the Declaration of Independence, they were signing a promissory note to which every American was to fall heir. This note was the promise that all men . . . would be guaranteed the unalienable rights of life, liberty, and the pursuit of happiness. . . . America has defaulted on the promissory note insofar as her citizens of color are concerned. . . . America has given the Negro people a bad check; a check which has come back marked "insufficient funds." (p. 13)

Like King, we refuse to believe that the bank of justice is bankrupt. We refuse to believe that there are insufficient funds in the great vaults of opportunity of this nation for every child in the United States. The need and the right to cash this check of freedom and justice are long overdue.

Selected Bibliography of Multicultural and Gifted Resources

We acknowledge and readers will notice that most of the literature focuses on African American students. This reality, which is troubling, is a function of the quantity and quality of literature written about and/or by groups of color.

Multicultural Literature for Students

The books in this section provide guidelines and strategies for selecting and using multicultural literature in school settings. A few of the books contain extensive annotated bibliographies.

Au, K. (1993). *Literacy instruction in multicultural settings.* Fort Worth: Harcourt Brace Jovanovich.

Beaty, J. J. (1996). *Building bridges with multicultural picture books: Skills for preschool teachers.* New York: Merrill.

Beaty, J. J. (1997). *Building bridges with multicultural picture books for children 3–5.* New York: Merrill.

Brown, J. E., & Stephens, E. C. (1996). *Exploring diversity: Literature themes and activities for grades 4–8.* Englewood, CO: Teacher Ideas Press.

Brown, J. E., & Stephens, E. C. (Eds.). (1998). *United in diversity: Using multicultural young adult literature in the classroom.* Urbana, IL: National Council of Teachers of English.

Campbell, D. E. (1996). *Choosing democracy: A practical guide to multicultural education.* Columbus, OH: Merrill.

Council on Interracial Books for Children. (1980). *Guidelines for selecting bias-free textbooks and storybooks.* New York: Author.

De Gaetano, Y., Williams, L. R., & Volk, D. (1998). *Kaleidoscope: A multicultural approach for the primary school classroom.* Columbus, OH: Merrill.

De Melendez, W. R., & Osterstag, V. (1997). *Teaching young children in multicultural classrooms.* Albany, NY: Delmar.

DeSpain, P. (1993). *Thirty-three multicultural tales to tell.* Little Rock, AR: August House.

Diamond, B. J., & Moore, M. (1995). *Multicultural literacy: Mirroring the reality of the classroom.* New York: Longman.

Finazzo, D. A. (1997). *All for the children: Multicultural essentials of literature*. Albany, NY: Delmar.

Gadsen, V. L., & Wagner, D. (Eds.). (1994). *Literacy among African-Americans: Issues in learning, teaching and schooling*. Creskill, NJ: Hampton Press.

Givens, A. (1997). *Spirited minds: African American books for our sons and our brothers*. New York: Norton.

Givens, A. (1998). *Strong souls singing: African American books for our daughters and our sisters*. New York: Norton.

Harris, V. J. (1993). *Teaching multicultural literature in grades K–8*. Norwood, NJ: Christopher-Gordon.

Harris, V. J. (1997). *Using multiethnic literature in the K–8 classroom*. Norwood, NJ: Christopher-Gordon.

Helbig, A. K., & Perkins, A. R. (1994). *This land is our land: A guide to multicultural literature for children and young adults*. Westport, CT: Greenwood Press.

Heltshe, M. A., & Kirchner, A. B. (1991). *Multicultural explorations: Joyous journeys with books*. Englewood, CO: Teacher Ideas Press.

Johnson, D. (1990). *Telling tales: The pedagogy and promise of African American literature for youth*. New York: Greenwood.

Lewis, N. (1995). *Novel extenders: African-American folktales for young readers*. San Antonio, TX: ECS Learning Systems.

Lewis, N. (1996). *Novel extenders: Multicultural collection, grades 1–3*. San Antonio, TX: ECS Learning Systems.

Lewis, N. (1996). *Novel extenders: Multicultural collection, grades 4–6*. San Antonio, TX: ECS Learning Systems.

Lind, B. B. (1996). *Multicultural children's literature: An annotated bibliography, grades K–8*. Jefferson, NC: McFarland.

Lindgren, M. (Ed.). (1991). *The multicolored mirror: Cultural substance in literature for children and young adults*. Fort Atkinson, WI: Highsmith Press.

McGowan, M., McGowan, T., & Wheeler, P. (1994). *Appreciating diversity through children's literature: Teaching activities for the primary grades*. Englewood, CO: Teacher Ideas Press.

Miller-Lachman, L. (1992). *Our family, our friends, our world: An annotated guide to significant multicultural books for children and teenagers*. New York: Bowker.

Moll, P. B. (1994). *Children & books I: African American storybooks and activities for all children*. Tampa, FL: Hampton, Mae Institute.

Muse, D. (Ed.). (1997). *The New Press guide to multicultural resources for young readers*. New York: New Press.

Nieto, S. (1996). *Affirming diversity: The sociopolitical context of multicultural education* (2nd ed.). New York: Longman.

Ramirez, G., & Ramirez, J. L. (1994). *Multiethnic children's literature*. Albany, NY: Delmar.

Rand, D., Parker, T. T., & Foster, S. (1998). *Black books galore! Guide to great African-American children's books*. New York: Wiley.

Rethinking Schools, Ltd. (1994). *Rethinking our classrooms: Teaching for equity and justice*. Milwaukee, WI: Author.

Roberts, P. L. (1998). *Multicultural friendship stories and activities for children ages 5–12.* Lanham, MD: Scarecrow Press.

Rochman, H. (1993). *Against borders: Promoting books for a multicultural world.* Chicago: American Library Association.

Rogers, T., & Soter, A. (Eds.). (1997). *Reading across cultures: Teaching literature in a diverse society.* New York: Teachers College Press.

Ryan, C. D. (1994). *Multicultural education: A resource book for middle and upper grades.* Torrance, CA: Frank Schaffer.

Schon, I. (1997). *Recommended books in Spanish for children and young adults, 1991–1995.* London: Scarecrow Press.

Shade, B., Kelly, C., & Oberg, M. (1997). *Creating culturally responsive classrooms.* Washington, DC: American Psychological Association.

Siccone, F. (1995). *Celebrating diversity: Building self-esteem in today's multicultural classroom.* Needham Heights, MA: Allyn and Bacon.

Sims, R. B. (1994). *Kaleidoscope: A multicultural booklist for grades K–8.* Urbana, IL: National Council of Teachers of English.

Slapin, B., & Seale, D. (Eds.) (1991). *Through Indian eyes: The Native American experience in books for children.* Berkeley, CA: Oyate.

Smith, K. P. (1994). *African-American voices in young adult literature: Tradition, transition, transformation.* London: Scarecrow Press.

Strickland, D. S. (1999). *Listen children: An anthology of Black literature.* New York: Yearling.

Tiedt, L., & Tiedt, I. (1990). *Multicultural literacy: A handbook of activities, information, and resources.* Needham Heights, MA: Allyn and Bacon.

Valdez, A. (1999). *Learning in living color: Using literature to incorporate multicultural education into the primary curriculum.* Boston: Allyn and Bacon.

Willis, A. (1998). *Teaching and using multicultural literature in grades 9–12: Moving beyond the canon.* Norwood, NJ: Christopher-Gordon.

Literature for Gifted Students

These annotated bibliographies have gifted students as the central characters or focus on issues of relevance to gifted students.

Baskin, B., & Harris, K. (1980). *Books for the gifted child.* New York: Bowker.

Halsted, J. W. (1994). *Some of my best friends are books: Guiding gifted readers from preschool to high school.* Dayton, OH: Ohio Psychology Press.

Hauser, P., & Nelson, G. A. (1988). *Books for the gifted child* (vol. 2). New York: Bowker.

Families and Children's Literature

Cecil, N. L., & Roberts, P. L. (1998). *Families in children's literature: A resource guide, grades 4–8.* Englewood, CA: Teacher Ideas Press.

Gifted Education

These books provide an overview of (or introduction to) gifted education. They are invaluable to schools and universities with gifted education programs and services.

Clark, B. (1998). *Growing up gifted: Developing the potential of children at home and at school* (5th ed.). New York: Merrill.

Colangelo, N., & Davis, G. A. (1997). *Handbook of gifted education* (2nd ed.). New York: Allyn and Bacon.

Davis, G. A., & Rimm, S. B. (1998). *Education of the gifted and talented* (4th ed.). New York: Allyn and Bacon.

Maker, J., & Shiever, S. W. (Eds.). (1989). *Critical issues in gifted education: Defensible programs for cultural and ethnic minorities* (vol. 2). Austin, TX: Pro-Ed.

VanTassel-Baska, J. (1998). *Excellence in educating gifted & talented learners* (3rd ed.). Denver: Love.

Multicultural Education

The following books provide a solid foundation for educators interested in infusing multicultural education into their curriculum. They include theory, research, and practice.

Banks, J. M. (1997). *Teaching strategies for ethnic studies* (6th ed.). New York: Allyn and Bacon.

Banks, J. M., & Banks, C. A. M. (Eds.). (1993). *Multicultural education: Issues and perspectives* (2nd ed.). Boston: Allyn and Bacon.

Banks, J. A., & Banks, C.A.M. (Eds.). (1995). *Handbook of research on multicultural education*. New York: Simon and Schuster.

Davidman, L., & Davidman, P. T. (1994). *Teaching with a multicultural perspective: A practical guide*. New York: Longman.

Derman-Sparks, L., and the ABC Task Force. (1989). *Anti-bias curriculum: Tools for empowering young children*. Washington, DC: National Association for the Education of Young Children.

Gollnick, D. M., & Chinn, P. C. (1998). *Multicultural education in a pluralistic society* (5th ed.). Columbus, OH: Merrill.

Grant, C., & Sleeter, C. E. (1989). *Turning on learning: Five approaches for multicultural teaching plans for race, class, gender, and disability*. Columbus: Merrill.

Grant, C., & Sleeter, C. E. (1998). *Turning on learning: Five approaches for multicultural teaching plans for race, class, gender, and disability* (2nd ed.). Columbus: Merrill.

Rodriguez, E. R., & Bellanca, J. (1996). *What is it about me you can't teach? An instructional guide for the urban educator*. Arlington Hills, IL: SkyLight.

Sleeter, C. E., & Grant, C. A. (1993). *Making choices for multicultural education* (2nd ed.). New York: Merrill.

Multicultural Counseling

The books in this section concern multicultural counseling theory and practice, particularly in school settings.

Pedersen, P. (1994). *A handbook for developing multicultural awareness.* Alexandria, VA: American Counseling Association.

Pedersen, P., & Carey, J. C. (1994). *Multicultural counseling in schools.* New York: Allyn and Bacon.

Ponterotto, J. G., & Casas, J. M. (1991). *Handbook of racial/ethnic minority counseling research.* Springfield, IL: Charles C. Thomas.

Ponterotto, J. G., Casas, J. M., Suzuki, L. A., & Alexander, C. M. (Eds.). (1995). *Handbook of multicultural counseling.* Thousand Oaks, CA: Sage.

Ponterotto, J. G., & Pedersen, P. B. (1993). *Preventing prejudice: A guide for counselors and educators.* Newbury Park, CA: Sage.

Sue, W., & Sue, D. (1990). *Counseling the culturally different: Theory and practice* (2nd ed.). New York: Wiley.

Gifted Counseling

Few books focus specifically on the counseling and affective needs of gifted students. Two are presented in this section.

Delisle, J. R. (1992). *Guiding the social and emotional development of gifted youth: A practical guide for educators and counselors.* New York: Longman.

Silverman, L. K. (Ed.). (1993). *Counseling the gifted and talented.* Denver, CO: Love.

Multicultural Research

Few books target research from a multicultural perspective. Two appear in this section.

Stanfield III, J. H., & Dennis, R. M. (Eds.). (1993). *Race and ethnicity in research methods.* New York: Sage.

Stanfield III, J. H. (Ed.). (1993). *A history of race relations research: First-generation recollections.* New York: Sage.

Gifted Education Research and Evaluation

The books below are appropriate for use in courses and schools committed to conducting research and evaluation in gifted education settings. Few books exist on this topic.

Buchanan, N. K., & Feldhusen, J. F. (Eds.). (1991). *Conducting research and evaluation in gifted education: A handbook of methods and applications.* New York: Teachers College Press.

Callahan, C. M., & Caldwell, M. S. (1995). *Practitioner's guide to evaluating programs for the gifted.* Washington, DC: National Association for Gifted Children.

Sample Multicultural Activities: Pre-Instruction or Reinforcement Exercises

The exercises below are useful pre-lesson and reinforcement multicultural activities. However, they cannot stand alone as strategies for integrating multicultural education into traditional curriculum and instruction.

- Make a book entitled *We All Look Special* about the physical characteristics of each child. Take color photos of each child and place each on its own page. Ask students to describe themselves and write what they say under the photo. Include skin color, hair, and eyes among the characteristics. When the book is complete, read it to students at circle time or some other time designated for group reading.
- As part of science, talk about skin and melanin, along with their functions. It might be helpful to provide students with skin-colored crayons. Help students to choose the crayon closest to their skin color and then draw pictures of themselves. In some instances, students may want to mix colors for painting pictures of themselves. Be creative and positive in talking about the beauty of each shade. Relative to skin tones, students can read *All the Colors of the Race* and *Black Is Brown Is Tan*. Similarly, students can read *Colors Around Me* (Church, 1971), which illustrates the variations of skin shades among minority children. It also emphasizes how they are all members of the same family of African Americans. This book can be used to help children explore the concept that people with different shades are still considered members of the same group. Have students make their own *Colors Around Me* book after reading such works as *Planting a Rainbow* (Ehlert, 1988). Read *Black Is Beautiful* (McGovern, 1969) and have children make a list of beautiful black, brown, and other colored objects. Make sure children use browns, blacks, and other tones in their artwork, play dough, paints, and so forth. Encourage positive feelings about brown and black. Talk with students about how colors are used in negative ways, and how to substitute the colors for other words (e.g., black sheep, dark mood, blackmail, blackball, in the red, etc.). Have them analyze the media for their use of these words in negative and positive ways. Students can write letters to newspaper editors, TV shows, and so forth, expressing their findings and concerns.
- Read children's books about families that reflect the ethnic groups in your class. Always read more than one book about each family. Talk about similarities and differences. Ask children to share, if they are comfortable, how they are different

from or similar to what is presented in the book. It may be helpful to have children locate and share the books that they prefer with classmates.

- Make sure that toys and objects in dramatic play come from different cultures (e.g., dolls, clothes, woks, bongo drums, tangrams, and chopsticks). Demonstrate how the objects are used and provide background information on them. Have children bring in and share items that are meaningful to them and their families. Teachers can bring in objects from home to set the tone and model of what is expected.

- Display different writing systems (Hebrew, Swahili, Chinese, etc.) and label materials in more than one language. Teach children how to make a few letters and their names in the different alphabets. For example, students can read *Jambo Means Hello* (Feelings, 1974) and *Moja Means One* (Feelings, 1971). Read children stories in different languages and ask them to help translate them. Further, read books with children that challenge stereotypes (*My Daddy Is a Nurse,* Wandro and Blank, 1981; *My Special Best Words,* Steptoe, 1974; *Don't Feel Sorry for Paul,* about a single father, Wolf, 1974; and *All Kinds of Families,* Simon, 1975).

- Read books about the beauty of black hair, such as *Cornrows* (Yarbrough, 1979) and *Honey, I Love* (Greenfield, 1978). In a class with minority students, these books nurture self-pride; in a class without minority students, the books increase children's awareness of diversity.

Multicultural Education Program Evaluation Guidelines and Checklist

1.0 Does ethnic and cultural diversity permeate the total school environment?

    1.1 Are ethnic content and perspectives incorporated into all aspects of the curriculum, preschool through 12th grade and beyond?

    1.2 Do instructional materials treat racial and ethnic differences and groups honestly, realistically, and sensitively?

    1.3 Do school libraries and resource centers offer a variety of materials on the histories, experiences, and cultures of many racial, ethnic, and cultural groups?

    1.4 Do school assemblies, decorations, speakers, holidays, and heroes reflect racial, ethnic, and cultural group differences?

    1.5 Are extracurricular activities multiethnic and multicultural?

2.0 Do school policies and procedures foster positive interactions among the various racial, ethnic, and cultural groups in the school?

    2.1 Do school policies accommodate the behavioral patterns, learning styles, and orientations of those ethnic and cultural group members actually in the school?

    2.2 Does the school provide a variety of instruments and techniques for teaching and counseling students of various ethnic and cultural groups?

    2.3 Do school policies recognize the holidays and festivities of various ethnic groups?

    2.4 Do school polices avoid instructional and guidance practices based on stereotypes and ethnocentric perceptions?

    2.5 Do school policies respect the dignity and worth of students as individuals *and* as members of racial, ethnic, and cultural groups?

3.0 Is the school staff (administrators, instructors, counselors, and support staff) multiethnic and multicultural?

    3.1 Has the school established and enforced policies for recruiting and maintaining a staff made up of individuals from various racial and ethnic groups?

4.0 Does the school have systematic, comprehensive, mandatory, and continuing multicultural staff development programs?

    4.1 Are teachers, librarians, counselors, administrators, and support staff included in the staff development programs?

    4.2 Do the staff development programs include a variety of experiences, such as lectures, field experiences, and curriculum projects?

    4.3 Do the staff development programs provide opportunities to gain knowledge and understanding about various racial, ethnic, and cultural groups?

    4.4 Do the staff development programs provide opportunities for participants to explore their attitudes and feelings about their own ethnicity and others?

    4.5 Do the staff development programs examine the verbal and nonverbal patterns of interethnic group interactions?

    4.6 Do the staff development programs provide opportunities for learning how to create and select multiethnic instructional materials and how to incorporate multicultural content into curriculum materials?

5.0 Does the curriculum reflect the ethnic learning styles of students within the school?

    5.1 Is the curriculum designed to help students learn how to function effectively in various cultural environments and learn more than one cognitive style?

    5.2 Do the objectives, instructional strategies, and learning materials reflect the cultures and cognitive styles of the various ethnic and cultural groups within the school?

6.0 Does the curriculum provide continuous opportunities for students to develop a better sense of self?

    6.1 Does the curriculum help students strengthen their self-identities?

    6.2 Is the curriculum designed to help students develop greater self-understanding?

    6.3 Does the curriculum help students improve their self-concepts?

    6.4 Does the curriculum help students to better understand themselves in light of their ethnic and cultural heritages?

7.0 Does the curriculum help students understand the wholeness of the experiences of ethnic and cultural groups?

    7.1 Does the curriculum include the study of societal problems, and some ethnic and cultural group members' experience, such as racism, prejudice, discrimination, and exploitation?

    7.2 Does the curriculum include the study of historical experiences, cultural patterns, and social problems of various ethnic and cultural groups?

    7.3 Does the curriculum include both positive and negative aspects of ethnic and cultural group experiences?

    7.4 Does the curriculum present people of color both as active participants in society and as subjects of oppression and exploitation?

    7.5 Does the curriculum examine the diversity within each group's experience?

    7.6 Does the curriculum present group experiences as dynamic and continuously changing?

    7.7 Does the curriculum examine the total experiences of groups instead of focusing exclusively on the "heroes"?

8.0 Does the curriculum help students identify and understand the ever-present conflict between ideals and realities in human societies?

8.1 Does the curriculum help students identify and understand the value conflicts inherent in a multicultural society?

8.2 Does the curriculum examine differing views of ideals and realities among ethnic and cultural groups?

9.0 Does the curriculum explore and clarify ethnic alternatives and options within U.S. society?

9.1 Does the teacher create a classroom atmosphere reflecting an acceptance of and respect for ethnic and cultural differences?

9.2 Does the teacher create a classroom atmosphere allowing realistic consideration of alternatives and options for members of ethnic and cultural groups?

10.0 Does the curriculum promote values, attitudes, and behaviors that support ethnic and cultural diversity?

10.1 Does the curriculum help students examine differences within and among ethnic and cultural groups?

10.2 Does the curriculum foster attitudes supportive of cultural democracy and other unifying democratic ideals and values?

10.3 Does the curriculum reflect ethnic and cultural diversity?

10.4 Does the curriculum present diversity as a vital societal force that encompasses both potential strength and potential conflict?

11.0 Does the curriculum help students develop decisionmaking abilities, social participation skills, and a sense of political efficacy necessary for effective citizenship?

11.1 Does the curriculum help students develop the ability to distinguish facts from interpretations and options?

11.2 Does the curriculum help students develop skills in finding and processing information?

11.3 Does the curriculum help students develop sound knowledge, concepts, generalizations, and theories about issues related to ethnicity and cultural identity?

11.4 Does the curriculum help students develop sound methods of thinking about issues related to ethnic and cultural groups?

11.5 Does the curriculum help students develop skills in clarifying and reconsidering their values and relating them to their understanding of ethnicity and cultural identity?

11.6 Does the curriculum include opportunities for students to use knowledge, valuing, and thinking in decisionmaking on issues related to race, ethnicity, and culture?

11.7 Does the curriculum include opportunities for students to take action on social problems affecting racial, ethnic, and cultural groups?

11.8 Does the curriculum help students develop a sense of efficacy?

12.0 Does the curriculum help students develop skills necessary for effective interpersonal and intercultural group interactions?

12.1 Does the curriculum help students understand ethnic and cultural reference points that influence communication?

12.2 Does the curriculum help students participate in cross-ethnic and cross-cultural experiences and reflect upon them?

13.0 Is the multicultural curriculum comprehensive in scope and sequence, presenting holistic views of ethnic and cultural groups, and an integral part of the total school environment?

    13.1 Does the curriculum introduce students to the experiences of persons of widely varying backgrounds in the study of each ethnic and cultural group?

    13.2 Does the curriculum discuss the successes and contributions of group members within the context of that group's values?

    13.3 Does the curriculum include the role of ethnicity and culture in the local community as well as in the nation?

    13.4 Does content related to ethnic and cultural groups extend beyond special units, courses, occasions, and holidays?

    13.5 Are materials written by and about ethnic and cultural groups used in teaching fundamental skills?

    13.6 Does the curriculum provide for the development of progressively more complex concepts, abilities, and values?

    13.7 Is the study of ethnicity and culture incorporated into instructional plans rather than being supplementary or additive?

14.0 Does the curriculum include the continuous study of the cultures, historical experiences, social realities, and existential conditions of ethnic groups within a variety of racial compositions?

    14.1 Does the curriculum include study of several ethnic and cultural groups?

    14.2 Does the curriculum include studies of both White ethnic groups and ethnic groups of color?

    14.3 Does the curriculum provide for continuity in the examination of aspects of experience affected by race?

15.0 Are interdisciplinary and multidisciplinary approaches used in designing and implementing the curriculum?

    15.1 Are interdisciplinary and multidisciplinary perspectives used in the study of ethnic and cultural groups and related issues?

    15.2 Are approaches used authentic and comprehensive explanations of ethnic and cultural issues, events, and problems?

16.0 Does the curriculum use comparative approaches in the study of racial, ethnic, and cultural groups?

    16.1 Does the curriculum focus on the similarities and differences among and between ethnic and cultural groups?

    16.2 Are matters examined from comparative perspectives with fairness to all?

17.0 Does the curriculum help students to view and interpret events, situations, and conflict from diverse ethnic and cultural perspectives and points of view?

    17.1 Are the perspectives of various ethnic and cultural groups represented in the instructional programs?

    17.2 Are students taught why different ethnic and cultural groups often perceive the same historical event or contemporary situation differently?

    17.3 Are the perspectives of each ethnic and cultural group presented as valid ways to perceive the past and the present?

18.0 Does the curriculum conceptualize and describe the development of the United States as a multidirectional society?

18.1 Does the curriculum view the territorial and cultural growth of the U.S. as flowing from several directions?

18.2 Does the curriculum include a parallel study of the various societies that developed in the geo-cultural U.S.?

19.0 Does the school provide opportunities for students to participate in the aesthetic experience of various ethnic and cultural groups?

19.1 Is multiethnic literature and art used to promote empathy and understanding of people from various ethnic and cultural groups?

19.2 Is multiethnic literature and art used to promote self-examination and self-understanding?

19.3 Do students read and hear the poetry, short stories, novels, folklore, plays, essays, and autobiographies of a variety of ethnic and cultural groups?

19.4 Do students examine the music, art, architecture, and dance of a variety of ethnic and cultural groups?

19.5 Do students have available the artistic, musical, and literary expression of the local ethnic and cultural communities?

19.6 Are opportunities provided for students to develop their own artistic, literary, and musical expression?

20.0 Does the curriculum provide opportunities for students to develop full literacy in at least two languages?

20.1 Are students taught to communicate (speaking, reading, and writing) in a second language?

20.2 Are students taught about the culture of the people who use the second language?

20.3 Are second language speakers provided opportunities to develop full literacy in their native language?

20.4 Are students for whom English is a second language taught in their native languages as needed?

21.0 Does the curriculum make maximum use of local resources?

21.1 Are students involved in the continuous study of the local community?

21.2 Are members of the local ethnic and cultural communities continually used as classroom resources?

21.3 Are field trips to the various local ethnic and cultural communities provided for students?

22.0 Do the assessment procedures used with students reflect their ethnic and community cultures?

22.1 Do teachers use a variety of assessment procedures that reflect the ethnic and cultural diversity of students?

22.2 Do teachers' day-to-day assessment techniques take into account the ethnic and cultural diversity of their students?

23.0 Does the school conduct ongoing, systematic evaluations of the goals, methods, and instructional materials used in teaching about ethnicity and culture?

23.1 Do assessment procedures draw on many sources of evidence from many sorts of people?

23.2 Does the evaluation program examine school policies and procedures?

23.3 Does the evaluation program examine the everyday climate of the school?

23.4 Does the evaluation program examine the effectiveness of curricular programs, both academic and non-academic?

23.5 Are the results of evaluation used to improve the school program?

Source: National Council for the Social Studies Task Force on Ethnic Studies Curriculum Guidelines (1992, Sept.), pp. 289–293.

Notes

1. The terms "minority," "racially and culturally diverse," and "students of color" are used interchangeably in this book.

2. At the time of this writing, the term "minority" is used connotatively for students who are Black, Hispanic American, American Indian, and Asian American. Thus, we use this term in the same manner. However, it is becoming inaccurate, for these students are becoming the majority.

3. The terms "multicultural education" and "education that is multicultural" are used interchangeably in this book. Some educators, however, argue that the former is too narrow, and is a component of the latter. These distinctions are not drawn in this chapter.

4. The students were formally identified as gifted by their school districts and were participating in gifted programs. A more complete description of the sample and study is given by Ford (1995a).

5. Berry (1984) is even more specific. Rural members of the Baganda tribe of Uganda think of intelligence (*obugezi*) as "slow, careful, active, straight-forward and sane" (p. 347). In Zimbabwe, the Mashona tribes value intelligence (*ngware*) and believe an intelligent person demonstrates prudence and caution. The Kispsigis of Kenya value intelligence (*ngon*) as social responsibility. More bluntly, definitions of intelligence depend on whom one asks, and their values and beliefs. Definitions are associated with the needs and purposes of a given culture.

6. The advanced mathematics assessment was administered to students who had taken or were taking pre-calculus, calculus, or AP calculus in the United States and to advanced mathematics students in other countries. The physics assessment was administered to students in the United States who had taken or were taking physics or AP physics and to advanced science students in other countries.

7. This figure is based on students who score in the top 3% to 5% on intelligence tests. It therefore underestimates the number of gifted students in general, as well as those not served. If one adopts a talent pool perspective, the number of gifted students would be greater. The figure also ignores gifted students with strengths in creativity, visual and performing arts, leadership, and academics.

8. For purposes of this chapter and because of our focus on school settings, we have replaced APA's use of "psychologists" with "educators" to refer to psychologists, counselors, teachers, and administrators.

9. Substitute, Combine, Adapt, Modify/Magnify/Minify, Put to other uses, Eliminate, Reverse.

10. We do not use the terms "literature-based" and "whole language" interchangeably. By literature-based, we refer to education that uses literature (books, poems, etc.) to convey important concepts and to reinforce and extend teaching and learning.

11. A third version of Little Red Riding Hood is *The Sun Girl and the Moon Boy* by Choi (1997).

12. Some publications use the term "Native American," and others use "American Indian." While our preference is "American Indian," we use the terminology of individual authors throughout this book.

13. According to Parker, tangrams are ancient Chinese puzzles. A tangram begins with a square that is then cut into seven standard pieces. Each piece is called a "tan." In creating a picture, all pieces must be used, they must touch, and none can overlap. When tangrams are used in storytelling, the storyteller arranges the tans to show the shape of a character in the tale. As new characters or story elements are introduced, the puzzle pieces are rearranged to represent the new character or element.

14. Where possible, we have presented the lessons as they appear in the original sources. In some cases, we made minor changes.

15. This lesson could be included in Van-Tassel-Baska's *What a Find!,* also discussed in this chapter.

16. A colleague recently told us of a student whose parents refused gifted education services for religious reasons. How could this information have been gathered early, prior to a placement decision?

17. We wish to thank Deborah Harmon for providing us with two case studies (Andrea and Marcus), as well as some of the recommendations for intervention.

18. One of our colleagues started such a program at a high school, which he called "Gentlemen on the Move." The Black males met after school one or two afternoons a week. They tutored each other, set aside time for homework, played sports, organized fundraisers, and visited nearby colleges and universities. Attendance rates were consistently high. Within a grading period, the Black males increased their school achievement and attendance rates.

References

Aardema, V. (1981). *Bringing the rain to Kapiti Plain*. New York: Dial.

Adoff, A. (1973). *Black is brown is tan*. New York: Harper & Row.

Adoff, A. (1982). *All the colors of the race*. New York: Lothrop, Lee, & Shepard.

Albert, R. S. (1969). Genius: Present-day status of the concept and its implications for the study of creativity and giftedness. *American Psychologist, 24,* 743–753.

Allard, H. (1977). *It's nice to have a wolf around the house*. New York: Bantam Double-day Dell.

Allport, G. (1979). *The nature of prejudice*. Reading, MA: Addison-Wesley.

American Association of Colleges for Teacher Education. (1994). *Teacher education pipeline III: Schools, colleges, and departments of education enrollments by race, ethnicity, and gender*. Washington, DC: Author.

American Association of Colleges for Teacher Education Commission on Multicultural Education. (1973). No one model American. *Journal of Teacher Education, 24*(4), 264–265.

American Educational Research Association, American Psychological Association, and National Council on Measurement in Education. (1985). *Standards for educational and psychological testing*. Washington, DC: American Psychological Association.

American Federation of Teachers, National Council on Measurement in Education, and National Education Association. (1990). Standards for teacher competence in educational assessment of students. *Educational Measurement: Issues and Practices, 9*(4), 30–32.

Anderson, B. L., Stiggins, R. J., & Gordon, D.W. (1980). *Educational testing facts and issues: A layperson's guide to testing in the schools*. Portland, OR: Northwest Regional Educational Laboratory and California State Department of Education.

Anderson, H. C. (1979). *The ugly duckling*. New York: Harcourt Brace Jovanovich.

Apple, M. W. (1993). *Official knowledge: Democratic education in a conservative age*. New York: Routledge.

Arce, C. A. (1981). A reconsideration of Chicano culture and identity. *Daedalus, 110,* 177–192.

Archambault, F. X., Westberg, K. L., Brown, S. W., Hallmark, B. W., Zhang, W., & Emmons, C. L. (1993). Classroom practices used with gifted third and fourth grade students. *Journal for the Education of the Gifted, 16,* 103–119.

Baldwin, J. (1962). *Nobody knows my name*. New York: Dell.

Banks, J. A. (1993). Approaches to multicultural curricular reform. In J. A. Banks &

C.A.M. Banks (Eds.), *Multicultural education: Issues and perspectives* (2nd ed.). Boston: Allyn and Bacon.

Banks, J. A. (1995). Multicultural education: Historical development, dimensions, and practice. In J. A. Banks & C. A. M. Banks (Eds.), *Handbook of research on multicultural education* (pp. 3–24). New York: Macmillan.

Banks, J. M. (1997). *Teaching strategies for ethnic studies* (6th ed.). New York: Allyn and Bacon.

Banks, J. M., & Banks, C. A. M. (Eds.). (1993). *Multicultural education: Issues and perspectives* (2nd ed.). Boston: Allyn and Bacon.

Banks, J. A., & Banks, C.A.M. (Eds.). (1995). *Handbook of research on multicultural education*. New York: Simon and Schuster.

Barnette, E. L. (1989). A program to meet the emotional and social needs of gifted and talented adolescents. *Journal of Counseling and Development, 67,* 525–528.

Baskin, B., & Harris, K. (1980). *Books for the gifted child.* New York: Bowker.

Baylor, B. (1972). *When clay sings.* New York: Aladdin.

Baylor, B. (1975). *The desert is theirs.* New York: Aladdin.

Baylor, B., & Parnall, P. (1980). *If you are a hunter of fossils.* New York: Aladdin.

Beecher, M. (1995). *Developing the gifts and talents of all students in the regular classroom.* Mansfield Center, CT: Creative Learning Press.

Bell, D. (1997). The world and the United States in 2013. *Daedalus, 116,* 1–31.

Bennett, C. I. (1990). *Comprehensive multicultural education: Theory and practice* (2nd ed.). Boston: Allyn and Bacon.

Berry, J. W. (1984). Toward a universal psychology of cognitive competence. *International Journal of Psychology, 19,* 335–361.

Betancourt, C. Y. (1991). *More than meets the eye.* New York: Bantam.

Bishop, C. (1938/1996). *The five Chinese brothers.* New York: Putnam.

Bloom, B. (Ed.). (1956). *Taxonomy of educational objectives. Handbook I: Cognitive domain.* New York: Wiley.

Bopp, J., Bopp, M., Brown, L., & Lane, P. (1989). *The sacred tree* (3rd ed.). Twin Lakes, MI: Lotus Light Publications.

Boykin, A. W. (1994). Afrocultural expression and its implications for schooling. In E. R. Hollins, J. E. King, & W. C. Hayman (Eds.), *Teaching diverse populations: Formulating a knowledge base* (pp. 225–273). New York: State University of New York Press.

Brown v. Board of Education of Topeka, Kansas, 347 U.S. 483 (1954).

Buchanan, N. K., & Feldhusen, J. F. (Eds.). (1991). *Conducting research and evaluation in gifted education: A handbook of methods and applications.* New York: Teachers College Press.

Callahan, C. M., & Caldwell, M. S. (1995). *Practitioner's guide to evaluating programs for the gifted.* Washington, DC: National Association for Gifted Children.

Carle, E. (1971). *Do you want to be my friend?* New York: Harper.

Carle, E. (1975). *The mixed-up chameleon.* New York: HarperTrophy.

Carson, B. S. (1992). *Gifted hands: The Ben Carson story.* New York: Harper.

Cherry, L. (1990). *The great Kapok tree.* New York: Gulliver Green.

Cherry, L. (1992). *A river ran wild.* New York: Gulliver Green.

Children's Defense Fund. (1998). Publications and reports. (25 E Street NW, Washington, DC 20001, Website addess: http://www.childrensdefense.org/)

Chinn, P. C., & Hughes, S. (1987). Representation of minority students in special education classes. *Remedial and Special Education, 8,* 9–16.

Chocolate, D. M. N. (1994). *Imani in the belly.* New York: Troll Medallion.

Choi, Y. (1997). *The sun girl and the moon boy: A Korean folktale.* New York: Random House.

Church, V. (1971). *Colors around me.* Chicago: African American Images.

Clark, B. (1997). *Growing up gifted* (5th ed.). Upper Saddle River, NJ: Prentice-Hall.

Clark, R. M. (1983). *Family life and school achievement: Why poor Black children succeed or fail.* Chicago: The University of Chicago Press.

Coerr, E. (1993). *Mieko and the fifth treasure.* New York: Putnam.

Colangelo, N. (1991). Counseling gifted students. In N. Colangelo & G. A. Davis (Eds.), *Handbook of gifted education* (pp. 271–284). Needham Heights, MA: Allyn and Bacon.

Coleman, E. (1996). *White socks only.* Morton Grove, IL: Albert Whitman.

Coleman, M. J., & Fults, B. A. (1985). Special-class placement, level of intelligence, and the self-concepts of gifted children: A social comparison perspective. *Remedial and Special Education, 6*(1), 7–11.

Coleman, M. R., & Gallagher, J. J. (1992). *Report on state policies related to the identification of gifted students.* Chapel Hill, NC: Gifted Education Policy Studies Program, University of North Carolina at Chapel Hill.

Coleman, M. R., Gallagher, J. J., & Foster, A. (1994). *Updated report on state policies related to the identification of gifted students.* Chapel Hill, NC: Gifted Education Policy Studies Program, University of North Carolina at Chapel Hill.

Coles, R. (1995). *The story of Ruby Bridges.* New York: Scholastic.

Comer, J. M. (1988). Educating poor minority children. *Scientific American, 259*(5), 2–48.

Cox, J., Daniel, N., & Boston, B. (1985). *Educating able learners.* Austin, TX: University of Texas Press.

Cross Jr., W. E. (1995). The psychology of Nigrescence: Revising the Cross model. In J. G. Ponterotto, J. M. Casas, L. A. Suzuki, & C. M. Alexander (Eds.), *Handbook of multicultural counseling* (pp. 93–122). Thousand Oaks, CA: Sage.

Davidman, L., & Davidman, P. T. (1994). *Teaching with a multicultural perspective: A practical guide.* New York: Longman.

DeCesare, A. (1996). *Anthony the perfect monster.* New York: Random House.

Diana vs. California State Board of Education, No. C-70-37 RFP, District Court of Northern California, 1970.

Diaz, E. (1998). Perceived factors influencing the academic underachievement of talented students of Puerto Rican descent. *Gifted Child Quarterly, 12*(2), 105–122.

Douglass, F. (1997). *Narrative of the life of Frederick Douglass, an American slave.* New York: Norton. (Original work published 1845)

Ehlert, L. (1988). *Planting a rainbow.* New York: Harcourt Brace.

Ehlert, L. (1992). *Moon rope.* New York: Harcourt Brace.

Ehlert, L. (1997). *Cuckoo/Cucu.* New York: Harcourt Brace.

Ellison, R. (1952). *The invisible man*. New York: Random House.

Emberley, R. (1990). *My house/Mi casa*. Boston: Little Brown.

Emberley, R. (1993). *My day/Mi dia*. Boston: Little Brown.

Epstein, J. L. (1997). *School, family, and community partnerships*. Thousand Oaks, CA: Sage.

Everett, G. (1993). *John Brown: One man against slavery*. New York: Rizzoli.

Feelings, M. (1971). *Moja means one: Swahili counting book*. New York: Dial.

Feelings, M. (1974). *Jambo means hello*. New York: Dial.

Ford, D. Y. (1992). Determinants of underachievement among gifted, above-average, and average Black students. *Roeper Review, 14*(3), 130–136.

Ford, D. Y. (1993). An investigation into the paradox of underachievement among gifted Black students. *Roeper Review, 16*(2), 78–84.

Ford, D. Y. (1994a). *The recruitment and retention of Black students in gifted programs*. Storrs: The University of Connecticut, National Research Center on the Gifted and Talented.

Ford, D. Y. (1994b). Promoting achievement among gifted Black students: The efficacy of new definitions and identification practices. *Urban Education, 29*(2), 202–229.

Ford, D. Y. (1995a). *A study of underachievement among gifted, potentially gifted, and general education students*. Storrs: University of Connecticut, National Research Center on the Gifted and Talented.

Ford, D. Y. (1995b). *Counseling gifted Black students: Underachievement, identity, and social and emotional well-being*. Research-Based Decision Making Series, The National Research Center on the Gifted and Talented. Storrs: The University of Connecticut.

Ford, D. Y. (1996). *Reversing underachievement among gifted Black students: Promising practices and programs*. New York: Teachers College Press.

Ford, D. Y. (1998). The underrepresentation of minority students in gifted education: Problems and promises in recruitment and retention. *The Journal of Special Education, 32*(1), 4–14.

Ford, D. Y., Grantham, T. C., & Harris III, J. J. (1996). Multicultural gifted education: A wakeup call to the profession. *Roeper Review, 19*(2), 72–78.

Ford, D. Y., Grantham, T. C., & Harris III, J. J. (1997). The recruitment and retention of minority teachers in gifted education. *Roeper Review, 19*(4), 213–220.

Ford, D. Y., & Harris III, J. J. (1995). University counselors' perceptions of factors incident to achievement among gifted Black and gifted white students. *Journal of Counseling and Development, 73*(4), 443–450.

Ford, D. Y., Harris III, J. J., & Schuerger, J. M. (1993). Racial identity development among gifted Black students: Counseling issues and concerns. *Journal of Counseling and Development, 71*(4), 409–417.

Ford, D. Y., & Webb, K. (1995). Desegregating gifted education: A need unmet. *Journal of Negro Education, 64*(1), 52–62.

Ford, M. A. (1989). Students' perceptions of affective issues impacting the social emotional development and school performance of gifted/talented youngsters. *Roeper Review, 11*(3), 131–134.

Fordham, S. (1988). Racelessness as a strategy in Black students' school success: Pragmatic strategy or pyrrhic victory? *Harvard Educational Review, 58*(1), 54–84.

Fordham, S., & Ogbu, J. U. (1986). Black students' school success: Coping with the burden of "acting white." *The Urban Review, 18,* 176–207.

Foster, M. (1992). The politics of race: Through the eyes of African-American teachers. In K. Weiler & C. Mitchell (Eds.), *What schools can do: Critical pedagogy and practice.* Albany: State University of New York Press.

Frasier, M. M., Garcia, J. H., & Passow, A. H. (1995). *A review of assessment issues in gifted education and their implications for identifying gifted minority students.* Storrs, CT: The University of Connecticut, National Research Center on the Gifted and Talented.

Frasier, M. M., Martin, D., Garcia, J., Finley, V. S., Frank, E., Krisel, S., & King, L. L. (1995). *A new window for looking at gifted children.* Storrs, CT: The University of Connecticut, National Research Center on the Gifted and Talented.

Frasier, M. M., & Passow, A. H. (1994). *Toward a new paradigm for identifying talent potential.* Storrs, CT: The University of Connecticut, National Research Center on the Gifted and Talented.

Freeman, D. (1968). *Corduroy.* New York: Viking.

Gallagher, J. J. (1988). National agenda for educating gifted students: Statement of priorities. *Exceptional Children, 55*(2), 107–114.

Garcia, F. (1994). *Understanding and meeting the challenge of student cultural diversity.* New York: Houghton Mifflin.

Gardner, H. (1983). *Frames of mind: The theory of multiple intelligence.* New York: Basic Books.

Gardner, H., Kornhaber, M. L., & Wake, W. K. (1996). *Intelligence: Multiple perspectives.* New York: Harcourt Brace.

Garrison, L. (1989). Programming for the gifted American Indian student. In J. Maker and S. W. Shiever (Eds.), *Critical issues in gifted education: Defensible programs for cultural and ethnic minorities* (pp. 116–127) (vol. 2). Austin, TX: Pro-Ed.

Gay, G. (1993). Ethnic minorities and educational equality. In J. A. Banks & C.A.M. Banks (Eds.), *Multicultural education: Issues and perspectives* (2nd ed.) (pp. 171–194). Boston: Allyn and Bacon.

Giroux, H. (1983). Theories of reproduction and resistance in the new sociology of education. *Harvard Educational Review, 52,* 257–293.

Glasser, W. (1986). *Control theory in the classroom.* New York: Harper & Row.

Gollnick, D. M., & Chinn, P. C. (1998). *Multicultural education in a pluralistic society* (5th ed.). New York: Merrill.

Gould, S. J. (1981). *The mismeasure of man.* New York: W. W. Norton.

Graham, S. (1992). Most of the subjects were White and middle class: Trends in published research on African Americans in selected APA journals. *American Psychologist, 47*(5), 629–639.

Grant, C., & Sleeter, C. E. (1989). *Turning on learning: Five approaches for multicultural teaching plans for race, class, gender, and disability.* Columbus: Merrill.

Grant, C., & Sleeter, C. E. (1998). *Turning on learning: Five approaches for multicultural teaching plans for race, class, gender, and disability* (2nd ed.). Columbus: Merrill.

Greene, M. (1993). The passions of pluralism: Multiculturalism and the expanding community. *Educational Researcher, 22*(1), 13–18.

Greenfield, E. (1978). *Honey, I love and other love poems.* New York: Crowell.

Grossman, H. (1991). Special education in a diverse society: Improving services for minority and working-class students. *Preventing School Failure, 36*(1), 19–27.

Halsted, J. W. (1994). *Some of my best friends are books: Guiding gifted readers from preschool to high school.* Dayton, OH: Ohio Psychology Press.

Hansen, J. (1989). *The gift-giver.* New York: Houghton Mifflin.

Harter, S. (1982). The Perceived Competence Scale for Children. *Child Development, 53,* 87–97.

Hawthorne, N. (1961). *The scarlet letter.* New York: Rinehart.

Hebert, T. (1991). Meeting the affective needs of bright boys through bibliotherapy. *Roeper Review, 13,* 207–212.

Heid, C. A. (Ed.). (1988). *Multicultural education: Knowledge and perspectives.* Bloomington, IN: Indiana University, Center for Urban and Multicultural Education.

Helms, J. E. (1994). Racial identity in the school environment. In P. Pedersen & J. C. Carey (Eds.), *Multicultural counseling in schools: A practical handbook* (pp. 19–37). Boston: Allyn and Bacon.

High, M. H., & Udall, A. J. (1983). Teacher rating of students in relation to ethnicity of students and school ethnic balance. *Journal for the Education of the Gifted, 6*(3), 154–166.

Hobson vs. Hansen, 269 F. Supp. 501 (D.D.C. 1967).

Hoffman, M. (1991). *Amazing grace.* New York: Dial.

Hollingworth, L. S. (1926). *Gifted children: Their nature and nurture.* New York: Macmillan.

Holmes, H., & Guild, S. (Eds.). (n.d.). *A manual of teaching techniques for intercultural education.* New York: United Nations Educational, Scientific, and Cultural Organization.

Howe, J. (1987). *I wish I were a butterfly.* New York: Harcourt Brace Jovanovich.

Irvine, J. J., & York, E. D. (1995). Learning styles in culturally diverse students: A literature review. In J. A. Banks & C. A. M. Banks (Eds.), *Handbook of research on multicultural education* (pp. 484–497). New York: Macmillan.

Jacobs, J. C. (1971). Effectiveness of teacher and parent identification of gifted children as a function of school levels. *Psychology in the Schools, 8,* 140–142.

Johnson, D. T., VanTassel-Baska, J., Boyce, L. N., & Hall, K. H. (1995). *Autobiographies: Personal odyssey of change.* Williamsburg, VA: College of William and Mary, The Center for Gifted Education.

Kaplan, S. N. (1979). *Inservice training manual: Activities for developing curriculum for the gifted/talented.* Ventura, CA: Ventura County Schools.

Karnes, F. A., & Marquardt, R. G. (1991). *Gifted children and the law.* Dayton, OH: Ohio Psychology Press.

Keeshan, B. (1996). *Books to grow by: Fun children's books.* Minneapolis, MN: Fairvew Press.

Kennedy, M. M. (1991). Policy issues in teacher education. *Phi Delta Kappan, 72,* 559–665.

Kim, J. (1981). *Process of Asian-American identity development: A study of Japanese American women's perceptions of their struggle to achieve positive identities.* Unpublished doctoral dissertation, University of Massachusetts, Amherst.

Kimmel, A. J. (1988). *Ethics and values in applied social research.* Newbury Park, CA: Sage.

King Jr., M. L. (1963/1997). *I have a dream.* New York: Scholastic Press.

Kirschenbaum, R. J. (1989). Identification of the gifted and talented American Indian students. In J. Maker & S. W. Shiever (Eds.), *Critical issues in gifted education: Defensible programs for cultural and ethnic minorities* (vol. 2) (pp. 91–101). Austin, TX: Pro-Ed.

Klausmeier, K., Mishra, S. P., & Maker, C. J. (1987). Identification of gifted learners: A national survey of assessment practices and training needs of school psychologists. *Gifted Child Quarterly, 31*(1), 135–137.

Kozol, J. (1991). *Savage inequalities: Children in America's schools.* New York: Harper-Perennial.

Krathwohl, D. R., Bloom, B. S., & Masia, B. B. (1964). *Taxonomy of educational objectives: Handbook II. Affective domain.* New York: David McKay.

Kyung-Wong, J. (1992). Bibliotherapy for gifted children. *Gifted Child Quarterly, 15*(6), 16–19.

Ladson-Billings, G. (1994). *The dreamkeepers: Successful teachers for African-American children.* San Francisco: Jossey-Bass.

Langdon, C. A. (1996). The third Phi Delta Kappa poll of teachers' attitude toward the public school. *Phi Delta Kappan, 78*(3), 244–250.

Larry P. v. Wilson Riles, 502 F. 2d 963 (9th Cir. 1974).

Lee, C. (1984). An investigation of psychosocial variables related to academic success for rural Black adolescents. *Journal of Negro Education, 53*(3), 424–433.

Lee, S. J. (1996). *Unraveling the "model minority" stereotype: Listening to Asian American youth.* New York: Teachers College Press.

Levine, E. (1988). *If you traveled on the underground railroad.* New York: Scholastic.

Li, A. K. F. (1988). Self-perception and motivational orientation in gifted children. *Roeper Review, 10*(3), 175–180.

Lionni, L. (1968). *Swimmy.* New York: Pantheon.

Lionni, L. (1997). *A color of his own.* New York: Knopf.

Lipman, M. (1991). Philosophy for children. In A. L. Costa (Ed.), *Developing minds: Programs for teaching thinking* (rev. ed.; vol. 2) (pp. 35–38). Alexandria, VA: Association for Supervision and Curriculum Development

Lomotey, K. (1990). *Going to school: The African-American experience.* Albany: State University of New York Press.

MacLeod, J. (1995). *Ain't no makin' it: Leveled aspirations in a low-income neighborhood* (2nd ed.). Boulder, CA: Westview.

Madaus, G. F. (1994). A technological and historical consideration of equity issues associated with proposals to change the nation's testing policy. *Harvard Educational Review, 64*(1), 76–95.

Mahy, M. (1990). *The seven Chinese brothers.* New York: Scholastic.

Maker, J., & Shiever, S. W. (Eds.). *Critical issues in gifted education: Defensible programs for cultural and ethnic minorities* (vol. 2). Austin, TX: Pro-Ed.

Manning, M. (1994). *A ruined house*. Cambridge, MA: Candlewick.

Marland, S. (1972). *Education of the gifted and talented: Report to the Congress of the United States by the U.S. Commissioner of Education*. Washington, DC: U.S. Government Printing Office.

Maslow, A. H. (1954). *Motivation and personality*. New York: Harper & Row.

Maslow, A. H. (1968). *Toward a psychology of being* (2nd ed.). Princeton, NJ: VanNostrand.

McAdoo, H. P. (Ed.). (1993). *Family ethnicity: Strength and diversity*. Newbury Park, CA: Sage.

McGovern, A. (1969). *Black is beautiful*. New York: Four Winds.

McIntosh, P. (1988). *White privilege and male privilege: A personal account of coming to see correspondences through work in women's studies*. Working paper no. 189. Wellesley, MA: Wellesley College, Center for Research on Women.

McIntosh, P. (1990). *Interactive phases of curricular and personal re-vision with regard to race*. Working Paper no. 219. Wellesley, MA: Wellesley College, Center for Research on Women.

Mendez, P. (1989). *The black snowman*. New York: Scholastic.

Merton, R. K. (1949). Discrimination and the American creed. In R. M. MacIver (Ed.), *Discrimination and national welfare* (pp. 99–126). New York: HarperCollins.

Montgomery, D. (1989). Identification of giftedness among American Indian people. In J. Maker & S. W. Shiever (Eds.), *Critical issues in gifted education: Defensible programs for cultural and ethnic minorities* (vol. 2) (pp. 79–90). Austin, TX: Pro-Ed.

Moody, C. (1990). Teacher effectiveness. In J. G. Bain & J. E. Herman (Eds.), *Making schools work for underachieving minority students* (pp. 159–163). New York: Greenwood Press.

Moore, K. (1994). *If you lived at the time of the Civil War*. New York: Scholastic.

Murray, R. J., & Herrnstein, C. (1994). *The bell curve: Intelligence and class structure in American life*. New York: Free Press.

Muse, D. (1997). *The New Press guide to multicultural resources for young readers*. New York: The New Press.

Myers, W. D. (1993). *Malcolm X: By any means necessary*. New York: Sholastic.

Namioka, L. (1992). *Yang the youngest and his terrible ear*. New York: Brown.

National Association for Gifted Children. (1994a). *Competencies needed by teachers of gifted and talented students*. Washington, DC: Author.

National Association for Gifted Children. (1994b). *Differentiation of curriculum and instruction*. Washington, DC: Author.

National Association for Gifted Children. (1995a). *Addressing affective needs of gifted children*. Washington, DC: Author.

National Association for Gifted Children. (1995b). *Standards for graduate programs in gifted education*. Washington, DC: Author.

National Association for Gifted Children. (1997). *The use of tests in the identification and assessment of gifted students*. Washington, DC: Author.

National Center for Education Statistics (NCES). (1998). *The Third International Mathematics and Science Study (TIMSS)*. Washington, DC: Author.

National Commission on Excellence in Education. (1983). *A nation at risk: The imper-*

ative for educational reform. Washington, DC: United States Department of Education.

National Council for Social Studies. (1992). Curriculum guidelines for multicultural education. *Social Education, 56*(5), 274–294.

National Educational Association. (1991). *Status of American public school teachers, 1990–1991.* Washington, DC: Author.

Ogbu, J. U. (1988). Human intelligence testing: A cultural-ecological perspective. *Phi Kappa Phi Journal, 68,* 23–29.

Ogbu, J. U. (1994). From cultural differences to differences in cultural frame of reference. In P. M. Greenfield & R. Cocking (Eds.), *Cross-cultural roots of minority child development* (pp. 365–391). Hillsdale, NJ: Erlbaum.

Ortiz, S. (1988). *The people shall continue.* San Francisco: Children's Books.

Paley, V. G. (1989). *White teacher.* Cambridge, MA: Harvard University Press.

Pegnato, C. W., & Birch, J. W. (1959). Locating gifted children in junior high school: A comparison of methods. *Exceptional Children, 25,* 300–304.

Peters, L. W. (1995). *October smiled back.* New York: Henry Holt.

Peters, W. (1987). *A class divided then and now.* New Haven: Yale University Press.

Pinkney, A. D. (1994). *Dear Benjamin Banneker.* New York: Harcourt Brace.

Plisko, V. W., & Stern, J. D. (Eds.). (1985). *The condition of education.* Washington, DC: National Center for Educational Statistics.

Pogrow, S. (1991). HOTS. In A. L. Costa (Ed.), *Developing minds: Programs for teaching thinking* (rev. ed.; vol. 2) (pp. 62–64). Alexandria, VA: Association for Supervision and Curriculum Development.

Ponterotto, J. G., & Casas, J. M. (1991). *Handbook of racial/ethnic minority counseling research.* Springfield, IL: Charles C. Thomas.

Ponterotto, J. G., Casas, J. M., Suzuki, L. A., & Alexander, C. M. (Eds.). (1995). *Handbook of multicultural counseling.* Thousand Oaks, CA: Sage.

Ponterotto, J. G., & Pedersen, P. B. (1993). *Preventing prejudice: A guide for counselors and educators.* Newbury Park, CA: Sage.

Rahaman, V. (1997). *Read for me, mama.* Honesdale, PA: Boyd Mills Press.

Reis, S. M., & Dobyns, S. M. (1991). An annotated bibliography of nonfictional books and curricular materials to encourage gifted females. *Roeper Review, 13,* 129–134.

Renzulli, J. (1977). *The Enrichment Triad Model: A guide for developing defensible programs for the gifted and talented.* Ventura, CA: Office of the Ventura County Superintendent of Schools.

Renzulli, J. S., & Reis, S. M. (1977). *The schoolwide enrichment model: A how-to guide for educational excellence.* Mansfield Center, CT: Creative Learning Press.

Renzulli, J. S., & Reis, S. M. (1997). *The schoolwide enrichment model: A how-to guide for educational excellence* (2nd ed.). Mansfield Center, CT: Creative Learning Press.

Reynolds, C. R. & Kamphaus, R. W. (1990). *Handbook of psychological and educational assessment of children: Intelligence and achievement.* New York: Guilford Press.

Rodriguez, E. R., & Bellanca, J. (1996). *What is it about me you can't teach? An instructional guide for the urban educator.* Arlington Hills, IL: SkyLight.

Rosenthal, K., & Jacobson, L. (1968). *Pygmalion in the classroom: Teacher expectation and pupil intellectual development.* New York: Holt, Rinehart, & Winston.

Ross, T., & Barton, R. (1994). *Eggbert: The slightly cracked egg.* New York: The Putnam & Grosset Group.

Salomone, R. C. (1986). *Legal rights and federal policy: Equal education under law.* New York: St. Martin's Press.

Saracho, O. N., & Gerstl, C. K. (1992). Learning differences among at-risk minority students. In H. C. Waxman, J. Walker de Felix, J. E. Anderson, & H. P. Baptiste Jr. (Eds.), *Students at risk in at-risk schools. Improving environments for learning* (pp. 105–136). Newbury Park, CA: Corwin Press.

Sax, G. (1989). *Principles of educational and psychological measurement and evaluation* (3rd ed.). Belmont, CA: Wadsworth.

Sebestyen, Q. (1968). *Words by heart.* Boston: Little, Brown.

Shade, B. J. (1994). Understanding the African American learner. In E. R. Hollins, J. E. King, & W. C. Hayman (Eds.), *Teaching diverse populations: Formulating a knowledge base* (pp. 175–189). New York: State University of New York Press.

Shade, B. J., & Edwards, P. A. (1987). Ecological correlates of the educative style of Afro-American children. *Journal of Negro Education, 56*(1), 88–99.

Shade, B. J., Kelly, C., & Oberg, M. (1997). *Creating culturally responsive classrooms.* Washington, DC: American Psychological Association.

Siccone, F. (1995). *Celebrating diversity: Building self-esteem in today's multicultural classroom.* Needham Heights, MA: Allyn and Bacon.

Simon, N. (1975). *All kinds of families.* Morton Grove, IL: Albert Whitman.

Siomandes, L. (1997). *A place to bloom.* Honesdale, PA: Boyds Mills.

Sisk, D. A. (1989). Identifying and nurturing talent among the American Indians. In J. Maker & J. W. Shiever (Eds.), *Critical issues in gifted education: Defensible programs for cultural and ethnic minorities* (vol. 2; pp. 128–132). Austin, TX: Pro-Ed.

Sleeter, C. E., & Grant, C. A. (1993). *Making choices for multicultural education* (2nd ed.). New York: Merrill.

Steptoe, J. (1974). *My special best words.* New York: Viking.

Steptoe, J. (1984). *The story of jumping mouse.* New York: Lothrop, Lee, & Shepard.

Sternberg, R. J. (1985). *Beyond IQ: A triarchic theory of human intelligence.* Cambridge, U.K.: Cambridge University Press.

Sue, D. W., Arrendondo, P., & McDavis, R. J. (1992). Multicultural counseling competencies and standards: A call to the profession. *Journal of Counseling and Development, 70,* 477–486.

Taba, H., Levine, S., & Elzey, F. F. (1964). *Thinking in elementary school children.* U.S. Office of Education, Cooperative Research Project No. 2402. San Francisco: U.S. Office of Education.

Tabor, N. M. G. (1997). *We are a rainbow.* Watertown, MA: Charlesbridge.

Takaki, R. (1993). *A different mirror: A history of multicultural America.* Boston: Little, Brown.

Tanaka, K. (1989). A response to "Are We Meeting the Needs of Gifted Asian-Americans?" In J. Maker & S. W. Shiever (Eds.), *Critical issues in gifted education: Defensible programs for cultural and ethnic minorities* (vol. 2), (pp. 174–178). Austin, TX: Pro-Ed.

Terman, L. M. (1925). *Genetic studies of genius: Vol. 1. Mental and physical traits of a thousand gifted children.* Stanford, CA: Stanford University Press.

Title IV, Part B. [Jacob K. Javits Gifted and Talented Students Education Act of 1988], Elementary and Secondary Education Act of 1988, 20 U.S.C. § 3061 et seq.

Tompert, A. (1990). *Grandfather Tang's story: A tale told with tangrams.* New York: Crown.

Torrance, E. P. (1977). *Discovery and nurturance of giftedness in the culturally different.* Reston, VA: Council on Exceptional Children.

Torrance, E. P. (1998). *Multicultural mentoring of the gifted and talented.* Waco, TX: Prufrock Press.

Tuttle, F. B., Becker, L. A., & Sousa, J. A. (1988). *Characteristics and identification of gifted and talented students* (3rd ed.). Washington, DC: National Educational Association.

Udall, A. J. (1989). Curriculum for gifted Hispanic students. In J. Maker & S. W. Shiever (Eds.), *Critical issues in gifted education: Defensible programs for cultural and ethnic minorities* (vol. 2) (pp. 41–56). Austin, TX: Pro-Ed.

U.S. Bureau of the Census. (1993). *We, the first Americans.* Washington, DC: U.S. Government Printing Office.

U.S. Department of Education. (1992). *OCR elementary and secondary school civil rights compliance report.* Washington, DC: Office for Civil Rights.

U.S. Department of Education. (1993). *National excellence: A case for developing America's talent.* Washington, DC: Office of Educational Research and Improvement.

U.S. Department of Health, Education, and Welfare. (1971). *Education of the gifted and talented.* Washington, DC: Author.

VanTassel-Baska, J. (1991). Teachers as counselors for gifted students. In R. Milgrim (Ed.), *Counseling gifted and talented children: A guide for teachers, children, and parents* (pp. 37–52). Norwood, NJ: Ablex.

VanTassel-Baska, J. (1992). *Planning effective curriculum for gifted learners.* Denver, CO: Love.

VanTassel-Baska, J. (1997). *What a find! A problem-based unit.* Dubuque, IA: Kendall/Hunt.

VanTassel-Baska, J., Feldhusen, J., Seeley, K., Wheatley, G., Silverman, L., & Foster, W. (1988). *Comprehensive curriculum for gifted learners.* Boston: Allyn and Bacon.

Van Tassel-Baska, J., Patton, J., & Prillaman, D. (1989). Disadvantaged gifted learners at-risk for educational attention. *Focus on Exceptional Children, 22*(3), 1–16.

Wall Street Journal. (March 31, 1993). Book purchases grew, survey finds, p. B10.

Wall Street Journal. (December 13, 1994). Mainstream science on intelligence. p. A18.

Wandro, M., & Blank, J. (1981). *My daddy is a nurse.* Reading, MA: Addison-Wesley.

Weschler, D. (1991). *Manual for the Weschler Intelligence Scale–Third edition.* San Antonio, TX: Author.

Whitmore, J. R. (1980). *Giftedness, conflict, and underachievement.* Boston, MA: Allyn and Bacon.

Whitmore, J. R. (1986). Understanding a lack of motivation to excel. *Gifted Child Quarterly, 30*(2), 66–69.

Widman, C. (1990). *Housekeeper of the wind.* New York: Harper & Row.

Williams, J. (1976). *Everybody knows what a dragon looks like.* New York: Macmillan.

Williams, S. (1992). *Working cotton.* New York: Harcourt Brace Jovanovich.

Williams, V. (1986). *A chair for my mother.* New York: Greenwillow.

Williams-Garcia, R. (1988). *Blue tights.* New York: Dutton.

Williams-Garcia, R. (1991). *Fast talk on a slow track.* New York: Dutton.

Winebrenner, S. (1992). *Teaching gifted kids in the regular classroom.* Minneapolis, MN: Free Spirit.

Winter, J. (1988). *Follow the drinking gourd.* New York: Knopf.

Wolf, B. (1974). *Don't feel sorry for Paul.* New York: HarperCollins.

Woo, E. (1989). Personal reflections on the purpose of special education for gifted Asian Americans. In J. Maker & S. W. Shiever (Eds.), *Critical issues in gifted education: Defensible programs for cultural and ethnic minorities* (vol. 2) (pp. 179–181). Austin, TX: Pro-Ed.

Woodson, C. G. (1933). *The miseducation of the Negro.* Washington, DC: Associated Publishers.

Woodson, J. (1994). *Maizon at Blue Hill.* New York: Delacort.

Worthen, B. R., Borg, W. R., & White, K. R. (1993). *Measurement and evaluation in the schools.* New York: Longman.

Wrenn, C. G. (1962). The culturally encapsulated counselor. *Harvard Educational Review, 32,* 444–449.

Yarbrough, C. (1979). *Cornrows.* New York: Coward, McCann, & Geoghegan.

Young, E. (1989). *Lon Po Po: A red-riding hood story from China.* New York: Philomel.

Zirkel, P. A., & Stevens, P. L. (1987). The law concerning public education of gifted students. *Journal for the Education of the Gifted, 10*(4), 305–322.

Zolotow, C. (1995). *When the wind stops.* New York: HarperCollins.

Index

Williams, J., 73
Williams, S., 104, 117
Williams, V., 92, 180–181
Williams-Garcia, R., 146–148
Winebrenner, S., 102–105
Winter, J., 117
Wolf, B., 218
Woo, E., 10
Woodson, Carter G., 16
Woodson, J., 143–144
Words by Heart (Sebestyen), 145–146
Working Cotton (Williams), 117

Worthen, B. R., 19, 187
Wrenn, C. G., 128–129

Yang the Youngest and His Terrible Ear (Namioka), 145, 181–182
Yarbrough, C., 218
York, E. D., 74, 75
Young, E., 88–89

Zhang, W., 60, 61
Zirkel, P. A., 21
Zolotow, C., 100

About the Authors

Donna Y. Ford, Ph.D., is an Associate Professor in the Special Education Program at The Ohio State University College of Education. She teaches classes and conducts research in gifted education, and consults with school districts nationally. Her work focuses on identification and assessment of gifted minority students, correlates of underachievement among gifted African-American students, and urban and multicultural education, and has received several awards for her research. She is also the author of *Reversing Underachievement Among Gifted Black Students* (Teachers College Press, 1996).

J. John Harris III, Ph.D., is a Professor in the College of Education and a Scholar in the African-American Studies Program (College of Arts and Sciences) at the University of Kentucky. He teaches classes in and conducts research on educational law and administration, gifted education, and urban and multicultural education, and is widely published in these areas. Professor Harris has been a public school teacher and administrator in several urban districts, as well as Dean of two colleges of education.